Concise Guide to Paralegal Ethics

Concise Guide to Paralegal Ethics

Therese A. Cannon
Dean
John F. Kennedy University
School of Law

Educational Consultant
American Bar Association
Standing Committee on Paralegals

ASPEN
PUBLISHERS

111 Eighth Avenue, New York, NY 10011
www.aspenpublishers.com

© 2006 Aspen Publishers, Inc.
a Wolters Kluwer business
www.aspenpublishers.com

Aspen Publishers
Attn: Permissions Department
111 Eighth Avenue, 7th Floor
New York, NY 10011-5201

Printed in the United States of America.

2 3 4 5 6 7 8 9 0

ISBN 0-7355-5108-1

Library of Congress Cataloging-in-Publication Data

Cannon, Therese A.
    Concise guide to paralegal ethics / Therese A. Cannon.— 2nd ed.
        p.   cm.
    Includes index.
    ISBN 0-7355-5108-1
    1. Legal ethics—United States. 2. Legal assistants—United States. I. Title.

KF320.L4C365 2006
174'.3'0973—dc22

2005021039

About Aspen Publishers

Aspen Publishers, headquartered in New York City, is a leading information provider for attorneys, business professionals, and law students. Written by preeminent authorities, our products consist of analytical and practical information covering both U.S. and international topics. We publish in the full range of formats, including updated manuals, books, periodicals, CDs, and online products.

Our proprietary content is complemented by 2,500 legal databases, containing over 11 million documents, available through our Loislaw division. Aspen Publishers also offers a wide range of topical legal and business databases linked to Loislaw's primary material. Our mission is to provide accurate, timely, and authoritative content in easily accessible formats, supported by unmatched customer care.

To order any Aspen Publishers title, go to *www.aspenpublishers.com* or call 1-800-638-8437.

To reinstate your manual update service, call 1-800-638-8437.

For more information on Loislaw products, go to *www.loislaw.com* or call 1-800-364-2512.

For Customer Care issues, e-mail *CustomerCare@aspenpublishers.com*; call 1-800-234-1660; or fax 1-800-901-9075.

Aspen Publishers
a Wolters Kluwer business

This book is dedicated to the thousands of paralegals who work tirelessly to provide quality legal services to clients and who strive to make legal services more accessible.

Summary of Contents

Contents

4. Conflicts of Interest 63

5. Advertising and Solicitation 91

6. Fees and Client Funds 107

7. Competence   135

8. Special Issues in Advocacy   155

9. Professionalism and Special Issues for Paralegals

Appendices

Preface

Approach

This book is written for paralegal students, working paralegals, and the attorneys who employ paralegals. It is intended for use primarily as a text, but can be used as a reference manual by those in practice.

In the past nearly 40 years, the paralegal occupation has truly come into its own. Its growth in numbers, its expansion into all areas of law practice and all sectors of the legal services industry, and its general acceptance by the legal community and the public are impressive. The occupation continues to evolve into a true profession. One of the most critical aspects of any profession is its adherence to an accepted code of ethics. Legal ethics is now taught in virtually every paralegal program in the country. Because of the diversity in paralegal education programs in terms of content, length, and format, ethics is treated in a wide variety of ways in the curriculum. A growing proportion of programs has a separate course on ethics, but many programs include ethics as a short segment in another required course and/or teach ethics across the curriculum.

This text is a concise version of *Ethics and Professional Responsibility for Paralegals.* This concise version covers all the same subject matter as the full version, but in an abbreviated format that can be adapted to short courses and to use in several different courses.

Organization and Coverage of the Concise Edition

The content of this book is comprehensive. It covers all the major areas of legal ethics, placing special emphasis on how the rules affect paralegals. It begins with a chapter on the regulation of attorneys and paralegals, covering ethics codes, disciplinary processes for lawyers, and the variety of ways in which paralegals are regulated both directly and indirectly. Unauthorized practice of law is covered in Chapter 2, including the definitions of the practice of law, detailed descriptions of those functions that only lawyers are permitted to perform, and information on how UPL is evolving in view of the growing role of paralegals and nonlawyer legal service providers. Chapter 3 covers the duty of confidentiality and the attorney-client privilege, including common issues that arise in these areas, ways to prevent disclosure of confidential information, and the impact of technology.

Chapter 4 covers conflicts of interest, demonstrating how conflicts rules apply to paralegals, including the use of screens and conflicts checks. Rules regarding legal advertising and solicitation are covered in Chapter 5. Chapter 6 is devoted to financial matters, including billing and fees, fee agreements, statutory fee awards that include compensation for paralegal work, fee splitting, referral fees, partnerships between attorneys and nonlawyers, and handling client funds. Chapter 7 defines the concept of competence specifically in relation to paralegals and includes a discussion of malpractice. Special issues confronted by litigation paralegals are covered in Chapter 8. Finally, Chapter 9 examines professionalism, issues facing paralegals in today's law firm environment, and pro bono work.

Key Features

Each chapter begins with an overview that lists the topics covered in the chapter. The text of each chapter is divided topically. Key terms are spelled out in italics when first introduced and key concepts are noted in bold. At the end of each chapter are a few hypothetical fact situations that require the students to apply the rules and concepts covered in the chapter. These may be used in class discussion or for assignments. Review questions that test each student's memory and understanding of the material and discussion questions that call for in-depth analysis, legal research, or factual investigation are also included. Selected references, including cases and ethics rules, are found at the end of each chapter.

Recognizing that every paralegal program teaches ethics, but each in its own way, the concise version has been designed for use in short ethics courses or short segments of courses where there is not enough time to use case analysis as a teaching methodology or to pursue in-depth analysis of the ethics rules, including the history and evolution of those rules. Hypotheticals were added in place of actual cases to provide a method for students to test their understanding of the material by synthesizing it and applying it in a new context. Discussion of specific sections of the ABA Model Code and Rules has been abbreviated, as has coverage of trends.

Acknowledgments

Finally, many people must be thanked for their support and assistance. The American Association for Paralegal Education, National Association of Legal Assistants, National Federation of Paralegal Associations, International Paralegal Management Association, and my colleagues with the American Bar Association Standing Committee on Paralegals and Approval Commission. Special thanks go to the many students I have had the pleasure of teaching and the paralegals who have shared their experiences with me. My deepest appreciation must be extended to the wonderful people at Aspen, especially Betsy Kenny, whose patience, warmth, intelligence, and talents made this book possible.

I would like to thank the following copyright holders who kindly granted their permission to reprint from the following materials.

American Bar Association. Model Guidelines for the Utilization of Paralegal Services. Copyright © 1991 by the American Bar Association. All rights reserved. Reprinted by permission of the American Bar Association.

National Association of Legal Assistants, Code of Ethics and Professional Responsibility. Copyright © 1975, Revised 1979, 1988, 1995. Reprinted by permission of the National Association of Legal Assistants, 1516 S. Boston #200, Tulsa, OK 74119.

National Federation of Paralegal Associations, Model Code of Ethics and Professional Responsibility. Copyright © 1993 by the National Federation of Paralegal Associations, Inc. All rights reserved. Reprinted by permission of the National Federation of Paralegal Associations, Inc.

Therese A. Cannon

September 2005

Concise Guide to Paralegal Ethics

1

Regulation of Lawyers and Paralegals

This chapter provides basic background on the regulation of lawyers and paralegals. Paralegals/legal assistants, who work under the supervision of lawyers, need to understand the rules governing lawyer conduct and how those rules affect them. Also covered is a brief history of the paralegal profession and an explanation of how paralegals are regulated directly and indirectly by the states in which they work. Included is an overview of voluntary professional associations for paralegals and certification programs. Chapter 1 covers:

- the inherent power of the courts over the practice of law
- the organized bar's participation in lawyer regulation
- the role of the legislature and state statutes in governing the conduct of lawyers
- the American Bar Association and its influence on legal ethics
- the evolution of the paralegal profession
- professional associations for paralegals
- the status of paralegal regulation
- the distinctions between certification, licensing, and limited licensing
- the liability of paralegals and the lawyers who supervise them
- guidelines for the utilization of paralegal services
- ethics guidelines promulgated by paralegal associations

A. Regulation of Lawyers

1. State Courts and Bar Associations

Like other professions that affect the public interest, the legal profession is subject to regulation by the states. Unlike these other regulated professions, however, the regulation of the legal profession falls mainly to the judiciary rather than the legislature. Because of the function of lawyers in the court system and the separation of powers, the judiciary has historically asserted inherent authority over the practice of law.

The highest court in each state and in the District of Columbia is responsible for making rules related to law practice admission and to lawyers' ethical conduct. The codes of ethical conduct promulgated by the states' highest courts have mechanisms for disciplining lawyers who violate the codes. Most state legislatures have also passed statutes that supplement the ethics rules adopted by the courts. Some states consider legislative authority over the practice of law to be concurrent with the judicial authority; others consider legislative action to be only in aid of judicial action. In a few states, such as California and New York, substantial authority over the practice of law rests with the legislature. Sometimes the judiciary and the legislature have conflicting ideas about matters affecting the practice of law, and a court will be called on to strike down legislation. Several state supreme courts have held unconstitutional legislation that would have authorized nonlawyers to engage in conduct that the court considered to be the practice of law. Local court rules also govern attorneys' conduct in matters before the courts.

In practice, many state supreme courts rely heavily on state bar associations to carry out their responsibilities for regulating the practice of law. These courts have delegated authority to the bar as a way to relieve the ever-growing burden of handling these matters in addition to their caseloads.

Some state bar associations are *integrated* or unified, which means that membership is compulsory. In a state with an integrated bar, annual dues to renew the practitioner's law license carry automatic membership in the state bar. Some states have purely voluntary state bar associations; funds to operate the admissions and disciplinary functions in the state are derived from annual licensing or registration fees. Integrated bars generally play a more active role in the admissions and disciplinary functions of the court and in other matters relating to the legal profession.

2. American Bar Association

Most states have patterned their codes of ethics on the models of the American Bar Association (ABA). The ABA is a national voluntary professional association of lawyers currently with more than 400,000 members—nearly half of the lawyers in the country. Over 100 years old, the ABA is the chief national professional association for lawyers. The ABA carries a strong voice in matters affecting substantive law, the judiciary, and the administration of justice. Among the ABA's many contributions to the profession is the promulgation of model codes of ethics.

The ABA first published the **Canons of Professional Ethics** in 1908. These Canons were patterned after the first code of ethics for lawyers adopted in 1887 by the Alabama State Bar Association. Prior to the adoption of state codes, lawyer conduct was governed largely by common law and some statutes. The 1908 Canons consisted of 32 statements of very general principles about attorney conduct, mainly conduct in the courtroom. Many states adopted these ABA Canons through court rule or statute.

In 1969, the ABA published a new code, called the **Model Code of Professional Responsibility**, designed as a prototype for states to use in developing their own codes. The Model Code was adopted in whole or in part by every state and is still followed in a few states. After six years of study, debate, drafting, and redrafting, a new code, called the **Model Rules of Professional Conduct**, was adopted by the ABA in 1983.

In August 1997, the American Bar Association launched a new review of the Model Rules, designated **Ethics 2000**. Major revisions to the Model Rules were adopted in 2001 and 2003. The current versions of the Model Code and Model Rules are cited throughout this book. The relevant ethics rules in your jurisdiction should always be consulted for the current and accurate rules governing lawyer and paralegal conduct.

As of this writing, 43 states plus the District of Columbia and the Virgin Islands have adopted some version of the new Model Rules; six jurisdictions still have codes based on the Model Code. California has its own code, which is based on neither the Model Code nor Model Rules.

Model Code of Professional Responsibility
ABA's code of ethics, designed as a prototype for states to use in developing their own codes, adopted in 1969

Model Rules of Professional Conduct
ABA's revised prototype code of ethics, adopted by the ABA in 1983

3. State Statutes, Ethics Opinions, and Case Law

While the state codes of ethics contain most of the rules with which we are concerned in this text, statutes also govern attorney conduct. For example, some states have statutes that prohibit attorneys from engaging in certain conduct in their professional capacity as lawyers and provide for criminal and civil penalties. As we will see in Chapter 2, most states have laws that make the unauthorized practice of law a crime, usually a misdemeanor.

Usually not binding on attorneys but often consulted when ethical issues arise are *ethics advisory opinions* of state and local bar associations and the ABA. Bar associations have ethics committees that consider ethical dilemmas posed to them by attorney-members. The committees

Ethics advisory opinions
Written opinions from a bar association interpreting relevant ethical precedents and applying them to an ethical issue

write opinions that are published in bar journals and manuals to give additional guidance to other attorneys facing similar dilemmas. Courts sometimes cite advisory opinions as persuasive authority. Some state and ABA advisory opinions will be cited in this text.

Of course, **disciplinary cases** and **court decisions** involving lawyer malpractice, disqualification, and breach of lawyers' duties also contribute to the body of law that governs lawyer conduct.

4. Sanctions and Remedies

Disbarment
Rescinding of a lawyer's license to practice

Four main formal sanctions imposed on lawyers for ethical misconduct are available to a state's highest court or other disciplinary body. The most severe sanction is *disbarment*, in which a lawyer's license to practice law is revoked. Disbarment is only imposed for the most egregious violations or when there is a long-term pattern of serious unethical conduct. While disbarment is in theory "permanent," most admitting authorities do occasionally re-admit a disbarred lawyer after some period of time if the lawyer can demonstrate complete rehabilitation.

Suspension
Attorney is deprived of the right to practice law for a specified period of time

Probation
Attorney can practice, but certain requirements must be met

The second most severe sanction is *suspension*, in which the attorney is deprived of the right to practice law for a specified period of time. Some disciplinary authorities also have the option of imposing *probation*, under which the disciplined attorney may continue to practice on the condition that certain requirements are met, such as restitution to injured clients, passing an ethics examination, attending ethics "school," or participating in counseling. Sometimes a suspension is stayed but the attorney remains on probation for some period during which the disciplinary body may reinstitute the suspension if further ethical violations come to light.

Reprimand
Warning that ethical violations have occurred and will not be tolerated

The mildest sanction is a *reprimand*, sometimes called a *reproval*. This action represents a slap on the hand, a warning that the conduct will not be tolerated. Reprimands may be made public (placed in the public record and published in a bar journal) or private (confidentially communicated in writing to the attorney). In either case, the reprimand becomes part of the attorney's record. A reprimand is considered further in determining the appropriate sanction if other violations occur.

In deciding the appropriate sanction, the disciplinary body considers the nature and severity of the offense and whether the attorney has a record of prior misconduct. Other **aggravating and mitigating factors** may be taken into account, such as the extent to which the attorney cooperated in the investigation and appreciates the seriousness of the matter, the attorney's reputation and contributions to the community through public service and professional activities, the circumstances surrounding the offense and the extent to which these make the attorney more or less culpable for the conduct, and whether the offense was a one-time incident and is unlikely to be repeated or was pattern of misconduct over time. The attorney's remorse and willingness to remedy the problems that may have led to the conduct are critical in determining the sanction.

In addition to direct discipline by the court or state bar, an attorney may be **prosecuted criminally** for violations of statutes governing attorney conduct or conduct that may relate to an attorney's practice, such as laws prohibiting solicitation of clients in hospitals and jails and laws limiting the methods that can be used to collect debts. Civil *legal malpractice* lawsuits brought by former clients also constitute a major incentive for conforming to ethical requirements and standards of practice. (See Chapter 7 for more on legal malpractice.) The courts also exercise **contempt power** to sanction lawyers appearing before them who engage in improper conduct that affects the administration of justice and the smooth functioning of the courts. (See Chapter 8, Special Issues in Advocacy.) And the courts also play a major role in deciding on matters in the area of conflicts of interest because they rule on **motions to disqualify counsel**, which are usually brought by the opposing counsel who claims that a lawyer or law firm has a conflict of interest that jeopardizes client confidentiality. (See Chapter 4, Conflicts of Interest.) It should be noted that disciplinary action may be taken not only against lawyers who are directly involved with the conduct of paralegals, but also against those who have supervisory or managerial authority or are partners in a law firm. Under recent changes to the rules in many states, law firms may also be held responsible for ethical misconduct, depending upon the nature of the violation and the surrounding circumstances and actions by the firm. (See ABA Model Rule 5.3, discussed below.)

B.   Regulation of Paralegals

1.   A Brief History of the Paralegal Profession

The use of specially educated and trained nonlawyers to assist lawyers in the delivery of legal services is a relatively new phenomenon in the history of American law. The concept is only about 35 years old.

The paralegal field's **beginnings** can be traced directly back to the late 1960s, when the rapidly rising cost of legal services, combined with the lack of access to legal services for low- and middle-income Americans, caused government, consumer groups, and the organized bar to take a close look at the way legal services were being delivered. Many innovations were instituted, including legal aid clinics, storefront law offices, and prepaid legal plans. Private law firms expanded their use of technology and began to manage and plan their operations more carefully. The concept of using the services of trained nonlawyers to perform certain legal functions arose. In 1967, the ABA endorsed the concept of the paralegal and in 1968 established its first committee on paralegals, which has since become the **Standing Committee on Paralegals**.

During the late 1960s and early 1970s, the ABA and several state and local bar associations conducted studies on the use of paralegals. While many studies showed initial attorney resistance to the idea of paralegals, the actual use of paralegals rose. The first **formal paralegal training** programs were established in the early 1970s and have grown from 11 programs in 1971 to a thousand. In 1974, the ABA adopted guidelines for the paralegal curriculum, and in 1975 began to approve paralegal programs under those guidelines. There were nine paralegal programs approved that year and there are now over 250.

In the mid-1970s, the first professional paralegal associations were formed. Dozens of groups cropped up locally. The **National Federation of Paralegal Associations** (NFPA) and **National Association of Legal Assistants** (NALA) were established. Paralegal educators formed their own organization, the **American Association for Paralegal Education** (AAfPE). In the 1980s, a group of paralegal supervisors and managers started the **Legal Assistant Management Association,** which recently changed its name to the **International Paralegal Management Association** (IPMA).

In 1976, the first voluntary **certification** program was established by NALA, called the **Certified Legal Assistant** (CLA) program. It was also at about this time that the U.S. Bureau of Labor Statistics predicted that a paralegal career would be one of the fastest-growing occupations. Job opportunities expanded dramatically in the 1980s, especially in large private law firms, and paralegals started to work as independent contractors.

In the 1990s, NALA developed advanced specialist examinations in a variety of areas, which are taken by paralegals who have already earned the CLA designation. NALA recently adopted the designation **Certified Paralegal (CP)**, which CLAs can use instead of CLA if they prefer, in recognition of the trend toward greater use of this title. In 1996, NFPA developed a certification examination called the **Paralegal Advanced Competency Examination** (PACE). This program is designed for experienced paralegals who may use the designation **Registered Paralegal** upon passing the examination. In 2004, **NALS, the Association for Legal Professionals** (formerly the National Association of Legal Secretaries) launched the **Professional Paralegal (PL)** certification examination program.

NFPA's current membership is about 14,000, with more than 50 affiliated local associations. NALA has 6,000 individual members and more than 90 affiliates. Nearly 13,000 paralegals have been certified by NALA and another 1,100 have gone on to become certified in specialty

NFPA
National Federation of Paralegal Associations

NALA
National Association of Legal Assistants

AAfPE
American Association for Paralegal Education

IPMA
International Paralegal Management Association

NALS
An Association for Legal Professionals

areas. IPMA, representing supervisors of paralegals mainly in large law firms and corporate law departments, has about 500 members and has local chapters in major cities across the United States and in Canada. AAfPE now has more than 300 institutional members.

2.   Direct Regulation of Paralegals: Certification and Licensing

Definitions of Terms

Certification of an occupation is usually a form of voluntary recognition of an individual who has met specifications of the granting agency or organization. Both NALA's CLA program and the NFPA's PACE are forms of certification. *Licensing* is a mandatory form of regulation in which a government agency grants permission to an individual to engage in an occupation and/or use a particular title. Only a person who is so licensed may engage in this occupation. There is no licensing of paralegals at the present time in the United States. Attorneys are "licensed" by the state in which they practice. Typically, both licensing and certification require applicants to pass an examination and meet specified requirements regarding education and moral character.

The terms *paralegal* and *legal assistant* are used interchangeably in this book, but the term "paralegal" is favored because of the trend nationwide toward using this title. In recent years, all of the professional entities involved in the paralegal profession have recognized "paralegal" as the favored term, and many, including the ABA Standing Committee on Paralegals and the International Paralegal Management Association, have changed their own names to reflect the common usage. In part, the change has come about because lawyers in many firms started to give the title "legal assistant" to their legal secretaries. The movement away from the title "secretary" complicates the matter as no new title has emerged that fits this role in the legal services delivery team.

The ABA adopted a **definition** of *paralegal/legal assistant* in 1997, which reads:

> A legal assistant or paralegal is a person, qualified by education, training or work experience, who is employed or retained by a lawyer, law office, corporation, governmental agency or other entity and who performs specifically delegated substantive legal work for which a lawyer is responsible.

This definition recognizes the progress that has been made in the paralegal occupation and moves from a vision of lawyer supervision to "lawyer responsibility" for paralegal work. Some organizations, like NFPA, would like the definition to be broader so that it encompasses nonlawyers who provide legal services directly to the public under the authority of a statute or other law.

Certification
Voluntary recognition of an occupation based on a person's having met specified qualifications

Licensing
Mandatory form of regulation in which a government agency grants permission to engage in an occupation and/or use a title

Regulation of Supervised Paralegals

Throughout the history of the paralegal profession, the need for certification or licensing has been raised and debated. In the last 15 years, this debate has become intense, and for the first time some minimal forms of regulation have been adopted.

Early in the profession's evolution, Oregon had a **voluntary certification** program for legal assistants, which was abolished after a few years because of low participation. Texas adopted a voluntary certification program for paralegals in 1994. Texas administers its program through its Board of Legal Specialization. Certification examinations are given in a number of areas, including family law, civil trial practice, criminal law, and personal injury practice. Certification, valid for five years, is renewable upon demonstrated participation in continuing education, employment by a Texas attorney, and substantial involvement in a specialty area. Nearly a thousand paralegals have been certified since the program began. In 2004, the North Carolina Supreme Court adopted a similar voluntary certification program, which is being implemented at the time of this writing. Other states are working on voluntary certification plans as well, including New Jersey and Kentucky.

The national paralegal associations continue to promote voluntary certification—NALA through its CLA/CP and CLA Specialist program, NFPA through its PACE, and now NALS through its PP (Professional Paralegal) designation. On a national level, these organizations want to be poised for regulation if and when it comes by having proven examinations in place that can be adopted by states. At the state level, three statewide organizations have joined with NALA to develop state-specific certification examinations that can be taken by CLAs. These three organizations are the California Alliance of Paralegal Associations, Florida Legal Assistants, Inc., which has had an examination since the early 1980s, and the Louisiana State Paralegal Association.

A few states have taken steps toward the **regulation** of paralegals. In 1999, Maine adopted a statute that defines "paralegal" and "legal assistant" and restricts the use of the title to those persons. Anyone who does not fit the definition, which requires the person to work under lawyer supervision, may be fined. A South Dakota statute defines *legal assistant/paralegal,* sets up minimum qualifications, and delineates ethical guidelines for attorneys to follow in working with paralegals. The law subjects the supervising attorney to sanctions for failing to meet the ethical standards. Both Florida and Arizona limit the use of the title "paralegal" and similar titles by Supreme Court Rule to persons working under lawyer supervision. A proposal for mandatory licensing of Wisconsin paralegals has been working its way through bar committees and the state Supreme Court for about five years, and both Florida and Missouri currently have active proposals for licensing as well.

The biggest step toward regulation was taken by California in 2000 when it enacted a statute that defines who may use the title "paralegal" (and comparable titles) and sets qualifications and continuing education requirements. The statute requires paralegals to be supervised by lawyers and distinguishes them from "legal document assistants," a title used in other state legislation for nonlawyer legal service providers. This statute is not enforceable through any particular state agency and no registration or licensing is involved. Criminal penalties are available, however, for anyone using the title while providing legal services directly to the public.

The ABA has issued policy statements that reject the notion that paralegals should be licensed, indicating that the public is protected by the extensive ethical and disciplinary requirements to which lawyers are subject. In 1997, IPMA issued a statement in which it took the position that licensing of paralegals who work under lawyer supervision was unnecessary for the protection of the public and would unduly interfere with a lawyer's prerogative to hire the best-qualified person for the job. NALA is also against mandatory licensing, mainly on the basis that there is no need for it to protect the public. NFPA promotes regulation that would enhance and expand the role of the paralegal.

The Regulation Debate

Arguments **favoring licensing** of paralegals who work under lawyer supervision center mainly on the benefits to the paralegal occupation, in terms of establishing it as a separate and autonomous but allied legal career, one with its own identity and a concomitant increase in societal status and rewards.

Proponents believe regulation would:

- provide appropriate public recognition for paralegals as important members of the legal services delivery team
- ensure high standards and quality of work by paralegals
- expand the use of paralegals, thereby expanding access to legal services and lowering costs
- provide assurance to clients and employers of paralegals of their qualifications
- encourage needed standardization in paralegal education

Some proponents favor regulation only if it permits paralegals to expand their role by permitting them to engage in work that they are not currently permitted to do under state statutes and case law.

The primary arguments **against licensing** of traditional paralegals are that licensing would:

- not benefit the public because attorney-employers are already fully accountable to clients
- increase the cost of legal services
- stifle the development of the profession

- inappropriately limit entry into the profession
- unnecessarily standardize paralegal education
- restrict the movement of paralegals into new areas of practice or duties

One important concern cited by opponents is the practical difficulty of determining exactly what legal tasks and functions could be assigned exclusively to paralegals through this *regulatory* process.

Nonlawyer Legal Service Providers

In the last 25 years, we have witnessed a resurgence of interest in reforming the legal services delivery system as the lack of **access to legal services** by low- and middle-income Americans has become increasingly apparent. Study after study has indicated that the most Americans do not have access to legal services, cannot afford an attorney when they need one, and do not know how to go about finding an attorney. Low- and middle-income persons in particular are seeking other ways to access the legal system and are more frequently than ever representing themselves with or without the assistance of self-help manuals and nonlawyers. For example, in some parts of the country, more than three-quarters of marital dissolutions are handled in propria persona.

The ABA and some state supreme courts and bars have researched and studied access issues extensively, with an eye toward increased use of nonlawyers as one method of addressing the unmet need for legal services. Most studies find some form of nonlawyer practice in virtually every jurisdiction; many states have considered proposals related to the regulation of nonlawyer practice. Recommendations usually include expanding the role of supervised paralegals and granting limited authority to nonlawyers to provide legal services, with appropriate oversight and regulation to protect consumers.

In some states, court rules and legislation have authorized nonlawyers to perform certain tasks that might otherwise be reserved exclusively to lawyers. For example, some courts have ***court facilitators*** who assist persons who represent themselves in completing forms to be filed with the court, a function that might require the facilitator to give legal advice. Court facilitators have been widely used in family law courts. California has legislation that regulates nonlawyer legal services providers, called ***legal document assistants*** and ***unlawful detainer assistants***, by requiring them to register in the county in which they work. This statute does not, however, expand their role; in fact, it specifically prohibits them from providing legal advice. Similarly, Arizona recently adopted court rules much like California's statutes, which authorize ***legal document preparers*** to assist the public (without providing legal advice, of course). Illinois saw proposed legislation that would have created a system of legal document preparers, but it was not passed.

Legal document assistants/legal document preparers
Nonlawyers who are authorized to assist members of the public in representing themselves, but who are not permitted to give legal advice or represent clients in court

While not much progress has been made officially in expanding the role of nonlawyers in the delivery of legal services, nonlawyer practitioners continue to provide assistance to people who need legal help—and the debate continues. In one state, Washington, the Supreme Court created the Practice of Law Board with the purpose of increasing access to legal services. The Board is considering rules that would establish a system for limited nonlawyer practice in designated areas of need. This Washington program, if it is implemented, will be the most progressive plan anywhere for increasing access to legal services through the use of nonlawyers. (For more on nonlawyer practitioners, see Chapter 2, Unauthorized Practice of Law.)

3. State Guidelines for the Utilization of Paralegal Services

In an effort to promote the effective and ethical use of paralegals, some states have adopted guidelines to assist attorneys in working with paralegals. These guidelines, directed specifically to attorneys, highlight the key ethical matters that come into play when a nonlawyer is involved in the delivery of legal services, such as unauthorized practice of law, confidentiality, conflicts, and fee splitting.

At the time of this writing, about 30 states have some kind of guidelines. In a handful of states, the guidelines have been adopted by the highest court of the state. In a few states, the legislature has acted. In most states, the guidelines have been approved by the state bar association, a state bar committee on paralegals, or both. Some of the states that have adopted guidelines have also prepared accompanying statements on the effective use of paralegals.

In 1991, the ABA adopted **Model Guidelines for the Utilization of Legal Assistant Services**, which were revised and renamed as the **Model Guidelines for the Utilization of Paralegal Services**, in 2004. Included in Appendix A at page 197, these guidelines were written to provide a model for states that want to adopt such guidelines, and to encourage attorneys to use paralegals effectively and appropriately. Several jurisdictions have either adopted the ABA guidelines or amended their existing guidelines in response to the ABA model.

4. Paralegal Associations' Codes of Ethics and Guidelines

The two major national paralegal professional associations both have codes of ethics to guide the conduct of their members. NALA calls its code the **Code of Ethics and Professional Responsibility**, included in Appendix B at page 217. NFPA has a **Model Code of Ethics and Professional Responsibility**, which it encourages its affiliated local associations to adopt (included in Appendix C at page 221). It also has Guidelines for the Enforcement of the Model Code to establish mechanisms for enforcing the rules, which are not included in the appendices. These Guidelines set forth procedures for the investigation and prosecution of ethics code violations for hearings and appeals and for a system of sanctions.

NALA has both individual members and affiliated local chapters. Members sign a statement of commitment to NALA's code on their membership application, and a mechanism is in place at the national level to investigate allegations of code violations and to remove from membership or to remove the CLA designation from any member who has violated the code.

NFPA issues ethics opinions on current concerns of interest to practicing paralegals. These opinions have addressed such matters as communications over the Internet and the role of paralegals who work in the corporate setting.

Both organizations make literature on ethics available. Their addresses, phone numbers, and Web sites are:

- The National Association of Legal Assistants 1516 S. Boston, Suite 200 Tulsa, Oklahoma 74119 918-587-6828 www.nala.org
- The National Federation of Paralegal Associations P.O. Box 33108 Kansas City, Missouri 64114-0108 816-941-4000 www.paralegals.org

In addition to the two national organizations, some local and regional associations have created and adopted their own ethics rules, borrowed from NALA, NFPA, and the ABA. Examples of two excellent local codes are those of the California Alliance of Paralegal Associations and the Virginia Alliance of Legal Assistant Associations, whose guidelines also include educational standards for legal assistants.

5. Responsibility of Lawyers and Paralegals for Paralegal Conduct

Because paralegals are not lawyers, they are neither directly bound by state codes of ethics for lawyers nor subject to direct sanctions for breaches of those codes. Without certification, licensing, or some other form of direct regulation of the paralegal occupation, paralegals are bound to comply with high standards of professional behavior primarily because the attorneys for whom they work are responsible for any lapses in their behavior. Lawyers therefore have a strong incentive to ensure that the paralegals they employ are familiar with the state's ethics code and comply with it. Some states specifically require lawyers to take affirmative steps to educate the paralegals they employ about ethical obligations and to ensure their compliance.

The ABA Model Rules of Professional Conduct contain an important section on supervision, Model Rule 5.3, which requires partners, supervising lawyers, and lawyers with managerial authority to "make reasonable efforts" to ensure that nonlawyer conduct is compatible with the lawyer's ethical obligations. Further, a lawyer is responsible for a paralegal's unethical conduct if the lawyer ordered it or ratified it, or if the lawyer is a partner in the firm, has managerial authority, or is the paralegal's supervisor and fails to take remedial action. Most states follow the principles of this rule and hold lawyers responsible for the unethical conduct of paralegals and other nonlawyers who work for them. As a result, lawyers may be disciplined for the unethical conduct of their paralegals.

Lawyers are also liable in civil suits for the negligent conduct of paralegals that they employ or retain. Paralegals themselves are potential defendants in civil legal malpractice suits brought by clients who believe paralegals in their attorney's employment may have acted negligently. Paralegals are subject to the same general tort principles that apply to lawyers and other professionals; that is, they are liable for negligent or intentional misconduct that injures a client.

Because clients always name their attorney and rarely name paralegals as defendants in malpractice cases, there is little case law available defining the standards of conduct to which paralegals are held. As a general rule, paralegals would be held to the same standard of care, skill, and knowledge common to other paralegals, so long as they do not hold themselves out as attorneys and they perform typical paralegal tasks. Most lawyers carry insurance that provides coverage in the event that a client sues paralegals. This coverage ordinarily extends to all the nonlawyer personnel who are employed by the lawyer.

REVIEW QUESTIONS

1. When and why did the paralegal profession begin?
2. What are the two main professional associations for paralegals?
3. What is certification? What is licensing?
4. What state(s) have some form of voluntary certification of legal assistants?
5. What are the national associations' programs for paralegal certification called? How do they differ?
6. What is limited licensure? How do nonlawyer legal service providers differ from traditional paralegals who work under the supervision of attorneys?

7. What are the arguments in favor of the licensing of traditional paralegals? The arguments against?
8. To what extent are paralegals directly regulated at the present time?
9. How many states have guidelines for the utilization of paralegals? What is the purpose of these guidelines?
10. What are the ABA Model Guidelines for the Utilization of Paralegal Services?
11. Do NALA and NFPA have rules on the conduct of paralegals? If so, how are these rules enforced?
12. May a paralegal who is negligent while working on a client's case be held liable for malpractice? May this paralegal's attorney-employer also be held liable? If so, on what grounds?
13. Is an attorney responsible for a paralegal's breaches of conduct such that the appropriate state body may discipline the attorney? Can the same state body discipline the paralegal?

HYPOTHETICALS

1. Lawyer Ann Adams and paralegal Ben Burns have been hired by client Carl Carlson to sue a grocery store where Carl, who is 85, fell down when he slipped in a puddle of water in the produce aisle. Ann delegates the task of preparing the complaint to Ben. Ben mis-calendars the date that the answer must be filed and the statute of limitations passes. What are Carl's remedies? Can he name Ben as a defendant if he brings a lawsuit? What kind of lawsuit can he bring? What will happen if he reports the matter to the proper disciplinary authorities? Is the failure to file the complaint on time an ethical breach? Can Ann and/or Ben be disciplined for this conduct by the state supreme court or another disciplinary authority? What if Ann already has a private reproval on her record for a similar violation? What if three other clients have reported Ann for failing to return calls and show up for court dates?

2. The state of Aurora is determined to regulate paralegals. A group of paralegals is lobbying hard for regulation so that the paralegals can be distinguished from nonlawyer legal service providers who often use the title "paralegal." Two years earlier, the Aurora supreme court struck down legislation that would have allowed nonlawyers to represent clients in workers' compensation cases. The proposed legislation regulating paralegals is passed and signed into law. A group of lawyers files suit, requesting that the court declare the legislation invalid. Under what theory might the court strike down the legislation? Would the same result be likely in all jurisdictions? If the legislation is found unconstitutional and struck down, what should the paralegals do to get the regulation they want?

DISCUSSION QUESTIONS AND PROJECTS

1. Find out where you can locate the recent decisions of disciplinary cases in your jurisdiction. What are the usual reasons for discipline? Do any of these cases involve paralegals?
2. Research your state statutes to find where paralegals are mentioned.
3. Obtain the position papers on regulation of all the paralegal-related groups mentioned in this chapter and compare their views. Have a debate in class. Bring in representatives of the local paralegal associations to discuss their views.
4. Research in phone books and other resources to see how many nonlawyer legal service providers are working in your area. How many are there? Who uses their services? What titles do they use? In what areas of law practice do they work?
5. Does your state or local bar association allow paralegals to join as associate members? Does your state or local bar have a committee that concerns itself with paralegals? Does your state or local bar have guidelines for attorneys who work with paralegals? Has it considered licensing of traditional paralegals or independent paralegals who provide services directly to the public?
6. Who is covered and not covered by the ABA definition of *paralegal/legal assistant*? Do you like this definition? Why or why not? How would you change it?
7. Is voluntary certification through NALA or NFPA popular in your state or local area? Why or why not?

SELECTED CASES

Bennion, VanCamp, Hagen & Ruhl v. Kassler Escrow, Inc., 96 Wash. 2d 443, 635 P.2d 730 (1981) (case in which state supreme court struck down legislation relating to the practice of law).

Florida Bar v. Lawless, 640 So. 2d 1098 (Fla. 1994) (freelance paralegal whose mistakes resulted in lawyer discipline).

Musselman v. Willoughby Corp., 230 Va. 337, 337 S.E.2d 724 (1985) (paralegal involved in malpractice).

Unauthorized Practice of Law Committee v. State Department of Workers' Compensation, 543 A.2d 662 (R.I. 1998) (case in which state supreme court upheld legislation relating to the practice of law).

SELECTED REFERENCES

ABA Model Rules of Professional Conduct, Rule 5.3 Also see your jurisdiction's rules of professional conduct and guidelines for paralegals, if any.

Unauthorized Practice of Law

This chapter outlines the limitations on who can practice law, especially those limitations that most affect paralegals. Chapter 2 covers:

- the history of the unauthorized practice of law from the colonial era to the present
- definitions of the practice of law
- the attorney's ethical responsibility to prevent the unauthorized practice of law and to supervise paralegals
- key areas of concern to paralegals in the unauthorized practice of law, including:

  - court appearances, depositions, pleadings, and giving legal advice
  - establishing the attorney-client relationship and setting fees
  - job functions that may constitute the unauthorized practice of law
  - nonlawyer practice before administrative agencies
  - disclosure of the paralegal's status

A. A Brief History of the Unauthorized Practice of Law

Limitations on who can practice law in the United States can be traced back to the **colonial era**. At that time a proliferation of untrained practitioners caused local courts to adopt rules requiring attorneys who appeared before them to have a license granted by the court. Additional rules adopted during this period limited the amount of fees that could be charged and dictated that an attorney could not refuse to take a case. The stated purposes of these rules were to prevent stirring up of litigation by unscrupulous "pettifoggers" and "mercenary" attorneys, to stop incompetence that harmed not only the clients but the administration of justice and dignity of the courts, and to prevent exploitative, excessive fees.

The rules establishing entry to the practice of law evolved slowly and unevenly through most of the nation's history. In the **mid to late 1800s**, state and local bar associations began to gain strength, and the first **unauthorized practice of law** (UPL) statutes were passed. These laws prohibited court appearances by anyone not licensed as an attorney, prohibited the practice of law by court personnel such as bailiffs, and made it illegal for an unlicensed person to hold himself or herself out as an attorney and for a nonlawyer to form a partnership with a lawyer.

UPL
Unauthorized practice of law

The definition of *practice of law* being formulated in these cases was gradually broadened to cover activities beyond court appearances. Most early cases defined the term as the preparation of documents by which legal rights are secured. New justifications for restricting the right to practice law to licensed attorneys emerged, including the lawyer's professional independence, moral character, and special training, as well as the fact that, unlike unlicensed practitioners, lawyers are subject to sanctions for breaches of duty or competence.

Some legal historians and commentators believe that the height of unauthorized practice restrictions came during the **Depression**, when lawyers needed most to protect their economic interests from competition. Bar associations became especially powerful trade organizations during this era. Unauthorized practice statutes were passed in virtually all states, which made it a crime to practice law without a license. The definition of *practice of law* was further expanded to include "all services customarily rendered by lawyers." In the **1930s**, the ABA and state bars entered into agreements with accountants, collection agencies, insurance adjusters, life insurance underwriters, publishers, realtors, and other professionals that delineated the law-related activities that nonlawyers could perform without moving into the lawyer's realm of the practice of law. These agreements were rescinded in the 1970s when it became apparent that they would be found illegal under the Sherman Antitrust Act.

Criminal prosecutions and civil suits to restrain unauthorized practice also slowed during this period. The courts in several states found that the sale of legal self-help kits and books did not constitute the unauthorized practice of law. And the movement to expand access to legal services by alternative means started to take hold.

The **1980s and '90s** saw a resurgence of unauthorized practice prosecutions because of the increased number of independent "paralegals" providing low-cost legal services directly to the public. In a 2005 study, nearly half the states reported active enforcement of the unauthorized practice of law, although ten states indicated that they do little or no enforcement. Florida leads the nation in UPL enforcement, spending more than a million dollars annually.

B.   Trends in the Unauthorized Practice of Law

1.   Nonlawyer Legal Service Providers and Lawyers Aiding in the Unauthorized Practice of Law

Many factors together have created the need for *nonlawyer legal services providers*: the decrease in funding for the legal services corporation that formerly supplied legal services to persons of low and moderate incomes; the increase in the need for legal services because of the proliferation and complexity of laws; and the rising cost of legal services provided by lawyers, which makes it difficult and sometimes impossible for even middle-income Americans to employ a lawyer when they need one.

Most nonlawyer legal service providers work in the **areas of practice** in which low- and moderate-income people need assistance, such as in landlord/tenant matters, divorce, child support, bankruptcy, and immigration. Some run "typing services" that assist persons only by typing documents, usually to be filed with the court, after the "customer" fills in the blanks. Others provide more complete information and assistance, helping the customer decide what forms to use, what information to include on the forms, and where to file them. Nonlawyer legal service providers use a variety of titles, including "independent paralegal," "legal technician," or "document preparer." As noted in Chapter 1, California uses the titles "**legal document assistant**" and "unlawful detainer assistant" in statutes that require such persons to register with the county in which they work. Similarly, Arizona uses "**legal document preparer**" as the designation for its nonlawyer legal service providers.

Legal document preparer/assistant
A nonlawyer legal service provider who is authorized by court rule or statute to assist persons in representing themselves, without being authorized to give legal advice or appear in court

While the unmet need for legal services is well documented, lawyers are largely **opposed** to giving up any of their traditional functions to nonlawyers. Clearly, lawyers have both monopolistic and economic reasons for this stance and legitimate professional and societal concerns about the quality of legal services that someone not trained as a lawyer can provide.

Defendants in widely publicized **prosecutions** in several states have argued unsuccessfully that they are not giving legal advice but are simply assisting laypersons in the preparation of legal documents. Some defendants in unauthorized practice prosecutions have argued that a statutory power of attorney from a client gives a nonlawyer the authority to represent the client in litigation although this argument has not met with success either. Some defendants have argued, to no avail, a public necessity defense based on the lack of availability of legal services for their clients.

Meanwhile, several states have seen proposed **legislation** that would define the practice of law more expansively or would institute harsher penalties for the unauthorized practice of law, or have stepped up their efforts to prosecute unauthorized practice cases. Bankruptcy reform legislation adopted in the 1990s contains provisions that limit the role of nonlawyer practitioners in Chapter 7 filings, including barring the use of the terms "legal" or "paralegal" in business names. Several states have taken action to regulate nonlawyers who assist persons with immigration matters. While federal statutes establish nationwide standards for accredited visa consultants, some immigration "consultants" do not fall within the reach of these federal laws, and widespread abuses of clients have been documented in the immigrant community.

Several states have determined that the **preparation of living trust documents** constitutes the practice of law, thus paving the way for the prosecution of many companies that market living trust plans. Most decisions hold that the client's decision on whether a living trust is appropriate, the attendant preparation and execution of documents, and the funding of the trust are functions that require an attorney's judgment and involvement. Lawyers in several jurisdictions have been disciplined for aiding in the unauthorized practice of law where they have participated in businesses that promoted and sold living trusts. Most courts find that these lawyers have abdicated their responsibility to advise clients about the ramifications of such an important legal decision as making a living trust. The lawyers in these cases either failed to supervise the work of their employees in counseling clients and preparing the documents for them or were asked to review documents by the nonlawyer operators who had already advised the clients and prepared documents for them with no attorney involvement whatsoever.

Finally, there is a growing trend toward the **discipline of lawyers** who are running large-volume practices and inadequately supervising

their paralegals and other employees. In most of these cases, the paralegals are accepting clients, having them sign retainer agreements,
preparing legal documents for them, and counseling them about their
legal rights with little or no lawyer involvement and no direct relationship between the lawyer and the client. In some cases, there has also been
unlawful solicitation of clients by the nonlawyers, coupled with compensation arrangements that violate rules against fee splitting and/or
with partnerships between lawyers and nonlawyers to engage in the
practice of law. These fee-related and solicitation issues are covered in
Chapters 5 and 6.

2.   Multijurisdictional Practice Issues

In the last few years, the legal community has seen growing concern about **lawyers who are providing legal services across state
lines** — that is, engaged, sometimes unethically, in *multijurisdictional
practice*. Under longstanding traditions and rules, lawyers may be admitted *pro hac vice* by courts to represent clients in litigated matters in states
in which they are not licensed to practice. This special court permission
to practice in the state applies only to the case in which the lawyer is
acting. In other situations, the out-of-state lawyer employs co-counsel
who is licensed in the state where the matter is being worked on.
However, other less clear situations are arising more frequently because
of the global nature of the economy and the mobility of lawyers and
clients.

pro hac vice
Special rules that allow
a lawyer to represent a
client in a state court
in a state where the
lawyer is not licensed
to practice

For example, a lawyer who represents a corporation may have to
handle litigation and transactional work that is done partially or wholly
in another state or relates to an incident or transaction in another state.
The issue arises as to whether the lawyer is engaging in the unauthorized practice of law when this work is undertaken. The recently ABA
Model Rules (Model Rule 5.5) have addressed this by providing **"safe
harbors"** for lawyers who are in these situations. In addition to these
traditional exceptions, lawyers may participate in alternative dispute resolution in one state if related to work in the state where they are
licensed, may do other work reasonably related to work where they
are licensed, and may advise corporate clients in a state where they are
not licensed, unless it would require pro hac vice admission.

Many states have adopted some version of this new rule, but some
states are not as generous as these rules are with out-of-state lawyers. At
the time of this writing, about ten states have passed rules that require
out-of-state lawyers who work for corporations to obtain a "limited
license," which permits them to practice only for their corporate
employer. It looks like several more states will follow this model as they
examine the changes proposed by the revised ABA Model Rules. On the
other hand, an ABA resolution was passed in 2000 calling on lawyers to

be vigilant in reporting instances of unauthorized practice of law arising from lawyers practicing in states where they are not licensed.

C. The Practice of Law Defined

No one definitive list of activities constitutes the practice of law. As you can see from the foregoing history, the concept is actually a somewhat flexible one that has changed over time by the push and pull of economics, political and professional activity, public pressure and consumerism, and the complexity of laws. The oft-quoted ABA Model Code of Professional Responsibility (ABA Model Code) EC 3-5 states: "It is neither necessary nor desirable to attempt the formulation of a single, specific definition of what constitutes the practice of law." Court rules, court decisions, statutes, and advisory opinions have produced several tests for determining what defines the practice of law. A few unauthorized practice statutes attempt to define the practice of law; most do not. About 13 have a definition in a court rule. The ABA established a task force in 2002 to create a model definition of the practice of law and found the task fraught with so many differences of opinion that it eventually gave up, and recommended that each state adopt its own definition. The cases interpreting the unauthorized practice of law statutes analyze the facts in determining if specific conduct constitutes the practice of law. In doing so, they may consider:

- Whether the services required the skills and knowledge of an attorney
- Whether the activity is one that is traditionally performed by a lawyer
- Whether the services are essentially legal or are "incidental" to some other transaction

Most comprehensive **definitions** of the practice of law contain some of the foregoing language, and some specifically prohibit anyone but a lawyer from doing the following:

- Preparing pleadings and legal instruments, such as wills, contracts, deeds, leases, trusts
- Preparing any document by which legal rights are secured
- Preparing documents for or making statements to a client that contain legal opinions, arguments, or interpretations of the law
- Appearing in court on behalf of clients or acting as an advocate in a representative capacity
- Giving legal advice — that is, applying knowledge and judgment to a client's particular situation and advising of rights and responsibilities and possible courses of action

The unauthorized practice of law is a **misdemeanor** in more than 30 states and subjects a person to civil contempt proceedings in more than 25 states. A common remedy is **injunctive relief**, which may be requested by prosecutors, bar associations, or courts to stop someone from engaging in activities believed to be the practice of law. This remedy is available in at least 40 jurisdictions. Additional **deterrents** to unauthorized practice include liability for negligent performance, unenforceability of the contract for legal services, court dismissal of an action, and a court's voiding of a judgment in which a nonlawyer represented the prevailing party.

Injunctive relief
A court order to stop someone from engaging in certain conduct; in this chapter, the unauthorized practice of law

D. The Attorney's Responsibility to Prevent the Unauthorized Practice of Law

Rules that prohibit the unauthorized practice of law affect both paralegals who work under lawyer supervision, and nonlawyer legal service providers who deal directly with the public. Ample opportunity exists in a traditional legal setting for a nonlawyer—especially a paralegal—employed by a lawyer to overstep the accepted boundaries into the practice of law.

Lawyers are obligated by various rules not to **aid the unauthorized practice of law**. In many states, a statute prohibits a lawyer from aiding unauthorized practice. Also, in many states, the ethics code contains such a restriction. This prohibition makes attorneys responsible for the training of, supervision of, and delegation of legal work to the nonlawyers whom they employ. The obligation of adequate supervision applies to all areas of ethics—such as confidentiality, conflicts, and competence—but carries special force in the area of unauthorized practice. Allowing a nonlawyer under a lawyer's supervision to engage in the practice of law is considered an abdication of the lawyer's obligation to "exercise independent professional judgment" on behalf of the client. Forming a partnership and dividing legal fees with a nonlawyer are also forbidden under this restriction. Chapter 6 discusses these topics in more depth.

ABA **Model Rule 5.3**, adopted in most states, establishes the duty of a partner, lawyer with managerial authority, and supervising lawyer to make "reasonable efforts to ensure that the firm has in effect measures giving reasonable assurance that the [nonlawyer assistant's] conduct is compatible with the professional obligations of the lawyer." Lawyers with managerial authority and the law firm as a whole were added to the list of lawyers who are ethically responsible for paralegal conduct in the Ethics 2000 revisions. The rule also makes any lawyer who employs or directly retains the nonlawyer responsible for the nonlawyer's ethical breaches if the lawyer orders, knows of, or ratifies the conduct. Partners and supervising and managing lawyers are also responsible if they learn of the conduct and do not take remedial action. The comment to Rule 5.3 speaks to the lawyer's duty to instruct and supervise assistants, especially with regard to confidentiality.

Guideline 1 of the **ABA Model Guidelines** for the Utilization of Paralegal Services phrases this responsibility a bit differently, stating that a lawyer is "responsible for all of the professional actions of a paralegal performing services at the lawyer's direction...." The comment to Guideline 1 emphasizes the lawyer's duty to provide instruction to paralegals concerning ethics and to supervise paralegals. Most state guidelines also refer to the lawyer's responsibility for paralegals' conduct.

Guideline 2 provides an expansive definition of the permissible functions of a paralegal by allowing lawyers to delegate any task except "those tasks proscribed to a nonlawyer by statute, administrative rule or regulation, controlling authority," or the relevant ethics rules.

E. What Constitutes the Unauthorized Practice of Law

1. Making Court Appearances

The one lawyering function that is universally considered to be the exclusive province of licensed attorneys is the representation of a client in court proceedings. You will recall from the brief history of unauthorized practice at the beginning of this chapter that this was the first kind of restriction placed on nonlawyer practitioners in the early days of the United States.

The rationale for this rule is strongly supported by the avowed purposes of unauthorized practice rules generally. Presumably, a court appearance, especially an adversarial one such as a pre-trial motion or a trial, requires **knowledge and skills** that only a lawyer possesses by virtue of long and specialized education, training, and experience. In addition to benefiting from an attorney's special competence, the client is protected by evidentiary rules relating to **attorney-client privilege**. A court appearance is the legal event that decides a client's rights and responsibilities; the client deserves the best protection and most highly **qualified representation** at this critical moment. Further, incompetent representation in court harms not only the client but also the administration of justice.

Attorney-client privilege
Rule of evidence that protects confidential communications between a lawyer and client during their professional relationship

Depositions

The rationale for prohibiting nonlawyer representation in court appearances extends to another aspect of the litigation process: the taking of depositions. In a ***deposition***, one of the key discovery tools, the attorney asks questions in a face-to-face setting of an opposing or a third party. The responses are given orally under oath and are recorded by a court reporter/stenographer, who then produces a verbatim transcript of the questions and answers.

Deposition
Method of discovery in which a witness or party makes statements under oath in question-and-answer form

A deposition may be **introduced in court** as evidence. It carries the same weight as testimony given under oath in court. This testimony may be used at trial to impeach the credibility of a witness or party, or admitted in lieu of direct testimony if the person deposed is no longer available.

The attorney's role in representing a client being deposed includes **making objections** to questions on evidentiary grounds and preserving these objections for the record. Typically, objections are based on relevancy or privilege. The attorney who is deposing a party or witness is performing a task similar to that of direct examination in a trial and therefore must be familiar with the complex rules of evidence.

During a deposition, the attorney asking the questions wants to learn as much as possible about the facts of the case from the witness's perspective, especially if there is information that weakens the opponent's case. This requires not only a full understanding of the factual and legal issues, but also highly developed skills in phrasing **questions** so as to elicit candid and thorough responses.

It is a well-accepted principle that paralegals may not conduct a deposition. State ethics opinions have advised that a lawyer may not allow a paralegal to conduct a deposition even where the paralegal has a written list of attorney-approved questions. The basis for this opinion is that the paralegal would not be qualified to answer any questions that might arise and may be called on to give legal advice.

Paralegals nonetheless play an active role in the discovery and trial phases of the litigation process. They are often the **factual experts** in cases and, as such, work with attorneys in preparing for depositions by assisting in identifying areas of questioning. Many paralegals help to **prepare clients** for the experience of being deposed or testifying at trial. Some accompany clients to independent medical examinations. It is common for paralegals to attend depositions and trials, where they take notes, assist with the introduction of evidence, and otherwise handle last-minute details or unanticipated matters that arise during trial. One open question is whether paralegals can **attend the deposition** of a witness without a supervising lawyer present for the sole purpose of observing the witness. Most ethics experts believe that this is acceptable but a few do not on the basis that the paralegal must state for the record the party he or she is "representing."

Pleadings

In addition to being restricted from representing clients in court and taking depositions, paralegals cannot **sign pleadings** or other documents

Pleading
A written document filed with a court that sets forth the facts of a party's case or the defendant's grounds for defense

filed with the court on behalf of a client. A *pleading* constitutes a written **"appearance"** in court that only a licensed attorney can undertake. Paralegals often prepare pleadings and other documents that are filed with courts. Lawyers must review these documents so that, in essence, the lawyer adopts the paralegal's work and it merges into the lawyer's.

Exceptions

Despite the clear rules and strong rationale for these prohibitions on the nonlawyer's role in court-related matters, a few notable exceptions do exist. Perhaps most important is the general rule of *self-representation*. The right of self-representation in federal courts is guaranteed by statute (28 U.S.C. §1654). Any doubt about the constitutional right to represent oneself in state court was resolved in *Faretta v. California,* 422 U.S. 806 (1975). However, cases in federal and several state courts have determined that the right to self-representation does not encompass a right to be represented by a nonlawyer.

pro per/pro se
A nonlawyer representing himself or herself in a legal matter

Some states have carved out narrow exceptions for the **marital relationship**. A California statute, for instance, permits one nonlawyer spouse to represent the other if both are joined as defendants in the same case and are appearing in **propria persona** (sometimes called *pro per* or *pro se*). However, parents cannot generally represent their children in actions before the courts, nor can a nonlawyer plaintiff represent other nonlawyer co-plaintiffs. In a recent California case, a court held that a nonlawyer representing an estate in pro per could not act for the estate in a nonprobate matter.

All jurisdictions have rules permitting **law students** to engage in limited practice under a lawyer's supervision, and nearly all allow law students to represent clients in court. This exception has been created for the dual purposes of providing practical training for law students and increasing the availability of legal services. Rules governing law student practice vary from jurisdiction to jurisdiction. Most states' rules identify specific qualifications that the law student must meet, require certification of the student by the law school dean and attorney-sponsor, and impose strict limitations on the kind of court appearances that the law student may make without being accompanied by the supervising attorney.

In some local courts, paralegals are allowed to make appearances for their attorney-employers in uncontested matters. A growing number of enlightened state courts permit **paralegal appearances under local court rules**. These rules usually permit paralegals who are registered with the local bar or court to present stipulated, ex parte, and uncontested orders in court when such orders are based solely on the documents in the record. Paralegals must meet specified educational and work experience requirements and must be sponsored by the employing lawyer.

Administrative Agencies

An *administrative agency* is created by state and federal legislatures to provide for the regulation of certain highly specialized fields. A few examples of administrative agencies are the Immigration and Naturalization Service, Patent Office, Social Security Administration at the federal level, and workers' compensation, unemployment insurance, public utility, and disability boards at the state level. Many administrative agencies handle an extremely large volume of cases that do not require much more than a mechanical application of rules. The volume of cases and the specialized nonlegal subject matter involved make it impractical and inefficient to adjudicate disputes in these fields through regular court procedures.

Administrative agencies are **quasi-judicial** in nature, which means that disputes before these agencies are resolved through a hearing similar to though less formal than a trial court. These proceedings are conducted before an administrative law judge or hearing officer or examiner, with advocates representing the parties. Procedures include the issuance of subpoenas, testimony under oath, admission of evidence, and oral and written arguments.

From even this brief description, it should be fairly clear why practice before administrative agencies constitutes the practice of law without some specific **exception** carved out for it. Someone representing a client before an administrative agency needs similar advocacy skills to those required of an attorney representing a client in a trial. The representative must have knowledge of the law and of the procedures used by the agency; must be able to apply this knowledge to the specific facts and context of the case, using the proper analytical and judgmental abilities in doing so; and must be able to advocate the client's case competently in an adversarial setting. While the area of law might be narrower and the rules of evidence and procedure more informal than in a court, the functions of the advocate-representative and the skills necessary for success in this setting are similar to a trial lawyer's.

Despite these similarities, many administrative agencies do not require persons appearing before them to be attorneys. And lawyers and the organized bar have not fought very hard to keep administrative agencies within the exclusive domain of the practice of law. Many administrative cases involve low-income individuals and small amounts of money. The fees paid or awarded by the agencies are also relatively small and provide little economic incentive for a turf battle over unauthorized practice.

The **federal government** has long permitted nonlawyer practice before many of its administrative agencies. The purpose of doing so is twofold: to allow easy access to these agencies and to make the process as informal, efficient, and inexpensive as possible. The Administrative Procedure Act, 5 U.S.C. §555(b) (1994), specifically authorizes individual

Administrative agency
A government body responsible for control and oversight of a particular activity, usually in a highly specialized field

federal administrative agencies to permit nonlawyer practice. It states that persons compelled to appear before an agency may be "accompanied, represented, and advised by counsel or, if permitted by the agency, by other qualified representative." This provision leaves the decision about nonlawyer practice to the agency itself. Some agencies have set very specific criteria (for example, a degree such as a JD or a license as a lawyer or certified public accountant, the recommendation of others admitted to practice, or an exam that must be passed) for nonlawyers to practice before the agencies. A few such federal agencies are the U.S. Patent Office, Internal Revenue Service, and Interstate Commerce Commission. Other agencies allow all nonlawyer representatives without requiring them to meet any specific standards. Examples of these agencies include the National Labor Relations Board, Small Business Administration, Social Security Administration, and Bureau of Indian Affairs.

There is no consistency among the **states** about nonlawyer practice before administrative agencies. Some state statutes authorize representation by nonlawyers before the state's agencies, and some do not. In states that have a strong judicial history supporting the inherent power of the court to oversee the practice of law, legislation authorizing nonlawyer practice before state administrative agencies has been struck down. Most states that have considered the matter endorse a lawyer's use of a paralegal employee to represent a client before an administrative agency when a nonlawyer is otherwise allowed to make such appearances, with the proviso that the paralegal be adequately supervised.

There is occasionally a conflict between the states' authority to regulate the practice of law and the federal government's authority over its administrative agencies. While the Supremacy Clause would appear to preempt state attempts to regulate practice before federal agencies, some states have brought unauthorized practice charges against nonlawyer practitioners who appeared before federal agencies in that state.

2. Establishing the Attorney–Client Relationship

The lawyer–client relationship is a **fiduciary relationship** that is held sacrosanct under ethics rules and statutes that relate to lawyers. Lawyers are held to a high standard of care in serving clients and are bound by duties of loyalty and confidentiality. The lawyers' communications with clients are protected by the attorney-client privilege, discussed in Chapter 3. The privilege and the duties of the lawyer generally begin with the formation of the relationship, which is therefore a very critical matter.

Only the lawyer should agree to represent a client. A paralegal should not state orally or in writing to a prospective client that the lawyer will represent the client and should not sign a retainer or other agreement on behalf of the lawyer. The lawyer must be personally involved in making the decision to undertake the representation and in making the arrangements with the client concerning the **scope of the representation** and the **fees** to be paid for the work. Chapter 6 has a comprehensive discussion of what should be contained in the agreement between the lawyer and the client.

The prohibition on a paralegal establishing the lawyer–client relationship is sometimes stated in terms of the paralegal not **"setting fees"** or **"accepting cases."** One distinction that needs to be made is between "setting" fees and "quoting" fees. The prohibition on "setting fees" does not preclude a paralegal from quoting standard fees to a prospective client or a client, with the proviso that only the attorney can actually contract with the client for legal services and determine the fee that will be charged to handle the client's case.

The ethical violation of setting fees or accepting cases usually arises in combination with other **unauthorized practice** matters. For example, there have been disciplinary cases in which a lawyer is operating a law firm with many nonlawyer employees who handle the cases completely on their own up until the time the case goes to a hearing or to court. Typically, these firms operate in the bankruptcy field. In some of these cases, the nonlawyers (called "paralegals" whether trained as such or not) interview the prospective clients and have them sign a standard retainer agreement without the lawyer's involvement. The nonlawyers usually prepare and file all the documents with little or no lawyer review. The clients do not meet the lawyer until they have to go to court.

Bear in mind that this ethical prohibition on forming the lawyer-client relationship does not protect the lawyer if the client later claims that no relationship was formed. There are cases in which the lawyer was found to have formed the lawyer–client relationship because of the **apparent authority** of the nonlawyer employee to establish that relationship.

Finally, paralegals should be aware that lawyers have **duties to prospective clients**, including the duty not to reveal information learned in a consultation and not to agree to represent a client if there is a conflict. (See Chapters 3 and 4.)

3.   Giving Legal Advice

The prohibition against nonlawyers giving legal advice has its foundation in the same precepts as the prohibition against court appearances by nonlawyers. Formulating a **substantive legal opinion** that will guide a client's conduct is one of the most important and critical functions an attorney undertakes. The attorney's advice lies at the heart of his or her value in society and to the client. Arriving at that legal advice requires the application of the attorney's knowledge of law gained through extensive formal education and experience, judgmental and analytical abilities, and an understanding of the client's situation, context, and goals.

Defining the parameters of "giving legal advice" is complex and contains a lot of gray. In general, giving legal advice may be any of the following:

1. **directing or recommending** a course of action to a client about how to proceed in a matter that may have legal consequences;
2. **explaining** to a client his or her legal rights and responsibilities;
3. **evaluating** the probable outcome of a matter, including litigation;
4. **interpreting** statutes, decisions, or legal documents to a client.

In practice, many paralegals and other nonlawyers in legal settings have frequent contact with clients, which may open the door to potential problems. Paralegals often cite **client contact** as an area of their work that affords considerable job satisfaction. That an important role for paralegals is acting as a liaison with clients deserves no argument. The benefits to the firm and the client are many. Paralegals are often easier to reach by telephone than attorneys, who are frequently unavailable because they are in court or at meetings. Because most paralegals enjoy client contact, they may be more patient with clients than attorneys are, especially with clients who need a lot of attention. Paralegals may use less legal jargon than lawyers and may be able to explain matters in simple language. Finally, it is more cost-efficient for the client and the firm to have the client speak with a paralegal rather than a lawyer.

It is not uncommon for a client to develop an especially strong rapport with a paralegal who works with that client over time, and for the client to **ask questions** of the paralegal that would require the paralegal to give legal advice in response. That the paralegal may know the answer to the question further exacerbates this dilemma. To avoid engaging in unauthorized practice, the paralegal must first consult with the attorney before relaying advice to the client. The paralegal may communicate such advice so long as it is the advice of the attorney. It must be the exact legal opinion of the attorney, however, without expansion or interpretation by the paralegal.

An attorney cannot avoid all client contact by delegating to the paralegal responsibility for all fact gathering and drafting. Attorneys must maintain a **"direct" relationship** with clients and must exercise independent professional judgment. Over-delegation creates great potential for ethical problems to arise, especially if a client becomes dissatisfied.

A Few Examples

There is general agreement that most common paralegal functions can be performed within the bounds of ethics so long as the functions are performed with appropriate supervision and a lawyer reviews the work. However, there are a few matters that not everyone agrees about. One of these is **will executions**. A *will execution* is a relatively simple but critical step in the process of estate planning. Whether by case law or statute, very specific rules exist in every state about the signing and witnessing of wills, including the number of witnesses, their relationship to the person(s) making the will, and their presence during the signing. In early ethics opinions, some state bars took the position that delegating the task of supervising a will execution is tantamount to having the paralegal counsel the client, and therefore constitutes the practice of law. The weight of opinions is now to the contrary, and most states that have addressed the matter say that a paralegal may oversee a will execution or serve as a witness to a will so long as he or she does not give legal advice.

Will execution
The formal process of signing and witnessing a will

Likewise, a few states prohibit attorneys from allowing a paralegal to appear at **real estate closings** without the supervising lawyer present, based on the rationale that the client is likely to ask the paralegal for legal advice, particularly for an explanation of the meaning and legal consequences of the various legal documents that must be signed. In addition, there is always the potential for last-minute disputes to arise over terms, disputes that require the services of the attorneys to resolve. A paralegal who gives legal advice by explaining the legal consequences of documents or by attempting to resolve a dispute over terms would likely be engaging in the unauthorized practice of law.

Real estate closing
The consummation of the sale of real estate by payment of the purchase price, delivery of the deed, and finalizing collateral matters

These concerns are addressed by bar association opinions that endorse the use of paralegals to attend real estate closings unaccompanied by a lawyer by placing certain conditions on the paralegal and lawyer. These conditions include attorney supervision and review up to the time of the closing; attorney availability to give advice during the closing if needed; client consent; a determination that the closing will be purely ministerial and that the client understands the documents in advance; and a prohibition against the paralegal giving legal advice or making legal decisions during the closing. Most ethics opinions now support this role for the paralegal.

Finally, paralegals sometimes are involved in **negotiating settlements**. Paralegals in personal injury firms frequently handle all the documentation for "working up" the case, such as collecting medical bills, assisting the client with medical insurance claims, and discussing the case with insurance claims adjusters. The paralegal often has extensive contact with adjusters and provides information on the nature of the client's injuries, his or her treatment, and property damage. The adjuster makes offers to settle to the paralegal. The paralegal must pass these offers on to the attorney, who discusses with the client whether or not to accept an offer. The paralegal may in turn relay the decision to accept or reject to the adjuster and handle follow-up negotiations or settlement paperwork. The paralegal may not accept a settlement offer on behalf of a client, however, even if the paralegal knows that it is an offer the client should or will accept.

Exceptions

One major exception to the prohibition against nonattorneys giving legal advice has been created in the criminal area for so-called *jailhouse lawyers*. In *Johnson v. Avery*, 393 U.S. 484 (1969), the Supreme Court held that a state may not bar inmates from helping one another to prepare postconviction writs unless the state provides a reasonable alternative. However, it should be remembered that communications between persons and their nonlawyer advisors are not protected by the attorney-client privilege. This important proviso applies to all nonlawyer representatives. Courts have consistently refused to extend the privilege to communications between nonlawyers of all kinds and their "clients" or "customers."

Jailhouse lawyers
Inmates who help other inmates prepare postconviction writs

The prohibition against nonlawyers giving legal advice has also been the basis for challenges to **do-it-yourself and self-help legal kits**, which now include books, forms, CD-ROMS and other computerized versions of instructions or forms. After years of state litigation over whether the sale of kits (such as divorce kits or books and forms to assist in preparing one's own will) is unauthorized practice, a few general rules have emerged. Distributing self-help materials does *not* constitute the unauthorized practice of law as long as the materials are not distributed in conjunction with direct personalized assistance in completing the forms or procedures. The cases about self-help legal materials make an important distinction between providing "legal information" that helps people handle their own legal affairs, and providing "legal advice" that is the application of legal knowledge and skills to a specific situation and client.

Nonlawyer Legal Service Providers and Related Trends

Typing services that type legal documents for laypersons are not engaging in unauthorized practice unless they select forms for the customer or assist the customer in deciding how and what to fill in on the forms. The line here is not always clear in practice and in the future may change with the growth of nonlawyer legal service providers.

There is a clear nationwide trend toward **expanding the role of nonlawyers** in providing legal advice to pro se litigants despite the unauthorized practice prohibitions. Most of the progress in this area has come about as the result of legislation that narrowly circumscribes the role of the nonlawyer to a particular area of law in which there is a great need for access to the legal system by persons who cannot afford attorneys and who therefore seek to represent themselves. For example, in some states, government-employed small claims advisers are authorized by statute to assist persons in filling out and filing forms and preparing for appearances. Legislation in several states permits private nonlawyer practitioners to assist litigants in unlawful detainer/summary ejection proceedings. In several states, court facilitators assist pro se litigants in divorce, restraining order, and child support proceedings. In at least one state, paralegals have been hired to assist prisoners in preparing their habeas corpus writs because it is less expensive than providing a full law library to serve the prisons.

Finally, **technological advances** that are being used to increase access to legal information are posing new challenges to the traditional notions of what it means to give legal advice. User-friendly computer programs have been set up in kiosks in courthouses in several states, enabling users to prepare court-approved forms in domestic relations, small claims, and landlord-tenant matters. Users answer a series of questions and forms and instructions are printed out. The individualized nature of this service raises new issues about the distinction between legal information and legal advice.

A related issue is giving out legal **information or advice over the Internet**. Giving out general legal information, such as that given in a newspaper column on law, not only is considered ethical, but is also encouraged by ethics codes. However, answering questions in a way that "customizes" the information to the specific person converts the legal information to "legal advice" and raises questions about whether a lawyer-client relationship has been formed and whether the person giving the advice is admitted to practice in the relevant jurisdiction. If a lawyer-client relationship is formed, the lawyer owes duties to the client and is liable if there is negligence. If the advice concerns a person or matter in a jurisdiction where the lawyer is not licensed, the lawyer may be committing UPL in that state. While most Web sites that give legal information have disclaimers about these matters, these issues have yet to be fully addressed by many bar associations and courts.

F.   Disclosure of Status as Paralegal and Job Titles

One of the main functions of many paralegals is acting as liaison to persons outside the law firm—clients, witnesses, opposing law firms, courts, and so forth. This contact may take the form of telephone conversations, correspondence, or meetings in person. A key ethical aspect of the liaison role is ensuring that the person with whom the paralegal is dealing is fully aware that the paralegal is not a lawyer.

A discussion of **disclosure** of one's status as a paralegal is appropriate in this chapter on unauthorized practice of law for two reasons. First, a nonlawyer may appear to be engaging in unauthorized practice if he or she seems to others to be an attorney. Not clearly identifying one's status as a paralegal may mislead the other party into believing that the paralegal is a lawyer. It is not difficult to see how someone, especially a layperson such as a client or witness, could misconstrue the status of a paralegal if the paralegal "sounds" like an attorney. To the other person, a paralegal's inadvertent lack of disclosure may appear to be intentional. If this conduct by the paralegal creates problems later, the paralegal could be charged with "holding himself or herself out as an attorney." This claim could give rise under many state laws to a criminal charge of unauthorized practice of law against the paralegal, against the paralegal's attorney-employer, or both. (In many jurisdictions, misrepresenting oneself as an attorney is itself a misdemeanor.) Disciplinary action against the attorney may also arise, as state ethics codes all have rules prohibiting attorneys from aiding in the unauthorized practice of law.

The second reason that disclosure of the paralegal's status relates to the unauthorized practice of law is that a paralegal who is mistaken for an attorney may be called on to perform functions that are tantamount to unauthorized practice of law. If a client mistakenly believes that a paralegal is an attorney, the client may ask for legal advice. This places the paralegal in the uncomfortable position of having to backtrack in the conversation to explain his or her status and how that status makes giving a legal opinion unethical.

Guideline 4 of the ABA Model Guidelines holds attorneys responsible for taking measures to ensure that clients and others are aware that the paralegal is not licensed to practice law. The comment to this guideline mentions several means by which this may be accomplished, including the attorney's oral and written communication to clients and third parties. Most state guidelines on paralegal utilization also cover disclosure. Many of the guidelines speak of **"routine, early disclosure"** or **disclosure at the "outset"** of the communication with the third party. Many ethics guidelines explain that this rule is intended to avoiding confusion or misleading of clients or the public.

Some advisory opinions and state guidelines have addressed the **titles** that paralegals may use. One specifically prohibits the use of the title "*associate*" for a paralegal because law firms commonly use this title to identify their attorneys. "Paralegal" and "legal assistant" are the most commonly used titles, although their use and shades of meaning vary across the country. "Lawyer's assistant," "nonlawyer assistant," and "attorney assistant" are also used. While the titles "paralegal" and "legal assistant" usually are used interchangeably, they carry different connotations in some regions of the country, and one or the other appellation may be preferred within the local legal community. Frequently, a legal specialty is attached to one of these titles to indicate more specifically the area of practice in which the paralegal works — for instance, "probate paralegal" or "litigation paralegal." As paralegals have become more specialized and firms have developed career paths for them, new titles have been created, such as "senior paralegal" and "litigation support specialist." As a general rule, any title that does not potentially mislead a third party into believing that the paralegal is an attorney is permissible.

One early ethics opinion (in Iowa) disallowed the use of the designation "Certified Legal Assistant" on the grounds that it may mislead the public into thinking the paralegal is state-certified, but this opinion was reversed in 2003 and other state ethics opinions endorse the use of this designation. New York endorses the titles "paralegal" and "senior paralegal" but finds unacceptable and ambiguous the terms "paralegal coordinator," "legal associate," "public benefits advocate," "family law advocate," "housing law advocate," "disability benefits advocate," and "public benefit specialist."

As a general rule, paralegals may sign **correspondence**, be listed on **firm letterhead**, and have their own **business cards**, so long as an appropriate and clear title is used. The ABA long ago issued ethics opinions endorsing these practices. In the major lawyer advertising case, *Bates v. State Bar of Arizona,* 430 U.S. 350 (1977), the Supreme Court held that the state could not impose blanket restrictions on lawyer advertising. In its opinion, the court emphasized that consumers need information about legal services in order to make them more accessible and to help consumers select a lawyer. After this decision, ethics rules and opinions were revised to allow nonlawyers' names on letterheads and business cards.

In general, most law firms who have paralegals on staff do provide them with business cards but do not list them on the firm letterhead or in other permitted places. Practice regarding paralegal listings on letterhead varies with the locale, the size of the firm, and the nature of its practice. Small and mid-sized firms are more likely to list paralegals than are large firms for both practical and firm-culture reasons. Most large law firms do not list all their partners' names on the firm letterhead because they could not possibly do so with the number of partners running into the hundreds. However, some mid-sized and small law firms do list paralegals on their letterhead, and many firms have individualized letterhead for each attorney and paralegal.

The NFPA Model Code addresses the issue of disclosure in DR 1.7, which requires that titles be fully disclosed. The ethical considerations that follow spell out the details, including the use of titles on business cards, letterhead, brochures, and directories, and in advertisements. Canon 5 of the NALA Code also requires disclosure "at the outset of any professional relationship. . . ."

G. A Word About Paralegals as Independent Contractors

Independent contractor paralegals
Paralegals who handle projects for attorneys on an as-needed basis
(Also **freelance paralegals**)

Paralegals now commonly offer their services as **independent contractors**, handling projects for attorneys on an as-needed basis. Early on, most of these *freelance paralegals* worked in the probate area, which lends itself well to the effective use of paralegals because the probate process is highly structured and procedural. In addition, many firms handle only a small amount of probate work—not enough to warrant having a full-time staff paralegal to perform the paralegal functions in this specialized area of practice.

Gradually, freelance paralegals began to offer their services in other areas of practice, especially litigation. Most **freelance litigation** paralegals are litigation support specialists who focus on trial preparation, usually in large civil lawsuits. Freelance litigation paralegals assist law firms in organizing, usually electronically, the sometimes-massive numbers of documents in a case. The use of independent contractors has become well accepted in the legal field, especially in large metropolitan areas. Many employment agencies place temporary or contract lawyers and paralegals in firms, as the growing use of part-time and freelance workers has become an essential feature of the economy.

Working as a freelance paralegal has ethical ramifications in many areas—such as confidentiality and conflicts of interest. One concern has been clarifying the difference between an independent contractor paralegal who provides legal services to an attorney, and a nonattorney who provides legal services directly to the public. The latter often call themselves *"independent paralegals,"* exacerbating the confusion between themselves and the paralegals who are acting under the supervision of lawyers.

A related concern involves the degree of **supervision** to which independent paralegals are subjected. Some state courts have expressed concern that a lawyer may not be properly reviewing the work performed by a freelance paralegal, especially if the lawyer is not conversant with the area of law in which the paralegal does the work. All courts and bars agree that lawyers who use the services of independent paralegals must exercise the same degree of supervision they would for an employed paralegal and are equally responsible for an independent paralegal's work.

REVIEW QUESTIONS

1. What were the purposes of the early unauthorized practice rules?
2. What was the role of bar associations in limiting the practice of law to licensed attorneys?

3. What kinds of legal functions do most nonlawyer legal service providers perform? Whom do they serve? In what areas of law do they work?
4. Give a complete and accurate definition of *practice of law.*
5. What are all the potential consequences of engaging in the unauthorized practice of law? Do most states address violations of UPL rules or statutes?
6. What are an attorney's responsibilities to prevent the unauthorized practice of law? What might happen to an attorney whose paralegal engages in the practice of law?
7. Make a list of the specific functions that constitute the practice of law and are prohibited to paralegals. What rationale lies behind each prohibition?
8. What are the exceptions to the general rule against a nonlawyer appearing in court on behalf of a client?
9. Give your best definition of what constitutes giving legal advice.
10. What are the exceptions to the general prohibition against giving legal advice?
11. Does selling a self-help divorce kit constitute giving legal advice? What about answering legal questions on the Internet? Why or why not?
12. What kinds of work can legal typing services perform without engaging in the unauthorized practice of law?
13. Why are paralegals prohibited from setting legal fees? From accepting cases?
14. May a paralegal supervise a will execution without an attorney present? Why or why not?
15. May a paralegal handle a real estate closing without the supervising attorney present? Why or why not?
16. Why are nonlawyers allowed to practice before some administrative agencies?
17. Why must a paralegal be careful to disclose his or her status?
18. Name some job titles that are appropriate for paralegals to use in identifying their status. Name some titles that are not appropriate and explain why.
19. May paralegals sign correspondence on firm letterhead? May paralegals have business cards? May their names be listed on law firm letterhead?
20. Is it ethical for paralegals to work as independent contractors for lawyers? What are the ethical concerns in working this way?

HYPOTHETICALS

1. Dean Downs has been working as a personal injury paralegal for a small law firm for six months. He specialized in litigation in

paralegal school and has never worked in another law firm or done any other kind of legal work. One of the lawyers in the firm, Enid East, is handling an appeal of a criminal case pro bono. Enid asks Dean to prepare the appellate brief in the case. Dean does not know where to begin. What should he do? Dean finishes the draft brief and gives it to Enid to review. Enid does not have any experience in criminal work either and gives the brief a cursory look before she approves it for filing with the court. What should Dean do now? Has Enid breached any ethical duties? What if the brief is terrible and the client loses because they missed a key case?

2. Fran Francis has just gone to work for a sole practitioner who is very disorganized. The lawyer, George Graham, has hired Fran in part to get him organized. Fran finds a file in the bottom drawer of a desk that relates to a case in which the statute of limitations is about to run. George is out of the country until next week, by which time the statute will have run. Fran knows how to prepare the standard form complaint for this kind of case and also realizes that if she makes any minor mistakes in the complaint, they can be remedied by amending the complaint later on. What should she do? Can she prepare the complaint? Sign it? File it? What are her other options?

3. Harold Homes is a family law paralegal. His best friend, Isabel Ivory, is getting a divorce. Isabel asks Harold to help her prepare the papers to file for divorce. Is it ethical for Harold to do this? How might he help her?

4. Joan Johnson is a paralegal for a large law firm that handles corporate and securities work. The lawyer for whom Joan works always introduces her to clients and encourages clients to call her for updates on matters. Joan enjoys this work and is good at it. One day a client, Ken Kaplan, calls her about a new corporate entity he is forming. He explains what the corporation will do and asks whether it would be better to incorporate in New York or in Delaware. Can Joan answer? What should she do?

5. Laura Lane is a business litigation paralegal for a firm that handles construction litigation. A prospective client comes in to see an attorney, Mary Moore, who is tied up in court and asks Laura to interview the client. The client, Nathan North, tells a story about the faulty construction done on the remodeling of his kitchen. He asks Laura, "Do I have a good case?" What should she say? He also asks: "Can I handle this myself, or do I need an attorney?"

6. Owen Olson, a paralegal in a personal injury firm, handles a lot of negotiations on cases. One day, an insurance adjuster, Peter Paul, calls to discuss a new case. After a few minutes, the adjuster says, "What if we just settle this for $20,000 right now?" What should Owen do? After more discussion, Owen realizes that Peter believes that Owen is a lawyer. Should Owen do anything about this?

DISCUSSION QUESTIONS AND PROJECTS

1. Does your state have a definition of the practice of law? Where is it—in a statute, court rule, or case? Does your state or local bar association have a UPL committee? Who prosecutes UPL in your state?

2. Do you think that a sole practitioner lawyer who has ten paralegals working in her or his office can adequately supervise these paralegals? What office procedures and policies might ensure adequate supervision? What if the lawyer is in court every day and only spends a few hours a week in the office?

3. Do you think that an attorney who hires a paralegal without any formal paralegal training is violating his or her duty to supervise? Why, or why not? Might this be appropriate or inappropriate depending on the circumstances? What factors would you consider in deciding?

4. Which of the following acts by a paralegal would be permissible and which prohibited under the definitions of *legal advice* given in this chapter?

   a. interviewing a client to obtain the facts relating to an automobile accident;

   b. telling the client that the firm probably would be able to get a $10,000 recovery;

   c. explaining to the client what happens at a deposition;

   d. explaining to the client the meaning of an affidavit given to the client for signature;

   e. telling a client that his or her case is likely to settle;

   f. telling a client that he or she would be best off to file a small claims action;

   g. answering a client's questions about the meaning of terms in a contract;

   h. giving a client the legal opinion that she or he knows the attorney would give;

   i. relaying a message from the attorney to the client that tells the client that it is okay to sign a contract.

5. In a personal injury law firm that takes every case that comes to it and that charges the same contingency fee, why should it be necessary for the lawyer to set the fee and establish the relationship with the client? Should this be an ethical rule, or is it really a matter of good practice? Suppose the initial contact between the attorney and client is a five-minute meeting to formalize the relationship and the client never speaks to the attorney again because the paralegal "works up" the case, negotiates the settlement, and has all the client contact. Is the attorney maintaining a direct relationship with the client?

6. What are the rules governing will executions in your state? Does the state or local bar association have an advisory opinion about paralegals supervising will executions without the presence of an attorney?
7. Do parties to residential real estate transactions in your state usually use the services of lawyers? If not, who does? If so, are paralegals who work for real estate lawyers permitted to handle closings without an attorney present? Is it common practice? Does the state or local bar have an opinion about it?
8. Has your state bar or supreme court studied the issue of providing access to legal services? If so, do any of its findings or recommendations relate to nonlawyer legal service providers or paralegals?
9. How can the prohibition against nonlawyers representing clients in court be reconciled with nonlawyer representation of clients before administrative agencies? Do you think that the differences in these two settings are substantial enough to warrant the difference in policy?
10. Are there any state administrative agencies in your area that permit nonlawyer practice? Do nonlawyers appear before these agencies frequently or infrequently? What about paralegals working under the supervision of lawyers? Are there any state or local bar ethics opinions on this matter? Do any statutes in your state disallow fees for nonlawyer representatives in administrative agencies?
11. How can independent paralegals who work under the supervision of lawyers distinguish themselves from those who serve the public directly? Would different job titles make a difference? For example, nonlawyer direct service providers have sometimes been called "legal technicians" and are called "legal document assistants" in California. Can a title be "forced" on the public and the occupation? Would it make a difference if the state regulated the occupation?
12. Are lawyers who use the services of independent contractors more likely to fail in their responsibility to select, train, supervise, and review the work of these paralegals than paralegals employed full-time by their firm? How would this happen? Are these risks significant enough to warrant a complete ban on independent contractor paralegals? What about other independent contractors who serve lawyers—for example, process servers, investigators, accountants, and experts?

SELECTED CASES

In re Anderson, 79 B.R. 482 (Bankr. S.D. Cal. 1987) (nonlawyer legal service provider and UPL).

Board of Commissioners of the Utah State Bar v. Petersen, 937 P.2d 1263 (Utah 1997) (nonlawyer legal service provider who had been to "paralegal school" and was "registered" as a paralegal is prosecuted for UPL).

Davies v. Unauthorized Practice Committee of State Bar of Texas, 431 S.W.2d 590, at 593 (Tex. Civ. App. 1968) (definition of the practice of law).

Drake v. Superior Court of San Diego County, 21 Cal. App. 4th 1826, 26 Cal. Rptr. 2d 829 (1994) (power of attorney).

Florida Bar v. Beach, 675 So. 2d 106 (Fla. 1996) (discipline of lawyer for relationship with nonlawyer legal service provider).

Florida Bar v. Brumbaugh, 355 So. 2d 1186 (Fla. 1978) (nonlawyer legal service provider and UPL)

Florida Bar v. Furman, 376 So. 2d 378 (Fla. 1979) (nonlawyer legal service provider and UPL).

People v. Landlords Professional Services, 215 Cal. App. 3d 1599, 264 Cal. Rptr. 548 (1989) (nonlawyer legal service provider and UPL).

In re Moffett, 263 B.R. 805 (Bankr. W.D. Ky. 2001) (nonlawyer bankruptcy preparer sanctioned by bankruptcy court for UPL and other statutory offenses).

In re Morin, 319 Or. 547, 878 P.2d 393 (1994) (supervised paralegals in estate planning practice and UPL).

UPL Committee v. State Department of Workers' Compensation, 543 A.2d 662 (R.I. 1998) (nonlawyer assistants in administrative agency proceedings).

In re Welch, 185 A.2d 458, 459 (Vt. 1962) (definition of practice of law).

SELECTED REFERENCES

ABA Model Rules of Professional Conduct, Rule 5.1 [lawyer responsibility for other lawyers]

ABA Model Rules of Professional Conduct, Rule 5.3 [lawyer responsibility for nonlawyers]

ABA Model Rules of Professional Conduct, Rule 5.5 [aiding in the unauthorized practice of law; multijurisdictional practice and safe harbors]

ABA Model Code DR 3-101(A) [aiding in the unauthorized practice of law]

NALA Code of Ethics and Professional Responsibility, Canons 1 through 5 [unauthorized practice of law, supervision, and disclosure of status]

NFPA Model Code of Ethics and Professional Responsibility, DR 1.7 and 1.8 [unauthorized practice and disclosure of status]

ABA Committee on Ethics and Professional Responsibility, Informal Opinion 1185 (1971) [business cards]

ABA Committee on Ethics and Professional Responsibility, Informal Opinion 1367 (1976) [signing correspondence] ABA Committee on Ethics and Professional Responsibility, Informal Opinion 1527 (1989) [letterheads and advertisements]

NFPA Informal Ethics Opinion 95-2 [letterhead]

3

Confidentiality

This chapter covers the rules relating to confidentiality, one of the most critical elements of legal ethics, and teaches how to identify and resolve issues related to confidentiality. Chapter 3 covers:

- foundations and basic principles of confidentiality
- the attorney-client privilege and the difference between the privilege and the ethics rules on confidentiality
- information that is privileged or protected by the rule of confidentiality
- how and when the privilege and the duty of confidentiality may be broken or waived
- the work product rule
- how the principles and rules of confidentiality come into play for paralegals in practice
- how to protect confidentiality of information and records
- special problems in maintaining confidentiality with technology

A. The Principle of Confidentiality

Confidentiality is one of the oldest precepts of legal ethics and is unquestioned in its importance. The principle of confidentiality is based on the notion that an attorney must know all the facts if he or she is to best serve the client, and that a client will not provide full disclosure without assurance that information that may be incriminating or embarrassing will not be revealed outside the attorney-client relationship. The principle of confidentiality is also based on agency law. A lawyer has a fiduciary relationship with the client that requires the lawyer's highest trust, which includes confidence, loyalty, and good faith.

The general duty of confidentiality encompasses both ethics rules and evidentiary rules relating to *attorney-client privilege* and *work product*. The attorney-client privilege is a rule of evidence that relates to what confidential information may be divulged in litigation by way of discovery or testimony. The ethics rules covering confidentiality are much broader than the attorney-client privilege, as they cover a lawyer's duty not to divulge information about a client in any context. The rules also extend to information that may not be covered by the privilege.

B. Attorney-Client Privilege

1. Defined Generally

All jurisdictions make provision for the attorney-client privilege by statute, court rule, or common law. The **general rule** is that a client who seeks a lawyer's advice or assistance may invoke an unqualified privilege not to testify and to prevent the lawyer from testifying as to communications made by the client in confidence to the lawyer. The privilege lasts indefinitely. The client is the holder of the privilege, and only the client may waive it, thereby consenting to the disclosure of the privileged communication. Although the client is the holder of the privilege, the attorney must advise the client of the privilege. It should be noted that the privilege only extends to the attorney-client relationship and does not cover nonlawyer legal service providers or jailhouse lawyers.

Case law has further **clarified the meaning** of the attorney-client privilege: The privilege covers confidential communications between lawyer and client—whether oral or written—so long as the advice sought by the client is legal; other kinds of advice—personal or business, for instance—are not covered. It also covers initial consultations even if the lawyer does not undertake representation, and it includes an attorney-client communication whether or not the attorney charges a fee.

The privilege does not cover material or information that is not classified as a communication. The privilege lasts after the representation of the client ends and even after the death of the client. There are very limited reasons for which the privilege will be waived, as noted below.

2.   Disclosure to Parties Other than Client's Lawyer: Waiver or Not?

One of the key aspects of the privilege for paralegals is that it extends to communications made directly to or in the presence of the **attorney's agents**, a category that includes colleagues and employees in the law firm who are working or may be working on the client matter. This principle also covers consultants, investigators, and outside agencies working with counsel on a case. For example, the privilege extends to an outside vendor, such as a data processing firm that stores confidential information.

Attorney's agents
Colleagues, vendors, and employees working at the behest or under the supervision of a lawyer to effectuate the representation of clients

Some state statutes on the privilege specifically extend its scope to employees of attorneys. Even without such statutory language, the privilege would be radically diminished were it not extended to persons other than attorneys who work on clients' matters as members of the legal services delivery team. Cases have confirmed that the communications between clients and paralegals are covered by the privilege.

Communications must be made in a **confidential setting** in order to merit the protection of the privilege. This means that the setting must be private—that is, one in which others cannot overhear—and there should not be any other persons present who would not otherwise be covered by the privilege—a friend of the client, for example. Under contemporary rules, an eavesdropper who listens in on a confidential communication will not destroy the privilege.

The **client can waive** the privilege by repeating the communication to nonconfidential third parties or expressing an intention to make the confidential information public. For example, if a client makes public disclosures of otherwise protected communications, the privilege is considered to be waived. However, the waiver applies only to the communications revealed, not to other related protected communications. It should be noted also that some disclosures are themselves protected and therefore do not result in a waiver of the privilege. For example, disclosures made during plea bargaining or settlement negotiations cannot later be admitted at trial to prove guilt or liability.

3.   Matters Not Covered by the Privilege

The privilege usually does not extend to **the identity of a client** or to **a client's whereabouts**. However, the Supreme Court has held that the identity of a client is privileged when a lawyer sends a payment to the Internal Revenue Service anonymously on the client's behalf for underpayment of federal taxes. Because revealing the identity of the client could have led to conviction of a federal crime, the client's identity was protected. However, only a few cases have followed this reasoning and then only when revealing the client's identity would lead to a criminal prosecution.

The **fee arrangement** between a lawyer and client has historically not been privileged, although some states now have statutes making fee agreements privileged. The only exception to this rule is triggered when details of the fee arrangement would reveal the identity of a client and the identity itself is privileged. This exception has been used in recent years by government prosecutors, grand juries, and the Internal Revenue Service in order to identify and then seize legal fees paid to attorneys with money or assets obtained through illegal activity, particularly in the drug trade. Criminal defense attorneys object to the exception and have challenged the government on the basis of the privilege. They contend that fee arrangements, payment records, and client names are privileged and that the government's actions constitute harassment and interference with the right to counsel. There is a split of authority in the courts that have decided cases on this issue.

Protection of confidential communications about a client's whereabouts is almost never extended. In such cases, the client is usually a fugitive, so the attorney's nondisclosure of the client's location would amount to assisting the client in committing a future crime, one of the traditional bases for an exception to the privilege.

A client cannot bring a **preexisting document** within the protection of the privilege simply by giving it to his or her attorney. However, if a preexisting document is covered by another privilege, such as the spousal privilege, it will continue to be privileged while in the attorney's possession. **Physical evidence** of a client's crime is not protected by the privilege, and an attorney who comes into possession of such evidence is probably required to turn it over to the prosecutor. The attorney may or may not be compelled to testify about the source of the evidence, depending on the attorney's role in obtaining the evidence. If the lawyer obtained the evidence illegally, a court would be more inclined to force such testimony.

4. Inadvertent Disclosure of Privileged Material

In addition to actual client consent to waiver of the privilege and consent implied from the actions of the client, inadvertent disclosure might destroy the privilege. For example, if a protected document is accidentally given to opposing counsel in a ***document production***, this document may be deemed by the court to lose its privileged status.

The cases across the country are not uniform: A few states consistently hold that such conduct constitutes a **waiver of the privilege**, with the majority of courts holding that inadvertent disclosure does not necessarily constitute a waiver. Most cases find that the disclosure is not tantamount to a waiver so long as the lawyer made reasonable good-faith measures to prevent disclosure. Some courts also look at the extent of the disclosure, the timeliness of attempts to rectify it, and the issue of fairness.

It has been argued that inadvertent disclosure by the attorney should not result in waiver of the privilege because the client is the holder of the privilege and would not consent to the revelation of damaging protected information. However, obvious practical difficulties arise with continuing protection of information once it is revealed, even if not admissible at trial, opposing counsel will have the benefit of the knowledge.

Incidents of inadvertent disclosure are not uncommon, in large part because of the increase in multiparty litigation, the large scale of discovery, and the use of electronic records and means of communication. Some compelling examples of damaging inadvertent disclosure do exist, e.g., a lawyer in a large law firm accidentally released sealed documents to a magazine; a firm inadvertently placed sealed records in an appellate file only to find them later published in a magazine; privileged documents were produced to opposing counsel when post-it notes marking them as privileged fell off the papers; and a lawyer's assistant accidentally sent a memorandum outlining legal strategy to the opposing lawyer. In yet another case, a trial judge dismissed a panel of prospective jurors when the defense firm inadvertently faxed a secret document on jury selection strategy to the plaintiff's firm.

Paralegals often have extensive responsibility for discovery, including responding to *subpoenas duces tecum* and handling document productions. When hundreds of documents are requested by opposing counsel, the paralegal is often the one to review, organize, and examine these documents to see that they are purged of privileged material before they are copied and provided to the opposing counsel. In addition to needing guidance from the supervising attorney as to what documents to look for, the paralegal needs a clear understanding of the privilege so that he or she can flag documents that may need to be protected and bring them to the attorney's attention.

Another important issue is what the paralegal should do if he or she **receives privileged documents** that were inadvertently sent. The ABA has issued two ethics opinions on the matter that have been followed in most jurisdictions where courts faced this issue. The general rule established in those opinions is:

1. to **refrain from reviewing** such materials as soon as it is evident that they are privileged

Document production
A form of discovery under which one party must provide copies of specified documents to the other side

47

2. to **notify the sender** (often the opposing counsel) about the materials
3. either to **follow instructions** of the sender, which will likely be to return the material immediately, or to **seek a resolution** of the disposition of the materials from a court

It should be noted that many jurisdictions have not addressed this issue and do not have a provision in their ethics rules to cover this situation. Some states, such as California, have case law that requires the lawyer to follow all three steps or risk being sanctioned by the court. In two recent California cases, lawyers and their experts were disqualified from a case after it was discovered that they had acquired privileged defense documents and attempted to use the information from those documents to impeach the defense experts.

5. Exceptions to and Waivers of the Privilege

An exception to or waiver of the privilege may occur when the client calls into question the **attorney's professional competence** through criminal charges, a malpractice suit, a disciplinary action, or a contention of ineffective counsel on appeal from a criminal conviction.

When an **attorney represents two clients** who later become adversaries, otherwise privileged communications relating to the joint matter are not protected. However, pooled information shared by counsel who represent different clients with common interests generally is protected, although it may be used by the parties in later litigation in which the interests of the parties are adverse.

Also, confidential communications about a **future crime or fraud** that a client is planning are not protected. Under the important crime-fraud exception, privileged communications can be disclosed if they were made in furtherance of a crime or fraud. What communications fall into this exception varies from jurisdiction to jurisdiction, but the trend allows more court-ordered disclosure. For example, in major tobacco litigation, the crime-fraud exception was used successfully in several cases to gain access to incriminating documents between the companies and their lawyers.

6. The Privilege in the Corporate Setting

Control group test
Limits attorney-client privilege to confidential communications between the attorney and top management personnel

Special problems in applying the attorney-client privilege inhere in the representation of corporations. Questions sometimes arise as to **who the "client" is** and, flowing from that, what communications are protected. Different jurisdictions use different tests to determine the application of the privilege. On one end of the spectrum is the *control group test,* which limits the privilege to confidential communications between the attorney and the management personnel responsible for acting in the legal matter being discussed. The broader *subject matter test* is followed in other jurisdictions. Under that test, all corporate employees are covered if they communicate in confidence with the attorney for the purpose of enabling the attorney to render legal services to the corporation.

Subject matter test
Applies attorney-client privilege to all corporate employees who communicate in confidence with the attorney for the purpose of enabling the attorney to render legal services

Another issue that arises in corporate representation relates to the **holder of the privilege**. The corporation, not the employee, is the client and thus the holder of the privilege; and only the corporation may waive it. The employee who communicates the information may not object to the corporation's waiver of the privilege. The current board of directors controls the exercise of the privilege. This leadership obviously changes over time and with modifications in the corporate structure. Such changes may alter the corporate policy on waiver as to any particular communication.

Finally, another issue that arises in the corporate setting is whether an **internal audit or investigation** conducted by a corporation's attorneys is protected under the attorney-client privilege. Whether or not a court will extend the protection of the privilege to such audits varies from state to state and depends to a large extent on how carefully the lawyers and their client constructed the audit to preserve the privilege.

Paralegals who work in house are covered by the privilege in the same way they would be if they worked in a private law firm; in essence the in-house counsel's office functions as a law firm with one client. However, paralegals in this setting must take care to ensure that they are fully and properly supervised by a lawyer, or a court may find that they are simply lay employees to whom the privilege is not extended. This scenario arose in a recent patent case in California, and while its reasoning has not been followed in other cases, it serves as a warning to paralegals who work in house.

Finally, the Sarbanes Oxley Act, enacted as a response to the latest round of corporate scandals, has resulted in the adoption of a new code of conduct for lawyers working with corporate securities. This code creates new duties concerning responsibility of lawyers for reporting of wrongdoing in ways that are not in alignment with the privilege or ethics codes in most states. While lawyers are alarmed about these inroads into the privilege, they are setting up systems to ensure compliance.

7.   Court-ordered Disclosure

If protected communications are sought, the attorney must respond to the court and invoke the privilege. If the court orders the attorney to testify or to produce documents, the attorney may do so or may refuse and appeal the ruling. Sometimes a court will order an *in camera* examination to determine whether to order disclosure in open court. If an attorney breaks the privilege without a client's consent or a court order, the client may seek to enjoin or suppress the attorney's testimony

in camera
Proceedings held in the judge's chambers without the jury or public present

49

or seek dismissal of the case. The client, of course, may sue the attorney for malpractice or file a complaint with the appropriate disciplinary authorities.

C. The Work Product Rule

Federal and state rules of evidence and discovery provide for the protection of materials prepared by lawyers in anticipation of litigation. This *work product doctrine* derives from the 1947 case of *Hickman v. Taylor,* 329 U.S. 495, in which the Court created a qualified immunity from discovery for a lawyer's trial preparation so as to allow each side to prepare fully and in private. This doctrine has been codified in the Federal Rules of Civil Procedure and in comparable state statutes.

Mental impressions
Lawyer's ideas on how to conduct the case

Informational material
Factual research material, such as witness interviews

The work product rule covers two kinds of trial preparation material: informational and mental impression. **Mental impressions**, which are covered by an unqualified privilege, are the lawyer's ideas on how to conduct the case — that is, his or her strategies, theories, and related legal research. **Informational material**, which is protected by a qualified privilege, covers factual research material such as witness statements. When the opposition finds such informational material critical to its case and does not have an effective substitute, it may convince a court to break the privilege and obtain access to the material.

Because only material prepared in anticipation of litigation is protected under the work product doctrine, some material, such as an investigator's report prepared before there has been a clear indication that a lawsuit would be filed, may be discoverable. Cases in this area vary widely, with some lending protection whenever an insurance company investigation is made, but others only after an attorney becomes involved and orders the investigation or report.

The work product doctrine has become increasingly critical with the advent of **electronic database management** systems. Discovery under the information prong of the rule is generally permitted if documents are input verbatim. However, paraphrased or summarized documents, selectively input documents, and documents sorted topically by means of an index of issues prepared by an attorney generally are protected because such information relates to case preparation, usually representing both strategy and legal theories that the lawyer is developing.

The life of the work product protection varies with the jurisdiction. Some states hold that the protection terminates with the end of the litigation; others continue it indefinitely; still others terminate it with the end of the litigation except as to future related litigation. As with the attorney-client privilege, work product protection can be waived by actual or implied consent of the client.

D.   Ethics Rules of Confidentiality

Broad protection for client confidentiality was included in the earliest codes governing attorney conduct and is included in the ethics rules in every state. In addition to requiring lawyers to protect client confidences, these rules also provide part of the foundation for conflict of interest rules, discussed in Chapter 4.

Canon 4 of the ABA Model Code of Professional Responsibility provides that "[a] lawyer should preserve the confidences and secrets of a client." The related Disciplinary Rule (DR 4-101) spells out the specifics of this requirement, including exceptions. A few states still follow this rule, which distinguishes between **confidences**, defined as information protected by the attorney-client privilege, and **secrets**, which include "other information gained in the professional relationship that the client has requested to be held inviolate or the disclosure of which would be embarrassing or would likely to be detrimental to the client." Under this rule, lawyers must protect all confidential information from release, may not use the information to the disadvantage of the client, and may not use the information to the advantage of the attorney or a third person without client consent after full disclosure. Confidentiality may be broken only: (1) with client consent; (2) when required by ethics rules, law, or court order; (3) to prevent the commission of a crime; and (4) to establish or collect a fee or to defend against an accusation of wrongful conduct. The rule also requires a lawyer to exercise reasonable care to ensure that employees and others involved in client matters do not disclose or use client confidences or secrets.

The ABA Model Rules, which now have been adopted in most jurisdictions, eliminate the distinction between confidences and secrets and contain a **general prohibition** against revealing "information relating to representation of a client" (Model Rule 1.6). Setting the parameters of what is confidential in this way means that virtually all information is covered, regardless of when and how it was learned by the attorney. No private setting is required; the information need not have been communicated directly by the client; and information learned either before or after the representation is covered. Further, the client need not request confidentiality, and the attorney must abstain from revealing information, whether or not it has potential to harm or embarrass the client. The Model Rules allow judicially ordered disclosure only in accordance with exceptions to the attorney-client privilege or work product rule, as noted above.

If confidential information becomes public, a paralegal is not relived of responsibility to protect the confidentiality of the information under the ethics rules; however, under the evidentiary privilege, the duty to protect the confidentiality of this information lapses. The rule provides for disclosure only if the client gives informed consent, unless implied authorization exists because the disclosures are necessary to carry out representation.

The ABA Model Rules permit, but do not require, a lawyer to reveal confidential information to prevent **death or substantial bodily harm**; to prevent a **crime or fraud** likely to cause serious harm; and to **prevent, mitigate, or rectify** a substantial financial or other injury. When a lawyer may reveal confidential information to prevent a future crime is the most controversial aspect of the ethics rules on confidentiality. Many states have adopted their own versions of this rule: Some *require* an attorney to reveal information to prevent the commission of a crime likely to result in death or substantial bodily harm; others follow the ABA exception *permitting* revelation of information to prevent commission of a crime without provision that the crime be serious. Still others allow the attorney discretion to reveal confidential information to prevent future crimes or fraud or acts only if they are likely to result in substantial injury to the financial or property interests of another. Other ethics rules that relate to this exception prohibit a lawyer from counseling a client to engage in criminal activity or from assisting a client in committing a crime. Lawyers may also reveal confidential information to **secure legal advice** about an ethical matter, **establish a claim or defense** in a controversy with the client, and comply with a **court order or law**.

E. Confidentiality and the Paralegal

1. Application of the Rule to Paralegals

Every state that has guidelines on the utilization of paralegals requires attorneys to ensure that paralegals preserve client confidences. The ABA Model Guidelines for the Utilization of Paralegal Services provide rules on confidentiality in Guideline 6: "A lawyer is responsible for taking **reasonable measures** to ensure that all client confidences are preserved by a paralegal." Most state guidelines speak in terms of the attorney "instructing" the paralegal to preserve client confidences or to "exercise care" to ensure that paralegals preserve client confidences. Some guidelines remind attorneys that the confidentiality duty covers everything from casual disclosure (for example, by common gossip) to intentional misuse (for example, insider trading).

NALA Model Guideline IV requires paralegals to preserve confidences and secrets using the terminology of the ABA Model Code. Canon 7 of the NALA Code calls for paralegals to protect client confidentiality and to uphold the laws on the attorney-client privilege. The NFPA Model Code requires paralegals to "preserve all confidential information provided by the client or acquired from other sources, before, during, and after the course of the professional relationship" (NFPA DR 1.5). The ethical considerations that accompany this rule set forth exceptions, cover the misuse of information, and establish a prohibition against "indiscreet" communications.

2. Protecting Confidentiality in Daily Practice

Law firms need well-established **policies and procedures** to help prevent inadvertent disclosure of confidential information. Some firms include these in their written manuals, orientation programs, and training videos.

Policies should be established to deny unauthorized personnel access to **files** and to the file room. Code numbers instead of names can be used on client files. Old files and papers (even scratch paper) concerning clients should be disposed of properly, preferably by shredding, so that no one outside the firm will have access to them. Electronic files should be purged so that they cannot be reconstructed. Computer screens should not be visible to those walking through the office. **Conversations** over intercoms and speakerphones should be limited to nonconfidential matters to prevent unauthorized personnel, clients, or others visiting the office from overhearing. Privileged documents should be labeled as such when they are created to lessen the risk that they will not be handled carefully. Privileged **documents** should also be segregated from nonconfidential documents in separate files whenever possible. Procedures should limit the personnel who have access to any privileged documents, whether in hard or electronic form.

The most common kind of disclosure of confidential information takes place in **conversations** about work outside the firm's offices. Like everyone else, lawyers and paralegals enjoy talking about their work. Casual conversations concerning clients that are held with coworkers and friends outside the firm are potentially serious breaches of ethics. Other participants in such conversations are not only receiving confidential information but may repeat these confidences to others and conversations can be overheard. While such improper disclosures take place often and rarely result in sanctions, the consequences — losing a client, having a court deny protection to the information, having a client bring a malpractice suit or initiate a disciplinary complaint — are serious and should provide a sufficient incentive to paralegals to exercise great discretion when discussing client matters.

Conversations with clients should never be had in the **presence of parties** who are not necessary to the representation. Such conversations should take place in the privacy of a closed office or conference room, not in the reception or secretarial area, lunchroom, hallway, or elevator. The presence of others should be limited to those attorneys and non-lawyer employees who are working on the client's case. Law firm employees, such as receptionists, file clerks, and mailroom personnel, should not be included in client conferences.

Paralegals should not take **calls** from a client while meeting with another client because the client that is present might overhear the para-legal's half of a confidential conversation. Likewise, when seeing a client or anyone else from outside the firm, a paralegal should not have any other clients' files exposed or an active computer screen visible to the visitor.

The privilege and the work product rule protect information in **databases**, including those used for litigation support. To ensure that the database is protected, lawyers must be involved in the design and planning of the database. Head notes should include their legal theories, opinions, conclusions, and strategies. Clients, witnesses, and others should not have access to the database. Full-text databases are most likely to be found discoverable. To prevent this, only selected material should be included, and headings or annotations to assist with searches should be developed cooperatively by attorneys and paralegals.

**Confidentiality
agreement**
Agreement between a
law firm and an
employee or vendor in
which the employee
agrees to keep client
information confidential

Confidentiality agreements are another means to protect against disclosures of confidential information. A confidentiality agreement should require the signer not to disclose and to prevent any disclosure of confidential information. It should also require the signer to return all documents acquired or developed during the course of work and admonish the signer not to remove any documents from the workplace. Such agreements should be signed by all employees, independent contractors, and outside agencies with access to privileged information. Access to extremely sensitive confidential information should be limited to as few employees as possible, preferably permanent staff members.

Finally, paralegals may have access to confidential information that they could **misuse** for their own gain. For example, if a paralegal learns that a real estate development being handled by a firm will result in dra-matic increases in property values in the surrounding areas, the paralegal should not misuse this information to buy property. Similarly, insider trading rules forbids using confidential information to benefit in stock trading. In addition to the individual's liability under securities law, the firm is also liable. Under the Insider Trading and Securities Fraud Enforcement Act of 1988, fines of up to $1 million may be levied against a law firm whose employee uses confidential or inside information to engage in unlawful securities transactions if the firm did not exercise appropriate supervision to prevent the unlawful trading. Many large firms that handle securities work screen paralegal employees very carefully and require them to sign agreements not to misuse confidential client information in trading.

3. Special Issues Relating to Technology

Technological advances that have changed the way law is practiced have also created new problems in protecting the confidentiality of information. **Electronic records** are more portable and accessible than paper; are easier to retrieve, copy, and transmit; are easier to alter and intercept; and are more difficult to delete. Firms must take special security measures to preserve confidentiality and to protect against potential claims that the privilege has been waived because communications were not treated as private and confidential.

Facsimile machines pose special risks to confidentiality. Generally, faxing confidential communications should be avoided; if time is short, courier service or overnight mail or delivery service should be used. If faxing is necessary, steps should be taken to ensure that the appropriate person is on the receiving end, to guard against third parties who are not covered by the privilege reading the communication. A notice of confidentiality should accompany the material on the cover sheet, and the word "confidential" or "privileged" should be stamped on every page.

Calls made on **cellular and cordless telephones**, especially analog versions, may be intercepted by special scanners, making them less secure for sensitive conversations than ordinary land-based telephone lines. Under the Federal Electronic Communications Privacy Act and some state statutes, an interception of any kind of communication made through these media does not destroy the privilege if the communication is otherwise protected by a privilege, such as the attorney-client privilege. Despite these statutes, caution should be exercised when using cordless or cellular telephones for privileged communications. While interception of cellular calls has been made more difficult by improvements in the technology, such communications are still not as secure as those made on land-based lines. A few state and local bar associations have issued opinions recommending that lawyers not use such telephones for confidential communications because of the risk of interception and the lowered expectation of privacy. These opinions also suggest that lawyers inform their clients of the risks involved and obtain their consent to use this means of communication to discuss confidential matters. The safest practice is obviously to limit the conversations on such phones and to communicate about sensitive and privileged matters only on a secure land-based phone. Because cell phones can be used anywhere, some people use them indiscriminately to have confidential conversations in public. Making a confidential call in a public place may violate the duty of confidentiality and jeopardize the privilege.

Special protections must be in place to ensure that privileged material on **computers** is not vulnerable. Physical security of computers and network servers is essential. Servers should be in a locked room and should be secured to the furniture or floor. Access to these areas should be restricted to those who must have it to service the equipment. All computers should also be bolted and have screensavers and panels that prevent anyone passing by from viewing the screen.

The system should be protected by requiring everyone to log in with **passwords**, which should be carefully chosen so that they are not obvious (avoiding passwords such as initials, birth dates, and the like) and should be frequently changed. Obviously, passwords should not be written down and left in an accessible place, and employees should be admonished not to reveal their passwords to anyone except their supervisor. As the technology is improving, more firms are starting to use electronic identification cards (**smart cards**) in conjunction with passwords. Everyone using the system should be required to log out if they leave their computer unattended. Some firms restrict what passwords can log on at different locations. A list of who has logged on and when should be maintained.

Anti-virus software must be used and disks and back-up tapes should be kept and stored in secure locations. Special software must be used to delete material; otherwise it may be subject to retrieval. The number of persons serving as **network administrators** should be small, and these persons should be especially screened and trained. The firm should establish policies that prohibit access to materials except to service the network. Laptop computers should require passwords and protective software so that if they are stolen, confidential information and/or the firm network cannot be accessed. Care should be taken when transmitting documents to opposing counsel by e-mail or disk because prior versions of these documents (metadata) may be reconstructed from these documents and because documents can be altered if not in read-only format. Lawyers and paralegals have an ethical duty not to reveal this confidential information and a number of methods are available to ensure that clean copies can be made and sent. Likewise, at least one bar association has issued an ethics opinion advising that it is unethical to extract and examine metadata.

Electronic mail has become the preferred method of communicating in law firms and businesses. Privileged e-mail communications are protected by the same federal and state laws as other forms of communication, as noted above. In the past, when e-mail was new, some commentators contended that using e-mail might be a breach of the duty of confidentiality because e-mail can be intercepted and is subject to being read as it passes through the system. Some early ethics opinions advised against using e-mail with clients; however, later ethics opinions, including a major opinion issued by the ABA, have endorsed the use of unencrypted e-mail with the advice to lawyers that they disclose the risks to clients and get their permission to use it and consider carefully whether to use it for especially sensitive communications.

There are a growing number of ways in which lawyers are using technology to protect the confidentiality of e-mail, including firewalls, closed networks with the client that use land-based phone lines, and encryption. Each new technological development, however, brings new risks. For example, some experts have warned that certain kinds of spam filters would give too much access to third-party vendors screening e-mail for spam. Likewise, wireless computers and networks create the possibility that someone outside the law firm can access data through the "wireless cloud." Protections must be in place when using wireless networks or the firm will not have met its duty of confidentiality, even if the information obtained illegitimately will not lose its privileged status.

Firms should use the following procedures to protect confidentiality in addition to those noted above that apply to computers generally:

- Inform clients about the risks of electronic communications and obtain their written **consent** to use electronic mail.
- Refrain from using e-mail for very **sensitive communications**.
- **Mark all confidential e-mails as privileged** and include a statement telling the reader what to do if the communication is inadvertently sent to the wrong person (that is, not to read it and to contact the sender).
- **Limit the recipients** of a privileged e-mail to those who are absolutely essential to the privileged communication and warn recipients not to send such communications on to other persons.
- Consider the use of **encryption** software that locks the message into unreadable form until it is unlocked by the intended recipient, who has the only "key" to decrypt the message.
- Consider **closed networks** using land-based lines with regular clients.

In addition, firms should have internal policies that employees are informed of and agree to in writing. These policies should prohibit employees from misusing e-mail to send personal, sexually explicit, or harassing material; prohibit accessing another person's e-mail; stress the importance of sending confidential material only to those who need to have it; and remind employees not to leave their e-mail access open and unattended and not to share their passwords.

REVIEW QUESTIONS

1. What is the basis for the principle of confidentiality?
2. Define the attorney-client privilege.
3. A client seeks advice from an attorney but later decides not to hire that attorney. Is the conversation they had about the matter privileged?
4. Are conversations that take place in the presence of law firm employees covered by the privilege?

5. Are communications privileged that are relayed to outside vendors hired by a lawyer?
6. Does the privilege cover communications in cases in which the attorney does not charge a fee?
7. Are conversations protected by the privilege if they take place in the reception area? In the lobby? Elevator? A restaurant? A cocktail party?
8. What happens to the privilege if the client tells a friend everything that was said in the privileged conversation with the attorney?
9. Does the privilege cover information about a client's identity? A client's whereabouts? The fee arrangement made with the attorney? Name the exceptions to these rules.
10. When are a client's written papers protected by the privilege? When are they not protected?
11. What does an attorney do when a court requests disclosure of information that the attorney believes to be privileged?
12. What happens when privileged information is inadvertently disclosed to opposing counsel?
13. What should you do if you receive a document that appears to be privileged and that has been sent to you by mistake by the opposing counsel?
14. When may an attorney disclose privileged information?
15. When the client is a corporation, what personnel are covered by the privilege? Describe the two approaches to answering this question.
16. Define the work product doctrine. What is the reasoning behind this rule?
17. Is the database in a computerized litigation support program protected as work product? Explain why or why not.
18. What work product is discoverable and under what circumstances?
19. If a nonlawyer helps a friend prepare divorce papers, are their communications covered by the privilege?
20. Should you use a cell phone to communicate with a client?
21. Should you use e-mail to communicate with a client?
22. What are some security measures that may protect against breaches of security in using computers?
23. What is a confidentiality agreement and when is it used?
24. Name some common law office procedures that should be used to protect confidentiality.

HYPOTHETICALS

1. Jan Jones works for a criminal defense attorney. One morning a man, Adam Anderson, comes into the office very distraught. He wants to see the lawyer, Bonnie Burns, who is not in the office.

He starts talking very loudly in the reception area about an incident the night before in which someone has apparently been killed. What should Jan do? Assume that Adam continues to tell Jan the whole story, which includes his participation in an attempted burglary. Is this information privileged? Why, or why not? What if someone followed Adam and was listening outside the office in the hallway?

2. Bonnie Burns decides to represent Mr. Anderson, who has subsequently been charged with several crimes. Ms. Burns asks Jan to assist in preparing Mr. Anderson for the upcoming trial. During Jan's discussions with Mr. Anderson, he hints that he might have an alibi for the time at which the crime was committed, which Jan knows not to be true. What should Jan do? What should Bonnie Burns do if Mr. Anderson proceeds to tell this story while testifying at the trial?

3. Karen Kent is a paralegal working on a large document production. Karen has no idea what the case is about but is asked to review and stamp some documents that will be copied and produced for the opposing counsel. What kind of documents should Karen look for that might legitimately be withheld from discovery? What is the best way to "flag" these documents? Should she attach post-it notes to them? Mark them in pencil? Remove them? What should she do after she has identified and isolated them?

4. Leonard Lessing is working on a top-secret corporate securities matter. The matter involves a corporate merger that could cause the value of one of the corporation's stocks to rise. Leonard overhears another paralegal, Tom Thompson, telling one of his friends about the matter over the phone. What should Leonard do? Is it okay for Tom or Leonard or Tom's friend to buy the stock involved?

5. Natalie Neari is working on some business litigation. She gets an e-mail from Cathy Cramer, paralegal for the opposing counsel, which is a letter to Dan Dinkel, who is "of counsel" to Ms. Cramer. Natalie is puzzled and starts reading the letter but quickly realizes it was sent by mistake, as it concerns the testimony of an expert witness in the case. What should Natalie do? Assume that she goes to the supervising lawyer in the case, Earl Everest, and he takes the letter and reads the whole thing. Has he done anything wrong? What should he have done? What should Natalie do now? What if the letter proposes that the expert be paid a bonus for a successful outcome in the case? (See Chapter 8 for a discussion of witnesses.)

6. Owen Oliphant is an in-house paralegal for Conklin Corporation. He has been with Conklin for 20 years and serves as a patent specialist. He confers with the research and development and marketing departments as they come up with new products and plans to

market them. He commonly drafts memoranda to the chiefs of these departments, explaining the results of research into the patents and providing information on how they can be marketed within the bounds of the law. Owen's supervisor, Pam Park, is general counsel for Conklin. She has been there about three years and knows little about patents. Pam meets with Owen monthly at staff meetings. Owen sends copies of all his memos to Pam. A lawsuit is filed against Conklin by Bizz, charging that Conklin has violated one of its patents. Bizz seeks to discover memoranda from Owen to the R&D department concerning this patent. Is this material discoverable? What might a court look at in deciding? What procedures should Owen and the legal department have in place to protect the privileged status of these materials? (See the *HPD v. Clorox* case cited below for some information.)

DISCUSSION QUESTIONS AND PROJECTS

1. Find the source of the attorney–client privilege in your state. Is it in the statutes? A case or series of cases? A court rule? How does it compare with the general definition of the privilege given in this chapter?
2. Are there any cases in your state relating to paralegals and the privilege?
3. Find the rule for the work product doctrine in your state. How does it compare with the provision in the Federal Rules of Civil Procedure?
4. You discover that opposing counsel has included clearly privileged documents in a document production. What would you do? What rule does your state follow in deciding whether an inadvertent disclosure destroys the privilege?
5. What would you suggest if a lawyer working on a civil lawsuit instructed you to have all the information your client had given you on the matter input electronically into a database verbatim in full text?
6. What is the ethical rule on confidentiality in your state's rules of professional conduct for lawyers?
7. What would you do as a paralegal if an attorney at your firm during the company's Christmas party introduced you to a client, who then proceeded to tell you the whole sordid story that led to his being represented by the firm?
8. What would you do if while attending a local paralegal association meeting you overheard a group of paralegals talking about a case on which you worked for opposing counsel? Would your answer be any different if you weren't working on the opposite side of the case?

9. What would you do if you overheard a paralegal in your firm discussing confidential information about a client with a paralegal in another firm? Would your answer be different if an attorney were doing the talking?

10. You happen to know that on Tuesdays and Fridays the file room personnel always have their friends (who do not work at the firm) eat lunch with them in the file room. What should you do? Would your answer be different if the friends were employees of another firm?

11. What would you do if you caught a client going through other clients' files on your desk while you were momentarily out of the room?

12. What should you do with handwritten notes of a confidential conversation once they have been typed up and put into a client's file?

13. Have any cases on inadvertent disclosure been decided in your jurisdiction? What about ethics opinions issued by the bar?

14. Contact some large law firms and find out what policies and procedures they have in place to protect client confidentiality, including policies relating to confidentiality agreements, cell phones, and e-mail.

15. Contact a corporate law department and see what procedures they follow when dealing with confidential legal matters in which they may have to talk with an employee.

SELECTED CASES

Baird v. Koerner, 279 F.2d 623 (9th Cir. 1960) (identity of client is privileged).

Berg Electronic, Inc. v. Molex, Inc., 875 F. Supp. 261 (D. Del. 1995) (inadvertently disclosed documents in document production).

Bloss v. Ford Motor Co., 126 A.D.2d 804, 510 N.Y.S.2d 304 (1987) (work product rule applicable to document indexes).

In re Cendant Corp. Securities Litigation, 343 F.3d 658 (2003) (trial strategy consultant's advice to corporate auditor communicated during confidential consultation with counsel is protected as work product).

In re Grand Jury Investigation of Ocean Transportation, 604 F.2d 672 (D.C.Cir. 1979) (inadvertently disclosed documents in document production).

HPD Laboratories, Inc. v. Clorox Co., 202 F.R.D. 410 (Cal. 2001) (communications of in-house paralegal not protected by the privilege).

People v. Mitchell, 86 A.D.2d 976, 448 N.Y.S.2d 332 (1982) (setting and presence of persons as factors in determining if communication is privileged).

Rico v. Mitsubishi Motors Corp., 116 Cal.App.4th 51, 10 Cal.Rptr.3d 601 (2004) (lawyer disqualified after he used confidential notes of opposing lawyers' conversations with experts to impeach experts).

61

Samaritan Foundation v. Superior Court, 844 P.2d 593 (Ariz. App. Div. 1 1992) (extension of privilege to paralegals).

Upjohn Co. v. United States, 449 U.S. 383 (1981) (control group and subject matter tests for determining client/privilege).

SELECTED REFERENCES

ABA Model Code of Professional Responsibility, Canon 4

ABA Model Code of Professional Responsibility, DR 4-101

ABA Model Code of Professional Responsibility, EC 4-2

ABA Model Rules of Professional Conduct, Rules 1.2 and 1.6

ABA Guidelines for the Utilization of Paralegal Services, Guideline 6

ABA Formal Ethics Opinion 88-356 [duty of confidentiality extends to freelance lawyers]

ABA Formal Ethics Opinions 92-368 and 94-382 [receipt of inadvertently disclosed privileged documents]

ABA Formal Ethics Opinion 99-413 [use of unencrypted e-mail to communicate with clients]

NALA Code of Ethics and Professional Responsibility, Canon 7

NFPA Model Code of Ethics and Professional Responsibility, DR 1.5

Conflicts of Interest

This chapter covers the rules and cases governing conflicts of interest and their application to paralegals, including the procedures that paralegals should follow to avoid conflicts and to handle conflicts that arise. Covered are:

- rules governing conflicts involving clients, including concurrent and successive representation
- rules governing personal and business conflicts, including:

  - business transactions with clients
  - publication rights
  - financial assistance to clients
  - lawyer's interest in litigation
  - gifts from clients
  - agreements with clients limiting malpractice liability
  - payment of attorney's fees by third persons
  - conflicts involving family members or relatives
  - sexual relations with clients

- disqualifications caused by individual conflicts of interest that are imputed to an individual's firm
- client consent to conflicts
- screens to protect against disqualification
- the use of conflicts checks and paralegals' responsibility to maintain records

A. Introduction

In the past 20 years, conflicts of interest have become one of the most troublesome areas of ethics for law firms and their clients. The growth in the size of law firms, the development of branch offices, the merger of firms, the increase in mobility from firm to firm, and greater legal specialization have made the potential for conflicts of interest an ever-present concern. The traditional, strict, straightforward rules governing conflicts are increasingly difficult to apply and in fact in some situations result in undue hardship on law firms, law firm employees, and clients.

The ethics rules governing conflicts of interest are based on the duties of **loyalty and confidentiality**. Both of these duties are threatened when an attorney or paralegal has an interest that is adverse to a client's, whether the adverse interest is a personal or business one or relates to the current or past representation of the client. For example, a lawyer or paralegal who has received confidential information from one client that may help another client may feel compelled to use that information to help the second client. An attorney who represents two clients, even if in different matters, may not represent them both with equal zeal, especially if one is a favored client (perhaps because this client brings more business to the attorney).

Ethics rules governing conflicts of interest have existed since the first codes of lawyer conduct came into being, and conflicts are included in the ethics rules of every jurisdiction. While these rules form the basis for attorney discipline, they are supplemented by **court interpretations** in cases in which a party has moved to disqualify a lawyer or a law firm because of a conflict of interest. The courts have seen many more conflict dilemmas than have disciplinary bodies and have had to flesh out the rules to apply them to growing numbers of complicated conflict situations.

The ethics rules cover:

- **concurrent representation** of adverse interests
- representation that is **adverse to a former client**
- **representation of clients whose interests are aligned**
- lawyer's **financial, personal, or business interests** that are or may be adverse to a client

Imputed/vicarious conflicts
The conflict of interest of one person in a law firm is imputed to everyone in the firm, causing the whole firm to be disqualified

Finally, the rules and cases cover *imputed* or *vicarious conflicts*, a principle under which the conflict of interest of one person in a firm is imputed to the firm and all its lawyers, causing the whole firm to be disqualified. Paralegals must pay special attention to this rule because it may apply to a paralegal's conflicts, also causing a law firm to be subject to disqualification.

Guideline 7 of the ABA Model Guidelines for the Utilization of Paralegal Services advises attorneys to take reasonable measures to prevent conflicts resulting from a paralegal's other employment or interests. Personal and business interests are covered, in addition to conflicts created by work on two or more different clients' matters. The ABA Guidelines and an important ABA ethics opinion endorse the use of screening of paralegals in cases in which a conflict exists. About half of the states that have guidelines on paralegals refer to paralegal conflicts of interests and call on the lawyer generally to ensure against conflicts impinging on the services rendered to a client. Most states endorse screening of paralegals.

The NFPA Model Code includes an extensive section on conflicts of interest (Disciplinary Rule 1.6). The NALA Code of Ethics and Professional Responsibility does not refer directly to conflicts of interest, although general language about confidentiality and adherence to ethics codes for lawyers covers conflict situations. (See Canon 3(c) and Canon 7.)

B. Conflicts Involving Representation of Clients

1. Concurrent Representation

General Rules

The most clear-cut case of a conflict of interest is an attorney's **concurrent or *simultaneous representation*** of two clients whose interests are adverse to one another. The most obvious and extreme example of this is an attorney attempting to represent both the plaintiff and the defendant in the same lawsuit. However, concurrent representation problems arise in other less blatant situations, such as in nonlitigated matters and when the adverse representation involves the same client or clients but in a different case.

The ABA Model Code and Model Rules permit concurrent representation only if:

1. The lawyer can **adequately represent** the interests of each client (under Model Code) or the lawyer reasonably believes that he or she can provide **competence and diligent representation**, the dual representation is not prohibited by law, and the representation does not involve the same litigation (under Model Rules); and
2. Each client **consents after full disclosure** (under Model Code) or **informed written consent** (under Model Rules).

ABA Model Code 5-101(A) and ABA Model Rule 1.7.

Both configurations have a twofold test: first, an assurance of adequate representation of both clients and, second, client consent. The

Concurrent representation
Where an attorney represents two clients whose interests are adverse to one another

65

latest revisions to the Model Rules added the requirement that consent be in writing. Some states had already adopted that requirement for consents, and others will undoubtedly follow.

The courts generally have treated simultaneous representation as improper on its face and start with the **presumption that disqualification is required**. The more remote the adverseness, however, the less stringently the rule is applied. For example, it is not considered a conflict of interest per se for an attorney to represent business competitors simultaneously in unrelated matters.

Consents

Determining whether there has been client **consent** (called **"waiver"** by many firms) is critical. Whether a court honors a client's consent depends on a number of circumstances, including:

- the extent of the **disclosure** and discussions with the client about the implications of the dual representation
- whether the consent was truly **voluntary** and not given under pressure from the attorney or others
- **when** the attorney raised the issue with his or her client
- the **capacity** of the client to understand fully the implications of the dual representation and consent
- whether or not the client consulted with and relied upon **independent counsel**
- whether the consent is **written and signed**

These factors suggest some guidelines that should be followed to ensure that consents will be upheld. Thorough written disclosures are highly recommended and are required in some states. The lawyer should provide in writing to the client information on the circumstances giving rise to the potential conflict and the actual and reasonably foreseeable consequences to the client if the lawyer undertakes or continues the representation. If independent counsel is consulted, the consulting counsel should not be from the same firm or be recommended by the firm. Consents should also include:

- **consideration** for the consent (that is, future or continued representation)
- procedures to **screen** appropriately to protect confidentiality
- procedures to follow if a client decides to **withdraw consent**

Finally, it should be kept in mind that courts sometimes will not honor a consent if the two clients' interests are so clearly adverse that the court believes the attorney cannot adequately represent them.

Withdrawal to Avoid Conflicts

Sometimes an attorney will attempt to avoid the strict rule against concurrent representation by dropping one client in order to represent the other, more favored client. This may seem desirable for the attorney because the rules governing representation of interests that are adverse to former clients are not as strict (see Section B below). However, a court may not allow continued representation under these circumstances. The court will look to see if representation was concurrent at any time. Improper concurrent representation generally results in disqualification of the attorney from representing *either* client unless, of course, there is proper consent under the rules.

Imputed Disqualification in Concurrent Conflicts

Imputed disqualification rules are applied strictly in cases of concurrent representation. These rules have been held to apply to branch offices of the same firm. A screen to protect against improper access to confidential information will not overcome the rule, as it might in cases involving former clients. Fortunately for paralegals, the courts have been more lenient in applying these rules to situations in which the paralegal carries the concurrent conflict to a new firm. (See Section D in this chapter.)

Issue Conflicts and Other Indirect Concurrent Conflicts

Another kind of concurrent conflict that is not fully addressed in the ethics rules is *issue conflicts*. An issue conflict occurs when an attorney is representing two clients in unrelated cases and is urging a legal position in one case that, if the attorney prevails, will have negative consequences for the other client. In general, representation of both sides is permitted in different **trial courts**, but some commentators believe it is improper in cases pending at the same time in **appellate court**. The Comments to the ABA Model Rules indicate that withdrawal from one case should be undertaken if an action in one matter will "materially limit" the lawyer's effectiveness in the other. Some advisory opinions refuse to apply prohibitions against conflicts to the issue conflict situation even where the attorney would be arguing opposite positions before the same judge; however, others recommend against lawyers handling cases that present issue conflicts at the appellate level or recommend consent only after full disclosure. Related to issue conflicts is the representation of **competitors**. The ethics rules do not prohibit such representation, but some firms have internal policies that prohibit the same attorney from handling competitors to protect their relationships with valued clients.

Issue conflicts
Occurs when an attorney argues opposing sides of a legal issue, the result of which may be that one client's interests are harmed

The Model Rules further prohibit concurrent representation when a lawyer's responsibilities to one client may materially limit the lawyer's ability to represent the other client. In this scenario, the interests of the two clients are not adverse, but the attorney's **loyalty or zeal may be impaired** because of the demands of a case. For example, an attorney representing two criminal defendants with conflicting trial dates will have to delay one trial, possibly to the detriment of that client.

Examples of Conflicts in Litigated Matters

Concurrent conflicts of interests may arise in litigation in various ways. One of the most common and controversial is dual representation of a husband and wife in a **marital dissolution**. Many dissolutions that begin amicably and seem to lend themselves to resolution by one attorney for reasons of cost and efficiency still end up in court. Although the courts are not in agreement throughout the country, many lawyers refuse to represent both parties to a dissolution.

Similar problems can arise in representation of **co-parties** in litigation. While aligned initially, co-parties may become adversaries during the course of litigation if cross-claims are filed or another party seeks to realign the parties. For example, a passenger and driver who sue a third party may find themselves adversaries if the passenger sues the driver. Some jurisdictions, such as California, have case law that prohibits any joint representation of a driver and a passenger as an inherent conflict of interest.

Both the ABA Model Code (DR 5-106) and ABA Model Rules (Rule 1.8) prohibit a lawyer who is representing multiple clients from making an **aggregate settlement** of civil claims or a collective plea in a criminal case unless all clients give informed written consent. Representing seemingly aligned defendants in criminal cases is especially dangerous because the interests of the defendants are often potentially adverse. In addition to the ethical concerns, multiple representation may deprive one or both of the defendants of effective assistance of counsel, which constitutes grounds to overturn a conviction.

Other less obvious conflict traps arise in litigation and can result in further litigation and serious sanctions, including disqualification. For example, a firm may be disqualified for retaining an **expert witness** who was previously interviewed by the opposing counsel if confidential information was disclosed to the expert during the interview. Representing both present and future claimants in **class action suits** may also result in an allegation of a conflict if a settlement seems to favor one group over another.

Examples of Conflicts in Non-Litigated Matters

While litigation is the most obvious setting for conflicts of interest, many other kinds of cases can pose conflicts. An attorney may represent more than one party to a **negotiation** if the parties' interests seem aligned, but the attorney should be aware of the potential for adverse interests to arise if negotiations fail or the contract becomes the subject of a dispute. If litigation is the result, the attorney may not represent either of the parties against the other and may be sued by a former client for malpractice because of the conflict. For example, entertainment law firms that represent producers, directors, writers, and actors have been accused of favoring wealthier and more prestigious clients in negotiations on film deals, resulting in less advantageous positions for other clients. Clients of these firms do sign consent forms to the multiple representation, but later, when deals fall apart, complain that there was not full disclosure or that they would have been frozen out of deals if they had sought independent counsel.

Conflicts may arise in the **drafting of wills** for members of the same family if the family members are not in complete agreement about the disposition of the estate. Consents to such joint representation are essential. Similarly, conflicts between an estate and the heirs of the estate may prohibit representation of both parties. For other conflicts in a probate setting, see Section C.6, on gifts from clients.

An attorney who represents a **corporation** and serves on its board of directors may face conflicts if the corporation's and board's interests become adverse, such as in a derivative suit. The ABA Model Rules suggest that an attorney who is asked to serve on a corporate client's board should consider several factors, including the likelihood of a conflict arising, and should not serve as a director if there is a "material risk that the dual role will compromise the lawyer's independence of professional judgment." Serving on a corporate board increases an attorney's risk of being sued for malpractice and threatens the attorney-client privilege as well. Even without serving on a corporate client's board, a lawyer may find that the interests of the board, management, and shareholders often diverge. These interests become quite problematic in derivative suits, especially in cases of self-dealing, when there are allegations of fraud, and in corporate takeovers. While the attorney is bound to represent the corporate entity, identifying clearly who the attorney represents or how to act in the best interests of that entity is often complicated. Conflicts may also occur in the corporate setting if an attorney represents several entities within the corporate family (for example, parent, subsidiary, and "sister" companies) and these entities find themselves in an adversarial position.

A lawyer may be acting as an intermediary or representing multiple clients whenever he or she represents more than one party to a **transaction**, such as a real estate sale, a mortgage, a loan, or a contract. For example, a firm has been held to have acted improperly when it represented both a school district and the underwriters in a school bond issuance. Several states now have advisory opinions on the issue of representing both sides in a real estate transaction. Most opinions recommend against dual representation except in purely ministerial matters. As mentioned above, representing both spouses in a **divorce settlement** is generally not acceptable because the interests of the parties are inherently adverse, and the potential for a real dispute necessitating litigation is too great. It should be noted that this rule does not apply to situations in which an attorney is acting as a neutral **arbitrator or mediator** between or among parties who are not the attorney's clients, such as in a bar-sponsored divorce mediation program or in a court-appointed arbitration.

2.   Successive Representation

General Rules

The rules governing the conduct of lawyers who desire to represent a client in a matter that may be adverse to a former client—called *successive representation*—have been steadily evolving over the past 25 years, in large part because of the growth and complexity of law practice as a business. The ability of clients to be represented by the counsel of their choice and the increasing mobility of lawyers have been significant factors in recent court decisions that apply the conflict rules in cases of successive representation with a good deal more flexibility than ever before.

Successive representation
Conflict of interest situation involving a current matter and a former client

The general rule is that an attorney will be disqualified from successive representation only if the interests of the former and current client are **truly adverse** and if the past and current matters are **substantially related**. This formulation presupposes an attorney–client relationship with the former client within which the attorney would have learned confidential information. If the current representation relates to the same or a closely related matter, the attorney would be in a position to breach his or her duty of confidentiality to the former client by revealing the confidential information to assist the current client. (Remember from Chapter 3 that the duty of confidentiality continues after the termination of the attorney-client relationship.) The ABA Model Code did not have a specific provision covering conflicts of interest in successive representation, although it prohibited employment if it were likely to involve representing differing interests. As a result, some courts have relied on general language in Canon 9 of the ABA Model Code in deciding whether to disqualify an attorney or firm from successive representation. Canon 9 calls on lawyers to avoid even the **appearance of impropriety**. Most circuits and states, however, do not order disqualification solely on the basis of an appearance of impropriety; instead, they determine whether the former client's confidentiality is in jeopardy. Most commentators disfavor disqualification predicated solely on Canon 9 because an appearance of impropriety may be only that—an appearance. It does not mean that anything improper, such as revealing confidential information, has or will take place; it does not address directly the conflict problem; and disqualification can seriously harm the interests of the current client as well as the attorney.

The ABA Model Rules contain a clearer and more complete statement than the ABA Model Code. Rule 1.9 states the general rule that has been followed by most courts: A lawyer may not represent a person in a matter that is the **same or substantially related** to the representation of a former client in which the interests of the potential client are **materially adverse** to the former client. Such representation is permitted if the former client gives informed written consent.

A separate ABA Model Rule applies to **government lawyers**. Model Rule 1.11 allows a former government lawyer, with the government agency's informed written consent, to represent a private client in a matter that the lawyer previously participated in or obtained confidential information about while in government service. It further allows a screen to prevent firm disqualification in such a representation. A lawyer who moves to private practice from government service is prohibited from switching sides or from negotiating for private employment with a party or an attorney with whom the lawyer is dealing on a matter. The older ABA Model Code (DR 9-101) prohibits a former public employee from accepting "private employment in a matter in which he had substantial responsibility as a public employee." The more flexible approach for government lawyers who wish to move into private practice is predicated on the policy of not discouraging lawyers from entering less lucrative government and civil service.

Defining "Substantial Relationship"

As the courts have heard an increasing number of motions for disqualification, they have been faced with the challenge of applying these rules consistently to factual situations. In ruling on these disqualification cases, the courts have been somewhat inconsistent in deciding the question of whether a substantial relationship exists between the former and current clients' representations. Some courts have examined the **facts** of the two matters to see whether it is likely that the attorney would have learned confidential information that relates to both matters. Others look to the **legal issues** and require a clear or even identical congruence of the issues before ordering disqualification. If the court finds that the matters are not substantially related, the attorney and the attorney's firm will not be disqualified. If the matters are found to be substantially related, a presumption that confidential information was disclosed arises. Some courts have held that this presumption is irrebuttable, thereby precluding evidence to the contrary, such as evidence that the attorney did not learn any confidential information on the prior matter or has been screened, in which case disqualification is automatic. Other courts have held that this presumption is rebuttable and that the attorney may provide evidence to overcome the presumption that confidential information has been or will be revealed. The latter rule is the trend among the courts.

C.   Other Conflicts Rules

1.   Business Transactions with Clients

Business transactions between a lawyer and client contain tremendous potential for a conflict of interest in which a lawyer's interests will conflict with the client's and/or with the lawyer's role in representing the client. In addition to this inherent conflict in business dealings, clients rely on the lawyer's superior **legal knowledge** and are generally in a weaker **bargaining position**. The attorney's duties of loyalty, trust, and zealous representation are implicated whenever a lawyer enters into a business transaction with a client.

Both the ABA Model Code and Model Rules prohibit business transactions between lawyers and clients but provide for an exception with **client consent** (ABA Model Code DR 5-101 and ABA Model Rule 1.8(a)). The Model Rule affords protection for the client by requiring: that (1) the transaction and terms must be fair and reasonable to the client; (2) the client is advised in writing of the desirability of seeking independent counsel and be given a reasonable amount of time to do that; and (3) the client must give informed written consent.

In practice, lawyers and clients have many opportunities to enter into business transactions, not all of which are prohibited. **Commercial transactions** that clients in their business capacities may provide to the public — as well as to law firms — such as banking, medical services, products, and utilities are not prohibited.

Some examples of business transactions with clients that lawyers are prohibited from entering into without proper client consent are: (1) purchasing real estate from a client while also drafting the documents relating to the sale; (2) advising clients to make investments in businesses in which the lawyer has an interest; (3) borrowing money from a client and advising the client how to perfect the client's security interest; (4) going into business with a client, forming the corporation for the business that gives the lawyer an ownership interest while continuing to represent the corporation as its attorney; and (5) taking as his or her fee an interest in a business entity that he or she has formed or is advising.

Conflicts based on business transactions may arise also for **paralegals**. For example, a paralegal may be invited to invest in a client's business or may own stock in a client's company. Such conflicts are easier for paralegals to cure than they are for an attorney. Because it is the attorney who is relied on by the client for legal advice, it is the attorney who is more likely to have an unfair advantage over the client. However, paralegals should be aware of the general prohibition on business transactions with clients and take care to avoid dual roles that might create a conflict. If such a conflict arises, the paralegal should consult with the supervising attorney about obtaining client consent under the relevant provisions of the state ethics rules.

2. Publication, Literary, and Media Rights

Both the ABA Model Code and Model Rules prohibit an attorney from entering into an agreement that grants the attorney publication, literary, or media rights relating to the subject matter of his or her employment prior to the conclusion of the representation (ABA Model Rule 1.8(d); ABA Model Code DR 5-104(B)). This rule protects against conflicts that might arise during the representation about what is best for the client and what would enhance the value of the "story" — that is, the value of the lawyer's interests in the literary or media rights.

In addition to disciplinary action for violation of this rule (which is rare), this kind of conflict may be the basis of a motion to disqualify counsel or of an appeal in a criminal case based on ineffective counsel.

3. Financial Assistance to Clients

Whenever a lawyer lends funds to a client, a new dimension — that of **creditor and debtor** — is imposed on the attorney-client relationship. Because of the inherent conflict in representing the client while being the client's creditor, the ABA Model Code and Model Rules prohibit most kinds of financial assistance to clients.

In general, the rules prohibit a lawyer from giving a client financial assistance except for **advancing or guaranteeing expenses of litigation**. The ABA Model Rule is more liberal in that it allows repayment of the advanced costs of litigation to be contingent on the outcome of the litigation and allows an attorney to pay litigation costs outright for an indigent client. Several states adopted the ABA Model Rules without adopting these two notable exceptions.

It should be noted that advancing a client funds for living expenses is not covered by the rules allowing advances for "costs." Doing so is generally regarded as unethical conduct; however, a loan from attorney to client for living expenses may be evaluated separately under the rules relating to business transactions, rather than under the rules about advancing costs (Model Code DR 5-103(B) and Model Rule 1.8(e)).

4. A Lawyer's Interest in Litigation

Contingency fee
Fee depends on the successful outcome of a case and is based on a percentage of the recovery

Lawyers are prohibited from acquiring a proprietary interest in litigation in which they are involved (ABA Model Code DR 5-103(A) and ABA Model Rule 1.8(i)). *Contingency fees* in civil cases and *liens* to secure fees or expenses are excepted.

The rule prohibiting an attorney from obtaining an interest in litigation derives from the old prohibitions on maintenance, champerty, and *barratry*. Under English common law these were crimes concerned with "stirring up litigation." *Champerty* meant obtaining a financial interest in the litigation. It was long felt that such conduct encouraged unmeritorious litigation and dishonesty in the courtroom.

Obviously, attitudes have changed dramatically. The approval by the organized bar and the widespread use of contingency fees has undercut these ideas about fees, and certainly the more recent changes in rules relating to attorney advertising have further diminished whatever strength remained in these principles. The current rules against obtaining an interest in litigation are all that remain. These modern rules are founded not so much on concerns about "stirring up litigation," but on the conflict that arises when an attorney "owns" a lawsuit and may be tempted to favor his or her own financial interests in the outcome over the best interests of the client.

5. Gifts from Clients

Because of the inherent conflict in a lawyer's dual role of adviser to a client and recipient of a gift from a client, a longstanding rule strongly **disfavors such gifts** from clients to their lawyers. This rule is especially pertinent when a lawyer drafts a document under which he or she then receives a gift, such as a will or trust. The courts have long held that this scenario is rife with potential for undue influence, fraud, and overreaching, especially because the cases often involve elderly clients who are vulnerable to overreaching by their attorneys.

Inter vivos
During life

Testamentary
Takes place at the time of death, such as through a will

Courts frequently void both *inter vivos* and *testamentary* gifts in such cases, even without an affirmative showing of undue influence. Some courts will allow the attorney-beneficiary to present evidence showing the legitimacy of the gift. To do so, the attorney usually must show that the gift was fair and fully intended by the client, who had the requisite capacity and was not subject to undue influence by the lawyer. One serious additional problem sometimes results from such a gift: It may raise the question of the client's testamentary capacity, potentially voiding the entire estate plan, including the gift to the attorney. A particularly egregious abuse of these rules led the California legislature to adopt a statute that invalidates instruments that purport to make such gifts except for gifts to blood relatives or when independent counsel certifies that there was no fraud or undue influence.

An attorney may also be subject to discipline for accepting such gifts (ABA Model Code EC 5-5 and Model Rule 1.8(c)). The rules prohibit a lawyer from **soliciting a gift** or **preparing a document** in which the lawyer or a close relative of the lawyer is given a gift. Family members named include parent, child, grandparent, grandchild, spouse, and other relatives or persons with whom the lawyer "maintains a close familial relationship." An exception is permitted if the client is also a relative of the attorney-donee or beneficiary. "Simple gifts," such as a holiday present or token of appreciation, are permitted. In cases that require the attorney-donee to draft a document, **independent counsel** should be consulted.

Two unresolved issues that are handled in a variety of ways by different jurisdictions are gifts that do not require a conveyance document and situations in which the attorney is nominated in the document he or she drafts to perform additional services, such as those of **executor or trustee**. This second practice is common and is rarely questioned; more questionable is when an attorney nominated to such a position in a document he or she drafts also acts as his or her own counsel or has another attorney in the same firm act as his or her counsel. Some states prohibit this arrangement unless the court approves it upon a finding that it is in the best interests of the estate.

A paralegal should also be aware of the potential conflict created when a client gives him or her a **gift**. As with business transactions, there is less risk of undue influence when a gift is bestowed on a paralegal than on a lawyer, but the appearance of impropriety may be present nonetheless. In the case of a substantial gift, especially by an elderly or otherwise vulnerable client, the paralegal should be most cautious to see that the supervising attorney recommends independent counsel and to refrain from working on the gift document.

6.   Agreements with Clients Limiting Malpractice Liability

Both case law and the ethical rules prohibit attorneys from attempting to limit their liability for malpractice. The conflict in this situation is clear: The attorney is trying to protect his or her own interests at the expense of the client. A few cases deal with attorneys who attempt to limit their liability by asking their clients to sign a **disclaimer** before representation even begins; most cases deal with attorneys who exercise undue influence to pressure a client into signing a **release** after the alleged malpractice has taken place.

The ABA Model Code prohibits lawyers from attempting to exonerate themselves from or to limit their liability to clients for malpractice (Model Code DR 6-102). The ABA Model Rules prohibit a lawyer from attempting to limit his or her liability up front unless the client is represented by independent counsel in making the agreement. It also prohibits a lawyer from settling a malpractice claim unless an unrepresented client is advised in writing to seek independent counsel and has a reasonable opportunity to do so (Model Rule 1.8(h)).

A lawyer may not circumvent the rule against limiting liability by including in a retainer agreement provisions that relieve the lawyer from responsibility if the client takes certain actions. One such provision, for example, might relieve the attorney from further responsibility if the client fails to inform the attorney of a new address or phone number. Both case law and bar ethics opinions have consistently disallowed such provisions. Equally unacceptable as a means to limit liability is returning a client's fee with an endorsement releasing the attorney from liability.

It should be noted that lawyers can limit the **"scope" of representation** if the limitation is reasonable and the client gives informed written consent. Good engagement and retainer agreements state the exact nature and limits of representation for the protection of both the lawyer and the client (Model Rule 1.2(c)).

7. Payment of Attorney's Fees by a Third Party

If someone other than the client pays the attorney's fees, a conflict may arise over who is guiding the representation—the client or the payer. The attorney's loyalty and sense of responsibility may be divided and judgment clouded if the person paying the fee wants to be involved in making decisions about the case. The potential for harm to the client is greatest when the interests of the client and the one paying for the representation diverge. Some common instances of this kind of conflict occur when a parent pays the fee for a child, a spouse for the other spouse, a corporation for a director, and an employer for an employee.

There have also been instances in which the legal fees for the representation of **criminal defendants** in drug cases were paid by an unknown third party, very probably the operator of the criminal enterprise. It is likely that the unnamed third party sought to guide the defense by keeping the client quiet about matters that may have mitigated the defendant's guilt or lessened the sentence imposed while implicating the third party. This situation would not only result in an ethical breach, subjecting the attorney to a civil suit and disciplinary action, but also would constitute grounds for appeal based on ineffective assistance of counsel.

Generally, the ethics rules permit third-party payment of attorney's fees so long as the third party does not interfere with the exercise of the attorney's **independent professional judgment**, does not otherwise interfere with the attorney-client relationship, and there is informed **consent. Confidentiality** must be maintained as well (Model Code DR 5-107(A) and ABA Model Rules 1.8(f) and 5.4(c)).

Some thorny issues arise in the application of these rules. For example, the salary of an attorney in a public defender's office is paid by a government entity, not by the indigent client that the attorney represents. The courts have upheld this arrangement so long as those who have interests that may conflict with the client's do not either interfere with the attorney's professional judgment or control the lawyer's compensation. Similar issues are present in legal aid organizations that serve indigent and other nonpaying clients.

8. Relatives of Lawyers

When married or other closely related attorneys represent adverse interests, the possibility of a conflict that may harm a client clearly exists. Husbands and wives and other close family members naturally discuss their work with one another, giving rise to the **risk of disclosure** of confidential information, which is potentially quite harmful if the spouse who learns the information represents an adversary. Duties of **loyalty and zealous representation** are also implicated; an attorney-spouse may not fight as zealously for a client when the opposing counsel is his or her spouse. Last, because spouses have a financial interest in one another's income, the potential to increase the marital funds from a large fee may also influence an attorney-spouse's sense of loyalty or independent judgment.

The number of women entering the legal profession has increased dramatically since 1970, thereby expanding the potential for conflicts, but a provision was added to the later ABA Model Rules. In the recent revisions to the Model Rules, this provision was removed from the rule itself and added as a Comment (Model Rule 1.7, Comment 11). This Comment provides that lawyers should not represent clients in the same or a substantially related matter if they are "closely related by blood or marriage." Removed from this provision were references to specifically named categories of relatives: parents, children, siblings, and spouses. Each client must give informed consent; such conflicts are not imputed to the firm for which the lawyer works. Some jurisdictions may not adopt the revised rule as they prefer a specific rule, rather than the comment.

Some states, such as California, have expanded the scope of this rule to **specified non-relatives**, such as persons who live with or have an intimate personal relationship with the lawyer. Informed written consent is also required in California.

The ethics rules governing conflicts based on family relationships are also applicable to **paralegals**. The potential for conflicts and disclosure of protected information is great between married or related paralegals and paralegals married or related to lawyers or other law firm employees when they are working on opposite sides of a case. Law firms must check prospective employees for family conflicts, and paralegals and other affected persons covered by the rules should inform their firms fully of any situation that might give rise to such a conflict.

State ethics opinions that have addressed family conflicts involving paralegals advise that the firm does not have to withdraw as along as the paralegal in question does not work on the matter, no confidences are revealed, and the client is fully informed or consents with full disclosure.

9.   Sexual Relations with Clients

A new provision in the 2001 revisions to the ABA Model Rules prohibits lawyers from having sexual relations with clients unless a sexual relationship **predated** the representation (Model Rule 1.8(j)). Comparable provisions have already been adopted in several states. The basis for this rule is twofold: (1) a sexual relationship between lawyer and client has the potential to involve **exploitation** of the client, who is sometimes in a vulnerable state; and (2) the emotional involvement of the lawyer with the client may prevent the lawyer from exercising **objective and rational judgment** on the client's behalf. Consent is not acceptable in such cases, and a lack of actual prejudice to the client does not mitigate the lawyer's actions.

Because rules on sex with clients are new, there are no cases on record that involve paralegals having sex with clients. The basis for the rule is not as strong for paralegals because the paralegal is not the one who is required to exercise independent professional judgment about the client's legal matter.

D.   Imputed Conflicts and Disqualification

1.   General Rules

As mentioned above, the disqualification of one lawyer in a firm may cause the entire firm to be disqualified from representing a client — that is, the lawyer's conflict is imputed to the other persons in the firm. The principle of imputed or vicarious conflicts is based on the idea that all the lawyers in a firm know everything about all the clients and cases being handled by the firm. Particularly, the partners in a firm (rather than other employees, whether lawyers or nonlawyers) are believed to **share confidential information** about clients in order to best represent their interests. While collegial sharing to this extent no longer characterizes large law firms, consideration of **financial incentives** still supports the application of imputed conflict rules in some conflict situations. Although confidential information can be protected by careful screening, it is much more difficult to protect against the actual or perceived pressure to handle a case in a manner that will most benefit the firm and not necessarily be the most beneficial for the client.

It should be noted that when a firm is disqualified by a court, the firm may be required to **disgorge fees** paid for the legal services during the representation. This remedy is most often applied when the firm knew or should have known of the conflict and failed to disclose it to the client. A disqualification may also be the basis for a malpractice case against the lawyer and firm for breach of fiduciary duty.

The strict application of imputed conflict rules has created serious problems for law firms, individual lawyers, and clients, given lawyer mobility and clients' choosing representation on a matter-by-matter basis. Vicarious disqualification also poses special concerns for paralegals, whose job mobility is also threatened by an overly rigid application of the rules.

The ABA Model Code contains a strict rule that states if a lawyer cannot represent a client under the code because of a conflict or for any other reason, neither can any other lawyer affiliated with the tainted lawyer's firm, whether partner, associate, or of counsel. This sweeping rule does not allow screening or client consent to overcome the disqualification (Model Code DR 5-105). The ABA Model Rules, however, do not apply imputed disqualification equally to all kinds of conflicts situations. The rules cover client-based concurrent and successive conflicts, but not those based on the lawyer's personal or business interest; i.e., the Rule excludes business transactions, familial relationships, gifts from clients, literary rights, sexual relationships, and more (Model Rule 1.10). Recent revisions to Rule 1.10 prohibit representation in cases where a lawyer has changed firms only if the matter is the same or substantially related and the lawyer learned confidential information about the matter while with the previous firm. Clients may waive such conflicts with informed written consent. A new Comment (4) to Rule 1.10 states the ABA position that the conflicts of paralegals and other nonlawyer personnel are not imputed to the firm. (See discussion below under Use of Screens.)

Most court decisions on vicarious disqualification were made during the time that the ABA Model Code was followed by nearly all jurisdictions. As a result, the courts have frequently applied a per se rule of imputed disqualification. The trend, however, is toward a more flexible approach, under which the presumption of imputed disqualification may be rebutted by evidence that the person with the conflict did not have access to confidential information in working on the first matter, or that the affected person is being properly screened from any involvement in the matter. A few state courts have resisted this trend.

Disqualification motions are sometimes used as a **strategy to delay or harass the opposition**. Courts look askance at such motions, especially if they are not made as early as possible in the proceedings or are based more on appearance of impropriety than on any real danger of harm to a client or a likely breach of confidentiality or loyalty.

Firms and clients have also been known to use the disqualification rules as a strategy to prevent another firm from being able to represent a specific client on a specific matter. For example, a large corporate client may give minor matters to competitor firms so that, in the event of litigation, there is no qualified attorney without a conflict available to represent the opposing party—that is, all the attorneys are "conflicted out."

2. Use of Screens

The use of screening in the law firm to overcome imputed disqualification of the entire firm first arose in cases involving **former government lawyers**. While the risk of conflicts involving such lawyers is especially high because of their perceived inside knowledge, connections, and influence, the legal community has been concerned primarily about the ability of government lawyers to move into private practice. If conflicts rules are strictly applied and screens are not allowed to overcome them, government lawyers' employment options are quite limited. Going into government service would become a "permanent" career choice—a significant deterrent to entering government service in which salaries are substantially lower than in private practice.

Screening in private law firms, in cases involving attorney and nonlawyer employees not previously in government service, has become common practice. A *screen* (also called a *Chinese wall* or *cone of silence*) isolates the disqualified attorney or paralegal by setting up office procedures to prevent the disqualified person from having access to information, including case files and other documents, and from communicating with anyone in the firm about the case.

Screen
Isolates a disqualified person by setting up procedures to prevent the affected person from any involvement with or communication about the matter

These **procedures** should include:

- a **memorandum to all individuals in the firm** informing them of the conflict and screen and admonishing them not to discuss the matter with the disqualified person
- **markings on files and documents** to indicate the limitations on access
- programmed **computer warnings or blocks** to prevent screened employee's access to documents on the firm's computer network

The screen must be erected at the **time** the disqualified person begins employment with the firm or when work on the new matter is commenced. **Physical separation** of the disqualified person from those working on the case is also advisable. The firm may also require the disqualified person to **sign an agreement** in which he or she vows not to disclose any confidential information about the matter and not to discuss the matter with anyone at the firm. An attorney who is disqualified is not permitted to **share in fees** generated by the matter. This part of the screen is designed to prevent the disqualified lawyer from having a financial stake in the case.

Proving the **effectiveness** of a screen can be problematic. For the most part, a court evaluating the procedures must accept what the firm says by way of affidavits and testimony about the thoroughness and care of the measures taken and the extent to which they are observed. Screening procedures should be routine and careful records should be kept. A court will examine not only the specific procedures in place, but also the context of the situation. Is the firm large or small? Does the disqualified attorney or paralegal work in the same department or physical area of the office as the team representing the client in question? Where are the case files kept? Do the person with the conflict and the rest of the team working on the matter in question work together on other matters? Does the firm have sanctions for breaking the rules relating to the wall? How many other persons in the firm have access to the confidential information?

The extent to which conflict rules apply to paralegals and whether a screen will prevent a firm from being disqualified over a paralegal's conflict have been the subject of several cases and ethics opinions in the last decade. The ABA endorses **screening of paralegals** even in concurrent conflicts if the firm is strict in adhering to the screen, no confidential information is revealed, and the former employer admonishes the paralegal not to reveal any confidential information. This ethics opinion distinguishes between the application of a screen to an attorney's conflicts and those of a paralegal. When a lawyer moves to another firm, the new firm is ordinarily disqualified from representing an adverse interest of the attorney's former firm; a screen would not protect the firm from disqualification. However, a paralegal who previously worked on a matter adverse to his or her former firm may be screened effectively, thereby preventing the disqualification of the paralegal's new firm. The rationale for the more flexible application of screens in cases involving paralegal conflicts is based on protecting paralegals' employment mobility (ABA Ethics Opinion 88-1521).

The ABA Model Guidelines for the Utilization of Paralegal Services (Guideline 7) endorse the use of screens for conflicts involving paralegals, as do most state guidelines and proposed revisions to the comments to the ABA Model Rules. Most of the cases that address paralegal conflicts support the use of screens. The only state that clearly does not yet endorse the use of screens in paralegal conflict situations is Kansas.

There are also several important **cases on paralegal conflicts** and the use of screens. In *In re Complex Asbestos Litigation,* the plaintiff's attorney, a sole practitioner, was disqualified from a number of asbestos cases because his paralegal had previously worked for a firm representing several of the defendants in the case, and the attorney had made no attempt to screen the paralegal. The California Court of Appeals clearly endorsed the use of a screening procedure for paralegals to rebut the presumption that confidential information was shared (232 Cal. App. 3d 670 (1991)). The Texas Supreme Court endorsed the use of screens for paralegals in ongoing litigation in the case of *Phoenix Founders, Inc. v. Marshall,* 887 S.W.2d 831 (Tex. 1994). In a few other cases, the courts approved the use of screens but found the procedures employed by the firms to be inadequate (*Grant v. Thirteenth Court of Appeals,* 38 Tex. Sup. Ct. J. 12 (1994), and *Smart Industries Corp. v. Superior Court,* 876 P.2d 1176 (Ariz. App. Div. 1 1994)). In 1998, the Texas Supreme Court again addressed paralegal conflicts, finding in the case of *In re American Home Products,* 985 S.W.2d 68 (Tex. 1998), that conflicts rules apply to freelance paralegals who work on the opposite side of ongoing litigation. The firm in this case was disqualified. The minority view, stated in *Ciaffone v. District Court,* 945 P.2d 950 (Nev. 1997), was dealt a blow when in 2003 the Nevada Supreme Court overruled and clarified *Ciaffone* in *Leibowitz v. Eighth Judicial District Court of the State of Nevada,* 78 P.3d 515 (Nev. 2003). The court held that disqualification is required only if the former employee acquired privileged information in the previous employment.

Several state and local **ethics opinions** have addressed the issue. Most of the opinions endorse the use of screens and do not demand adherence to strict disqualification rules that would apply to lawyers in similar conflict situations. It seems likely that courts will continue to apply the conflicts rules flexibly because they have shown sensitivity to the different roles of the lawyer and paralegal and to the problems of job changing in an increasingly mobile legal business. The new comment to the revised ABA Model Rules may have some influence in encouraging the use of screens for paralegal conflicts in the few remaining states that are undecided or have found against screens.

E. Conflicts Checks

Conducting a conflicts check when a firm is considering hiring a new employee or undertaking a new matter is critical to identify and address potential and real conflicts. The ethics rules necessitate that lawyers adopt reasonable procedures to determine in both litigation and nonlitigation matters the parties and issues involved, and whether there are actual or potential conflicts of interest.

When a **prospective client** seeks representation by a firm, the attorney or paralegal should obtain first all the information necessary to conduct the conflicts check before the prospective client reveals confidential information about the matter for which representation is sought.

This gives greater protection of the confidential information in the event that the firm does not undertake representation. The new client information obtained should relate to the client's activities and the nature of representation sought. If the client is a business client, such as a corporation or partnership, the information should include the names of subsidiaries and other related businesses as well as principal shareholders, officers, directors, partners, and the like. The lawyer and client should discuss the nature of the legal services sought—for instance, whether representation is needed for a single matter such as a lawsuit or negotiation of a business deal, or whether representation is needed for an array of ongoing legal matters. If a lawsuit is contemplated, the names of potential adversaries should be obtained. If the client has other legal matters pending, basic information about these matters (such as the names of adversaries) should also be obtained. When an existing client seeks representation on a new matter, information relating to the nature of this matter and potential adversaries should always be obtained. It is good practice to update client information on existing clients regularly—names of officers and directors and the nature of business activities, for instance—to ensure the accuracy and currency of all information.

Similarly, **prospective employees**, including both attorneys and nonattorneys, must provide the firm with basic information about matters on which they worked in previous employment, major business or financial interests that have the potential to create conflicts, and personal and family relationships that may give rise to conflicts.

The firm then must process the information to determine if any conflicts or potential conflicts exist that would preclude representation or require the erection of a screen to isolate the disqualified employee. Many firms have **computer programs** that conduct searches more quickly and thoroughly than manual systems. Firms need an established procedure for evaluating conflicts that have been identified to decide how the firm should deal with them. Many firms have an **ethics or conflicts committee** or an ethics counsel to act on these matters. Prompt action on new clients and matters is essential to prevent a client or prospective client from delay in securing counsel. The conflicts committee should evaluate each new client, new matter, and new prospective employee—along with any potential conflicts they carry with them—applying the relevant ethical rules, case law, and firm policies that may impact their decision.

If a possible conflict exists, the firm examines the information relating to the new client, matter, or prospective employee to determine whether the conflict is one that could disqualify the firm. It may need to decide, for example, whether an apparent conflict with a former client concerns a "substantially related" matter. Once it is clear that a potential conflict of some type exists, the firm may recommend declining the representation, or it may accept the representation while seeking consent from the appropriate party or parties and/or creating a screen.

Avoiding conflicts of interest is a critical matter for paralegals. They have an ethical responsibility to keep good **records** of the matters on which they work and to be forthcoming with this information when appropriate. Generally, this information becomes pertinent when the paralegal prepares to make a job change, begins work on a new matter, or engages in freelance work, which in essence is a job change with every new assignment. **Freelancing** greatly increases the potential for conflicts. While it has become common practice for freelance paralegals and lawyers to handle assignments on a temporary, as-needed basis, this practice does necessitate careful monitoring. In providing prospective employers with information that enables them to conduct a conflicts check, paralegals must take care to protect client confidentiality as well. Information about matters on which the paralegal has worked should not be revealed until the firm is ready to make a firm job offer and should be limited to the minimum information necessary to conduct the check.

REVIEW QUESTIONS

1. On what principles are the conflicts of interest rules based?
2. Why are conflicts problems becoming more common?
3. What is the general rule about simultaneously representing two clients whose interests are adverse?
4. May clients consent to a concurrent conflict of interest? Under what circumstances may clients consent? Why might a court not honor this consent?
5. What are the requirements for a client's consent? What should be disclosed in a letter to a client regarding the potential conflict?
6. What do NALA and NFPA ethics rules say about conflicts?
7. What is an issue conflict? Are lawyers allowed to represent clients where these conflicts are present?
8. Would it be a conflict of interest for an attorney to represent two clients whose interests are not adverse but whose trial dates conflict? Would it be a conflict of interest if the attorney could obtain a postponement of one of the trials?
9. Is it ethical for a lawyer to represent both the husband and the wife in an uncontested divorce?
10. Is it ethical for an attorney to represent the passenger and the driver in a lawsuit against another driver?
11. Is it ethical for an attorney to represent codefendants in a criminal case?
12. May a firm represent more than one party to a business transaction?
13. Do the rules permit a firm to represent all the family members in creating an estate plan?

14. Can a lawyer with a conflict withdraw from representing one client and continue representing the other client?

15. What is the general rule about representing a client whose interests may be adverse to a former client?

16. How does a court decide if matters in successive representation are "substantially related"? If a court finds that matters are substantially related, is the attorney or firm automatically disqualified? In what two ways might the attorney or firm rebut a presumption that the confidentiality of information is at risk?

17. What is the general rule about business transactions between lawyers and clients? What are the conditions necessary for a business transaction to override the rule's prohibitions?

18. What is the general rule about an attorney being granted publication or media rights? What is the rationale behind it?

19. Are attorneys prohibited from paying clients' costs in a matter? From lending a client money? Why? Are there any circumstances under which a lawyer may cover a client's costs?

20. Why are lawyers prohibited from obtaining an ownership interest in a lawsuit they are handling? What are the exceptions?

21. Under what circumstances are gifts from clients prohibited? Explain the rationale. What steps should be taken to legitimize a gift to an attorney?

22. May an attorney attempt to limit his or her malpractice liability to a client? To settle a malpractice claim with a client?

23. What potential conflicts arise when a third party pays a client's legal fees? How can an attorney ensure against such conflicts?

24. What family relationships give rise to conflicts of interest rules? How do these rules apply to paralegals? Do the rules cover relationships outside of blood or marriage?

25. What is imputed disqualification? What is the basis for this rule? How does the rule apply to paralegals?

26. Describe how to create an effective screen that will withstand judicial scrutiny.

27. What do the majority of jurisdictions and the ABA say about the use of screens in conflicts cases involving paralegals? What jurisdictions do not follow this trend?

28. How should a conflicts check be conducted when a firm has a new client? A new matter or case? A new employee?

29. Do conflicts rules apply to freelance paralegals?

HYPOTHETICALS

1. Amy Anderson graduated from paralegal school in June and was immediately offered a position by one of the best firms in town, Xavier & Young. Her job is in the business litigation department.

The firm asks Amy to complete a conflicts check form in which she has to state the names and affiliations of her relatives who work in the legal field, stock she owns, and client matters she has worked on. She completes the form, and in the third section indicates that she has not worked on any client matters. On her second day at the job, Amy is assigned to work on the Toxall pharmaceutical litigation. She remembers that she worked briefly on the opposite side of this litigation for her internship sponsor, another large law firm, Abernathy & Crum. What should Amy do? Is there a conflict? Was Amy wrong not to report her internship work on her conflicts check form? Does it matter that it was not paying work? Does it matter that Amy only worked on the matter briefly and doesn't remember anything about it?

2. Bill Brown is a paralegal who works for a large firm that is handling some major products liability litigation involving Ford Motors. He knows that his job is being phased out and starts looking for another job. He likes one of the lawyers he has met working on the case; the lawyer, May Meredith, is one of the opposing counsel in the case. May's firm, Meredith and Lansing, handles real estate transactions, and Bill is interested in doing more real estate work and less litigation. Is it ethical for Bill to approach May about working at her firm? Is it ethical for May to hire Bill? Does May need to screen Bill in any way? What about after the Ford litigation is over?

3. Danielle Durham, a paralegal, works for Nally & Overland, a small law firm that handles family law, bankruptcy, and other small business and personal legal matters. She works for all three lawyers in the firm, each of whom specializes in one or two areas. The firm represented John and Katherine Jackson in a bankruptcy in 1997, and Danielle worked on that matter. Now the Jacksons are getting divorced and John wants the firm to represent him. May Nally & Overland represent John Jackson? May Danielle work on the case? May the firm represent both the Jacksons? Is a consent or screen needed?

4. Evelyn Ellerbe is a paralegal who works for an estate-planning lawyer, Timothy Taft. An elderly client, Sam Stone, comes in after his wife dies to have his will rewritten. It turns out that he is a neighbor of Evelyn, who takes a liking to Sam and begins to help him out by stopping by his house once or twice a week with groceries. After two years, during which Evelyn and Sam continue to be friends, Sam asks Timothy to rewrite his will for the purpose of leaving Evelyn half of his estate. Is it ethical for Tim to draft Sam's will with this provision? Is it ethical for Evelyn to assist in the preparation of the will? If the will is challenged, what will the court consider in deciding whether to void the gift? Would it make any difference to your answer if Sam had no other relatives?

Would it make any difference if Sam and Evelyn had a sexual relationship?

5. Frank Fink, an intellectual property paralegal, works in a boutique law firm, Edmund & Sun, which specializes in technology. The firm puts together its regular clientele of venture capitalist clients with clients who have ideas for high technology companies. The firm is often approached by start-up companies that need funding. Is it ethical for Edmund & Sun to represent both the venture capitalists and clients that need funding? How might the interests of these two clients conflict? Are consents needed? Assume that VC, a venture capitalist entity, and SU, a start-up company, are put together by Edmund & Sun and VC agrees to fund SU to the tune of $5 million. May Edmund & Sun draft the incorporation agreements, stock arrangements, and contracts involved? May Edmund & Sun take as its fee a 2 percent interest in the new company? If a dispute arises between VC and SU, may the firm mediate? May the firm represent one of the parties in the litigation that ensues? Both of the parties? May Frank invest his own money in the client's new company?

6. Jerry Jones works for Biotech Corp as an executive assistant to the president. She leaves company and works as a freelance secretary for executives. She is contacted by lawyer Bonnie Butler, who hires her to organize documents obtained in discovery from Biotech, who Jones is suing on behalf of another former employee. Has Butler done anything wrong? Is the information that Jones learned as an executive assistant confidential? What if she had signed a confidentiality agreement? What if Butler knew that she had obtained confidential information when she hired Jones? What will happen if Biotech brings a motion to disqualify Butler?

DISCUSSION QUESTIONS AND PROJECTS

1. If you worked in a law firm and were getting a divorce, would you find it acceptable to have two different lawyers in your firm represent you and your spouse? What if you were getting married and needed a prenuptial agreement?

2. Do you think firms should be bound by ethics rules against representing matters that create issue conflicts? Explain your reasoning.

3. What would you do if you worked for an attorney who had such a heavy court calendar that she or he was constantly rescheduling court dates and delaying motions and trials?

4. What would you do if you knew that your firm had a conflict of interest problem that it was not addressing internally? Would it make any difference in your actions if the firm was knowingly ignoring the problem?

5. Draft a letter to a client explaining a recently discovered potential conflict based on your previous employment.

6. What are your state's ethics rules on conflicts of interest?

7. Does your state or local bar have any special guidelines or ethics opinions on the application to paralegals of conflict rules? Are there any cases in your state involving firm disqualification because of a paralegal conflict of interest?

8. Do you think paralegals should be subject to the same rules on conflicts as those governing lawyers? Why, or why not?

9. What would you do as a paralegal if a client of an attorney with whom you work asked you to invest in his or her business? To buy property from him or her? Do you think that entering into these transactions would create a conflict of interest?

10. Do you think that a paralegal's obtaining the rights to a current client's story creates a conflict of interest?

11. Would you lend a client money for living expenses? Would your answer be different if lending the money would keep your client from accepting a low settlement offer because of the client's dire financial condition?

12. What would you do if an elderly client wanted to leave you a substantial gift in his or her will? Would it make any difference if the client had no other living relatives? If the client wanted to do this because of an estranged relationship with his or her children?

13. What would you do if a client gave you a valuable piece of jewelry? Would it make a difference if the gift was intended as thanks for your work on a case? What if the client promised to give you a personal "bonus" if your firm prevailed in the case?

14. What would you do if you worked for a firm that had all new clients sign an agreement limiting the firm's malpractice liability?

15. Do you think the rules prohibiting conflicts involving relatives should be extended to nonrelatives? What about roommates? Long-term live-in relationships? In-laws? Is it any "safer" for closely related lawyers and paralegals to work in the same firm? What kinds of problems might this situation create?

16. Interview paralegals at five local law firms and ask them about their policies and procedures for establishing screens and conducting conflicts checks. Also find out how effective they think screens are.

17. Do you think it is possible to screen an employee in a small law firm—for example, a firm with one lawyer, one paralegal, and one secretary? What if the firm had two lawyers, two paralegals, and two secretaries?

18. What should you do if a firm that has offered you a job does not request information to do a conflicts check?

SELECTED CASES

In re American Home Products, 985 S.W.2d 68 (Tex. 1998) (conflicts rules apply to freelance paralegals).

In re Complex Asbestos Litigation, 232 Cal. App. 3d 670, 283 Cal. Rptr. 732 (1991) (firm disqualified for paralegal conflict; screens endorsed).

Hayes v. Central States Orthopedic Specialists, Inc., 202 Okla. 30, 51 P.3d 562 (2002) (screening for paralegals allowed).

Leibowitz v. Eighth Judicial District Court of the State of Nevada, 78 P.3d 515 (Nev. 2003) (overturned strict rule of disqualification in cases of paralegal conflicts).

Phoenix Founders, Inc. v. Marshall, 887 S.W.2d 831 (Tex. 1994) (screen endorsed for paralegal conflict).

Smart Industries Corp. v. Superior Court, 876 P.2d 1176 (Ariz. App. Div.1 1994) (screen endorsed for paralegal conflict).

Zimmerman v. Mahaska Bottling Company, 19 P.3d 784 (Kan. 2001) (disallows screening for paralegals where screening would not be allowed for lawyers).

SELECTED REFERENCES

ABA Model Code Disciplinary Rules 5-101 through 5-107 ABA Model Rules 1.7 through 1.11

ABA Formal Opinion 88-356 (1988)

NFPA Ethics Opinion 93-3 [re conflicts of interest]

NFPA Model Code EC-1.6(a) through (g) [conflicts]

5

Advertising and Solicitation

This chapter explains the rules governing lawyer advertising and solicitation, how they evolved, and how they apply to paralegals working with lawyers. Chapter 5 covers:

- key cases affecting the ways that lawyer advertising is regulated
- the current status of legal advertising and marketing
- ethics rules governing advertising
- advertising rules as they apply to paralegals
- ethics rules prohibiting direct solicitation of clients
- limits on solicitation of clients
- advertising and solicitation on the Internet

A. Advertising

1. The Advent and Evolution of Lawyer Advertising

In 1977, the landmark case of *Bates v. State Bar of Arizona,* 433 U.S. 350, upset decades of ethics rules prohibiting lawyer advertising. These rules date back to the first state codes and first ABA Canons issued in 1908. The early rules prohibited virtually every form of advertising except business cards. Later, inclusion of biographical information on approved lists of lawyers was permitted.

The **political and social environment** surrounding the *Bates* decision was one of growing consumer awareness. Part of this general awareness was the recognition that most citizens did not have access to legal services, while at the same time the cost of legal services was rising dramatically. During the late 1960s and throughout the 1970s, new non-traditional methods of increasing access to legal services were being developed. Legal aid and public interest law firms began opening their doors. The first prepaid legal insurance plans were established. Storefront legal clinics that handled common legal problems at lower cost than traditional firms began to crop up. The organized bar and the public shared the realization that not only were most middle- and lower-middle income citizens unable to afford an attorney, but most did not even know how to go about finding one.

The ABA Model Code, adopted in 1969, contained the **traditional restrictions** on lawyer advertising. Only business cards, announcements of attorney personnel changes within a firm or of a new address, and Christmas cards to existing clients were permitted. The ABA had made some slight modifications in these rules in the mid-1970s to accommodate the special needs of legal aid organizations and prepaid legal insurance plans. It was not until *Bates* that sweeping changes were made in the ethics codes of every jurisdiction.

In the *Bates* case, two Arizona lawyers advertised low-cost legal services in a local newspaper and were disciplined by the state bar. Their challenge to restrictions on lawyer advertising was ultimately heard by the U.S. Supreme Court, which struck down such restrictions as violative of the First Amendment. The Court held that lawyer advertising — like other forms of commercial speech — was protected, and states could prohibit advertisements only in limited ways. States could prohibit **false, misleading, or deceptive ads** and could provide for **reasonable time, place, and manner restrictions**.

Several Supreme Court decisions that followed *Bates* struck down attempts by states to restrict lawyer advertising. In *In re R.M.J.,* 455 U.S. 1991 (1982), the Court held that a practitioner could advertise the **areas of law** in which he practiced in language other than that specified in the state ethics code because the language the lawyer used was not misleading and the code was unnecessarily restrictive. The court also allowed the lawyer to advertise the jurisdictions in which he was licensed to practice. In *Zauderer v. Office of Disciplinary Counsel of Supreme Court of Ohio*, 471 U.S. 626 (1985), the Supreme Court reversed the state supreme court's ruling that disciplined a personal injury attorney for placing a newspaper ad that pictured the intra-uterine device that was the subject of litigation. The Court held that the attorney had the right to publish ads **directed at readers with specific legal problems** so long as the ads were accurate and not misleading.

In 1988, the Supreme Court in *Shapero v. Kentucky Bar Association*, 486 U.S. 466, held that state ethics codes could not prohibit truthful and nondeceptive **direct mail advertising**. The language the Court found unconstitutional in the Kentucky code was identical to ABA Model Rule 7.3, which has since been revised. Prior to *Shapero*, ethics rules had classified direct-mail advertising with telephone and in-person solicitation and had prohibited it completely. In *Peel v. Attorney Registration and Disciplinary Commission of Illinois,* 496 U.S. 91 (1990), the Court struck down state prohibitions on statements on a lawyer's letterhead indicating the lawyer's **certification as a specialist**. While the certifying agency in the case—the National Board of Trial Advocacy—was not authorized by the state, the NBTA was shown to have objective and verifiable criteria for the certification of a civil trial specialist. This ruling resulted in changes in several state codes that had restrictions similar to those of Illinois.

Peel was followed by another case endorsing the use of a designation by an organization not approved by a state agency. In *Ibanez v. Florida Dept. of Business and Professional Regulation*, 512 U.S. 136 (1994), the Court held that an attorney/certified public accountant who advertised her certified public accountant (CPA) and certified financial planner (CFP) designations could not be reprimanded by the Florida Board of Accountancy for false, deceptive, and misleading advertising because the ad was truthful and the CFP designation was publicly recognized by potential clients.

The pattern of the court striking down state prohibitions on lawyer advertising was finally broken in 1995 in the case of *Florida Bar v. Went For It, Inc.*, 515 U.S. 618 (1995). In this landmark case, the Supreme Court upheld **restrictions on targeted direct mail advertising** sent to accident and disaster victims. Florida, like many other jurisdictions, had adopted a rule prohibiting such ads from being sent within 30 days of the accident or disaster. In upholding the prohibition, the Court cited heavily to bar studies that showed how negatively such letters were viewed by the public, which saw the lawyers' conduct as an invasion of privacy designed to take advantage of vulnerable people in tragic circumstances. This case could be viewed as marking a change in the way that restrictions on lawyer advertising are treated by the court or as one in a series of cases that are defining permissible limits since the *Bates* decision.

2. The Current Ethics Rules

The ABA Model Code was amended after *Bates* to comply with that decision (DR 2-101 through 2-105). The code prohibits false, fraudulent, misleading, deceptive, self-laudatory, or unfair statements or claims in public communications and delineates the specific information that may be used in print or broadcast media advertisements. The code requires ads to be "dignified," a requirement that would probably not be upheld by the Court. Special rules dictate that copies of broadcast and other ads be retained for stated time periods and that lawyers who advertise fees abide by the advertised fee for specified periods. Another provision prohibits a lawyer from compensating anyone in the media for giving him or her publicity. Some states adopted an alternative version of the ethics rules on advertising that permits any advertising except that which is false, fraudulent, misleading, or deceptive.

False/misleading communications
Contain material misrepresentations of fact or law or omit necessary material facts

The ABA Model Rules (7.1 through 7.5), which have been adopted in most states, follow a less restrictive and less specific approach to advertising, by prohibiting only **false or misleading communications.** The rule defines such communications as containing material misrepresentations of fact or law or omitting necessary material facts. The previous version of the rule, followed in many states, also prohibits communications that create an **unjustified expectation** about results or imply that results can be achieved by **violating the law** or ethics rules or statements that **compare** the lawyer's services to other lawyers' unless factually substantiated.

A few states specifically prohibit **testimonials**, contending that they are inherently misleading, create unjustified expectations, or are self-laudatory. A growing number of jurisdictions allow testimonials, usually with the requirement that they include information about payment to the endorser and/or the status of the endorser as a client, or have disclaimers to avoid unjustified expectations. The U.S. Supreme Court has refused the opportunity to review this issue twice. A **list of clients' names**, with their approval, may be used in advertising in all jurisdictions. **Dramatizations** in radio and television ads are also disfavored by many in the organized bar, but are becoming increasingly common and are tolerated in most states. Several states permit them, usually with disclaimers that advise the viewers that the ad is a dramatization and does not guarantee similar results.

Many states' rules are more restrictive than the ABA Model Rules. Some prohibit all lawyer **comparison advertising**. Other states prohibit statements regarding past performance on the grounds that they are inherently misleading and create false expectations. Several states specifically prohibit predictions of success; these claims would probably be found to be misleading even without a specific prohibition in the code. Claims about quality are generally prohibited because they are incapable of objective measurement. **Fee information** and comparisons are generally permissible, although some states have adopted specific language that may or may not be used to describe fees.

Lawyers may advertise through virtually any medium, including telephone directories, legal directories, newspapers, periodicals, outdoor signs, radio, television, direct mail, and the Internet. **Direct mail, e-mail, and recorded communications** must include the words **"Advertising Material"** at the beginning and end, and if the communication is direct mail, the words must appear on the outside of the envelope. Most states require lawyers to keep copies of ads and records on when and where they were used, whatever the method of advertising, for a stated period, usually between two and six years. Some also require that ads be submitted to a specified agency. Some states also require specifically worded **disclaimers** in ads. The rules also prohibit **payment** to a person for recommending legal services except for the cost of ads, charges for legal service organizations or lawyer referral services, or payment when a lawyer buys another lawyer's practice.

Certification may not be stated unless the lawyer is certified by a state- or ABA-accredited program and the name of the certifying entity is clear. Most states' rules prohibit the statement that a lawyer is "specialized" or a "specialist" in a practice area unless he or she is certified as such. Some states' rules and the proposed revisions to the ABA Model Rules allow the terms **"limited to"** or **"concentrated in"** to describe a lawyer's particular area of practice.

Trade names are permitted under ethics rules so long as they do not imply a connection to a government agency or legal services organization; however, some states have strict limits on the use of trade names. Firms with multijurisdictional practices may use the same firm name in all states but must show limits on listed lawyers' licenses to practice. Lawyers in public office cannot be listed in a firm's name or on its letterhead unless the lawyer is actively and regularly practicing with the firm. Finally, lawyers cannot state or imply that they practice with a partnership or organization unless they do in fact. For example, lawyers who share office space but are not partners cannot hold themselves out as partners by means of their firm name or letterhead.

As indicated in Chapter 2, paralegals' **names and titles** may be listed on letterheads and business cards in most jurisdictions. Earlier restrictions on nonlawyers being listed on letterheads and having business cards have been revised in most jurisdictions because of changes in the rules on lawyer advertising brought about by *Bates* and the cases that followed it. Paralegals' names may also be included in lawyer advertising of all kinds. The NFPA Model Code's DR 1.7 also endorses the use of paralegals' names and titles in lawyer communications. Three ethics opinions specifically endorse the use of "CLA" and "CLAS" on letter-heads and business cards.

Paralegal titles must clearly reflect the role of the paralegal and cannot mislead the public to believe that the paralegal is a lawyer. Some ethics opinions on the subject have been issued, including a fairly restrictive one issued in 1992 by New York State Bar Association Committee on Professional Ethics. Opinion 640, the first opinion issued by a bar on the **titles** that may be used by paralegals, endorsed the use of "paralegal" and "senior paralegal," which unambiguously convey the nonlawyer status of the paralegal. It recommended against the use of several other titles: "legal associate," "paralegal coordinator," "public benefits specialist," "legal advocate," "family law advocate," "housing law advocate," "disability advocate," and "public benefits advocate." The committee objected to these titles on the ground that they are likely to be confusing to the public, which would be misled about the nonlawyer status of someone with one of these titles.

A final concern about **letterhead and business cards** relates to their use by persons outside the firm, which should be carefully monitored. For example, several ethics opinions advise against allowing clients to use lawyers' letterhead to send correspondence without attorney review. Business cards, of course, must not be used for unethical solicitation.

3. Current Issues and Trends in Lawyer Advertising

The legal profession's initial resistance to lawyer advertising was tremendous, based mainly on the notion that it would de-professionalize and commercialize law practice. Strong support for these beliefs still exists in many segments of the legal community; however, studies show that at least half of the lawyers in the country engage in some form of advertising. More firms than ever are using advertising as part of a marketing plan that creates a firm's image to attract clients.

While many lawyers attribute the declining image of the legal profession to advertising, the public does not. The public considers advertising as a source of information and only begins to perceive it as objectionable when it becomes "invasive." It is also clear that an increasing number of people find lawyers through advertising.

Legal **marketing** has become a small support industry to the legal profession. Consultants, Web site designers, and legal public relations and marketing firms abound. Many larger firms have their own in-house legal marketing personnel. An organization of persons working in this niche, the National Association of Law Firm Marketing Administrators, has been around for twenty years. Many firms have become sophisticated marketers, using tactics to attract clients in ways never dreamed of when *Bates* was decided.

Legal advertising takes many forms and is designed to target many different kinds of potential clients. Larger traditional law firms have strategic marketing plans that identify potential clients and develop ways to attract their business. Most have **firm brochures** that describe the backgrounds of the firm's attorneys and the nature of their practice. Many also have regularly published **newsletters** for clients to update the clients on the latest firm triumphs and to inform them of changes in the law that may encourage the clients to have legal work done. Many hold social events and educational seminars for clients and send press releases to the media to announce significant events in the firm—for example, when the firm wins an important case or a prestigious new partner joins the firm.

Combined with the increased competition for corporate clients, the phenomenon of advertising has created a new atmosphere in larger law firms. New value is placed on **rainmakers** who can bring in business. A lawyer's ability to work well with clients and keep them satisfied is essential to success in a firm. Law firms try to establish a high public profile by donating funds to worthy causes, participating in community and civic activities, taking pro bono cases that will generate favorable publicity, and encouraging their lawyers and paralegals to participate in a wide variety of organizational activities outside the firm that are both professional and civic in nature. Many firms sponsor in-house seminars or send lawyers to continuing education programs that train lawyers how to better market their services and how to enhance client relations. Many firms give seminars at trade shows in industries from which they draw clients—an example of "niche marketing."

Some large firms use **client surveys** to assess the attitudes, needs, and levels of satisfaction of their clients. Surveys, conducted either orally through structured interviews or in writing, aim to identify the importance of various factors in meeting clients' needs and to find out how the firm's responsiveness, communication, services, and fee structure are perceived. Theoretically, client relations are improved simply by virtue of conducting the survey, and the information gained may be used to enhance services and to remedy weaknesses. Sophisticated research surveys are also being used by a few major firms, sometimes in conjunction with a client, to gain information about a particular industry or trend. The firms then use the results to sponsor firm events for clients and prospective clients and to craft press releases and articles for publication in bar, industry, or special-interest periodicals. Many firms have sought to **"brand"** themselves, making changes to the firm name to make it easier to recall (and eliminating the punctuation); developing taglines used in publications; promoting the values they hold or their specific expertise. Some firms have experimented with advertorials in major newspapers.

Smaller firms also engage in **advertising**. The more traditional small firms use the same kinds of marketing activities as large firms. But many small firms are specialized; they handle one or two kinds of legal matters and seek a clientele that might not otherwise have a ready referral to an attorney. Personal injury firms have led the way in lawyer advertising, most noticeably with television and radio spots, but also with billboards, flyers placed on cars or doorknobs, posters on telephone poles, and even ads on the backs of grocery store receipts. Firms that handle immigration, family law, workers' compensation, Social Security benefits, and bankruptcy frequently use these techniques as well. Direct mail advertising of targeted persons who may need a specific kind of legal service is employed by some firms. Some lawyers have 900 telephone numbers to dispense legal advice, and others have catchy 800 numbers that are included in print, radio, or television ads.

Paralegals can play an important role in marketing by serving clients efficiently, emphasizing the cost savings to the client from the use of paralegals, identifying sources for referrals, alerting attorneys to opportunities for rainmaking, and working with attorneys to develop a marketing plan and client surveys.

As the **Internet** has become such an important means of disseminating information, lawyers are using various kinds of Internet communications to reach prospective clients. Most law firms now have **Web sites** that, like firm brochures, provide background information on the lawyers in the firm and the areas in which the firm practices. Web sites also include articles about legal issues of interest to clients. Some have catchy names to draw in clients who are searching the Internet for a lawyer. Some lawyers participate in **chat groups** and have used direct e-mail to attract clients. Many lawyers post advertisements and articles on Internet bulletin boards and newsgroups and participate in trade group seminars on-line.

Chat group
Discussion carried on electronically over the Internet, which can be live or synchronous

Web sites that provide legal information have also sprung up. These sites have lawyers who answer questions from inquirers who have a legal problem. Lawyers sometimes answer these queries for free; other times they are paid by the Web site. Many lawyers who participate hope that they will gain clients this way. Another use of the Internet to increase access to legal services has been created by Web sites that **match up prospective clients with lawyers**. In these sites, the client usually spells out his or her legal problem, and participating lawyers "bid" for the case. Lawyers have to be careful about the sites they associate with or link to, as some have been less than scrupulous in the way that they advertise to clients. Some lawyers have been disciplined for running afoul of the rules; others have been badly and publicly embarrassed.

The use of the Internet to attract clients has raised **new ethical issues** that fall into many areas of the ethics rules. Are the lawyers who answer questions on Web sites for people with legal problems giving advice or providing legal "information"? If clients pay a fee to the Web site to have their questions answered, is the lawyer engaging in fee splitting with the Web site owner? Is direct e-mail of prospective clients advertising or solicitation, and which rules apply? Is a Web site more like a television ad or a firm brochure? If an attorney states a legal opinion in a chat group or a legal Web site, is the attorney forming an attorney-client relationship with the person posing the question? Is the attorney violating unauthorized practice rules in states in which he or she is not licensed to practice but where the opinion is read? Is it inherently misleading to advertise on the Internet when the attorney is not licensed in all the states where the ad may be read? Are firms that match up lawyers and clients acting as referral services that must be approved by the state bar or court?

Some states have issued ethics opinions or new rules that explain how the ethics rules on advertising and solicitation apply to electronic communications. At this point, a few generalizations can be made about the ethics of electronic advertising and solicitation:

- It is not unethical for a lawyer or law firm to have a **Web site** providing information about the firm so long as other ethics rules on advertising are followed. The applicable rules prohibit false and misleading statements, require lawyers to retain copies of the material for review, specify language about certifications, and mandate inclusion of the lawyer's name in the "advertisement."
- A lawyer's Web site must state the **jurisdictions** in which the lawyers in the firm are licensed to practice law and should contain disclaimers to warn prospective clients that they can practice only in those states. This information and the disclaimers are needed to prevent the public from being misled about where a lawyer can practice and to protect against UPL.
- Advertising on the Internet, including direct e-mail, constitutes **"advertising,"** not solicitation, so lawyers can use the Internet to advertise as long as the existing ethics rules on advertising are followed.

Most lawyers have **disclaimers** on their Web sites indicating that information provided therein is not legal advice and that no attorney-client relationship is established by virtue of the prospective client sending a lawyer an e-mail. Disclaimers also warn that such communications are not privileged and state the jurisdictional limits of the lawyer's practice.

The recent revisions to the ABA Model Rules classify **"real-time electronic contact"** with prospective clients, such as in live chats, as solicitation, not advertising, and it is therefore subject to the more rigorous restrictions that apply to that kind of communication. Another issue is when an attorney-client relationship is formed in electronic communication. Some experts believe that an attorney-client relationship may arise in **threaded discussions** and chat rooms if a lawyer gives advice that is specific to the client's problem. If a lawyer-client relationship does arise without the lawyer checking for conflicts, the lawyer could be placed in a conflict situation. If the client follows the advice and is harmed by the results, the lawyer may be sued for malpractice.

Spam
Direct unsolicited
e-mail to a large num-
ber of Internet users

At least one state, Tennessee, has disciplined a lawyer for soliciting on the Internet by sending a direct e-mail **"spam"** to more than 10,000 Internet users, including users in jurisdictions in which the lawyer was not licensed to practice. Some states have determined that lawyers are not permitted to be listed in lawyers' directories on the Internet, and several states classify fee-charging directories as profit-making referral services that lawyers are prohibited from using. Some firms use direct e-mail with current clients, sending newsletters and the like, but most are not ready to run the risk of ethics violations for direct e-mail solicitation or illegal spam.

Many commentators would like to see **uniform national ethics rules** concerning Internet communications. The great variation among states in their handling of advertising and solicitation exacerbates this already difficult new area of ethics; a lawyer may be in compliance with the local jurisdictional rules but in violation of the rules in another state where the communication is read. Further, the lawyers in states with more restrictive advertising rules are at a competitive disadvantage because they are more limited in what they can say, how they can say it, and where they can say it. Differences in rules on advertising in directories, how one's areas of expertise can be described, and whether extensive disclaimers are required make advertising on the Internet especially challenging for lawyers in restrictive jurisdictions.

B. Solicitation

The changes in ethics rules and practice relating to advertising have not had much impact on the rules restricting the conduct of lawyers in soliciting clients directly, either **in person or by telephone**. The foundation for these restrictions is strong and remains virtually unquestioned by the profession. The rules reflect concerns about the intimidation, undue influence, and unfair bargaining position that a lawyer may have when he or she confronts a prospective client face-to-face or on the phone. Related to this is the longstanding prohibition against "ambulance chasers" or "**runners and cappers,**" agents of lawyers who prey on accident victims by soliciting them directly at the scene of an accident or while they are in a hospital as the result of an accident. This kind of overreaching conduct, especially when it is directed toward clients who are vulnerable and not in a position to make a rational or well-thought-out choice about selecting counsel, clearly offends most lawyers and the public.

Runners and cappers
Agents of lawyers who prey on accident victims by soliciting them directly, usually at the accident scene or hospital

Several cases have addressed this issue. The leading case upholding restrictions on direct solicitation is *Ohralik v. Ohio State Bar Association,* 436 U.S. 447 (1978), which was decided at about the same time as the

Bates case. This case involved an attorney who solicited an accident victim both by telephone and in person, including making a visit to the victim in the hospital. Aggravating the solicitation violation was the attorney's refusal to stop the solicitation after the potential "client" refused representation.

The U.S. Supreme Court case of *Edenfield v. Fane,* 507 U.S. 761 (1993), caused speculation that the Court might strike down some of the restrictions against direct solicitation by lawyers. In that case, a Florida CPA sought relief from regulations that prohibited direct solicitation of clients. The Court held that such restrictions are a violation of free speech in a business context where prospective clients are sophisticated and experienced business executives. This decision has not, however, caused any jurisdiction to do away with prohibitions on lawyer solicitation of clients.

An **exception** to rules against direct solicitation of clients is made in cases involving organizations that seek to represent plaintiffs in cases that further a specific **political principle**, such as freedom of speech or association, or civil rights. Examples of such organizations are the National Association for the Advancement of Colored People and American Civil Liberties Union. The leading cases in this area are *NAACP v. Button,* 371 U.S. 415 (1963), and *In re Primus,* 436 U.S. 412 (1978).

The ABA Model Code prohibits lawyers from soliciting employment **in person** or by **telephone.** The recent revisions to Model Rule 7.3 qualify telephone solicitation as **live telephone** and add **real-time electronic contact**. In order to meet the definition of solicitation, the lawyer's financial gain has to be a significant motive. Exceptions are carved out for other **lawyers, family members, close personal friends,** and **clients.** Speaking or writing about legal matters is not considered soliciting employment so long as the lawyer is not emphasizing his or her own experience or reputation or giving individual advice. The Model Rules also prohibit lawyers from soliciting when the prospective client has asked not to be solicited or when the solicitation involves "coercion, duress or harassment." Some states have adopted an alternative provision that takes a different approach to the exception for politically motivated solicitations. This version of the rule allows personal contact with the prospective client if "under the auspices of a public or charitable legal services organization; or . . . a bona fide political, social, civic, fraternal, employee or trade organization" whose purposes include providing or recommending legal services. Generally, courts have also carved out an exception for attorneys seeking to contact members of a class in a *class action suit*.

Some states have also adopted additional provisions that prohibit any direct or written solicitation of persons who are in a **vulnerable physical, emotional, or mental state**. California, for example, adds that communications transmitted at the scene of an accident or en route to a health care facility are presumed to violate rules against solicitation.

Finally, there is a split in the jurisdictions over the use of **pre-recorded telephone messages**. Some states classify these messages as direct telephone solicitation and prohibit them while others find this method to be more like direct mail advertising and do not prohibit them per se. The ABA rules classify them as "communications," i.e., advertising, not solicitation, as these messages are much like direct mail.

A lawyer who attempts to use **agents** or intermediaries to circumvent rules against solicitation will be held responsible in a disciplinary action for the conduct of his or her agents, under general principles of agency law and ethics rules. Despite these very clear rules, instances of unethical solicitation are not that uncommon, especially by lawyers using agents. For example, agents of lawyers, including accident investigators, have been found soliciting business at the scene of airline crashes and other major accidents. Some states are attempting to overcome the difficulties inherent in stopping unlawful solicitation by creating disaster response teams of volunteer and staff lawyers who go to the scenes of major accidents and disasters to warn victims about unlawful solicitation and to deter lawyers from engaging in such conduct.

A few state bars have found arrangements where **independent nonlawyers** providing legal services have referred clients to lawyers to constitute unlawful solicitation, usually coupled with fee splitting. Some personal injury lawyers offer a referral fee to anyone who brings a new case to the firm, often accomplished through the agent's unethical in-person or telephone solicitation. These violations are not often the subject of discipline because only the parties involved are aware of them, and none is willing to report them and thus lose a source of income.

The NALA and NFPA ethics codes do not address advertising and solicitation directly, but do prohibit a paralegal from engaging in any act that is unethical (see NALA Canon 3(c) and NFPA DR 1.3). Likewise, the ABA Model Guidelines for the Utilization of Paralegal Services require the lawyer to ensure that the paralegal's conduct is compatible with ethical rules (see Guidelines 1 and ABA Model Rule 5.3).

REVIEW QUESTIONS

1. When were prohibitions on lawyer advertising lifted? Under what leading U.S. Supreme Court case?
2. How did the recognition in the 1960s and 1970s that many Americans do not have access to legal services affect the movement toward acceptance of lawyer advertising?
3. What kinds of lawyer advertising were permitted under the 1969 ABA Model Code?
4. What kinds of restrictions may states place on lawyer advertising after the *Bates* case?
5. Why do many lawyers dislike lawyer advertising?

6. What kinds of advertising do lawyers most commonly use?
7. What do the key court decisions since *Bates* say about lawyer advertising?
8. What kinds of restrictions do some states place on lawyer advertising?
9. Do lawyer ads have to be "dignified" under ethics rules?
10. In what media can lawyers advertise under the ethics rules?
11. What are the rules governing lawyer advertising of specialization and certification?
12. What are acceptable restrictions on direct mail ads to accident victims?
13. Are law firms allowed to use trade names? Under what circumstances?
14. May paralegals be listed on lawyers' letterhead? Their business cards?
15. Are lawyers prohibited from soliciting clients in person? On the telephone? Why?
16. What are the exceptions to the direct solicitation rule?
17. May lawyers use paralegals to solicit clients directly?
18. How common are violations of the ban on direct solicitation?
19. What job titles for paralegals are and are not acceptable?
20. What role can a paralegal play in marketing?
21. What kinds of advertising and solicitation are being done on the Internet? What do ethics rules say about it? Are on-line chats considered to be communications/advertising or solicitation? What about threaded discussion?

HYPOTHETICALS

1. A group of lawyers and nonlawyers form a profit-making company that is called "Foreclosure Fighters." The company represents people whose houses are being foreclosed. Foreclosure Fighters has a strong public interest mission to help people who are being treated unfairly, but it does charge a fee to the client. The goal of the representation is to forestall or stop the foreclosures. Are there any ethical issues involved in this scenario? May the company advertise its services using its name? May it solicit clients directly under the public interest exception to the solicitation rules? Would it make any difference if it were a nonprofit company?

2. Pam Pearson is a paralegal who works for a small personal injury law firm called Jones & Johnson. Her cousin, Marge Marshall, is injured in a car accident and is in the hospital. Pam asks Jan Jones, one of the name partners in the firm, for permission to leave an hour early to go see Marge in the hospital. Jan says yes, and adds, "Be sure to tell Marge that we can represent her." Should Pam do this? Is it unethical? Does it make any difference that Marge is in the hospital? Does it make any difference that Marge is a relative of Pam's?

3. Nathan Norris, a business paralegal, goes to work for Ollie Owen, who handles small business matters, including some that are litigated. Ollie wants to run an ad in the local business newspaper and asks Nathan to research the ethics rules and opinions to be sure that the ad is okay. The proposed ad would say: "Ollie Owen, experienced business and trial lawyer. Never lost a case. Handles some matters on contingency—no recovery, no fee." Examine each aspect of this ad and determine if there are any ethical violations. Would it matter if Ollie had only been in practice a year? Would it matter if Ollie settled all his cases and had never done a trial? Note that in most contingency cases, the client has to pay the costs even if he or she loses. What advice should Nathan give Ollie? How should the ad read?

4. Ruth Reardon works for a criminal lawyer, Sammy Swanson. As a paralegal, Ruth sometimes goes to the county jail to talk with clients who are awaiting release. One day when Ruth is going to the courthouse, Sammy hands her a stack of flyers about his services and asks her to hand them out in front of and inside the courthouse and jail. The flyer is on letter-size paper and looks like a business card. It has Sammy's name, address, telephone number, and e-mail address and the words, "Specializing in criminal defense work. Call collect any time night or day. Free initial consultation. $150/hour." May Ruth hand out these flyers? May she post them on bulletin boards and walls in the courthouse or jail? If the state has a certification program and Sammy is not certified as a criminal defense specialist, may he use the word "specializing"? If not, what alternative language may he use? Is it okay for the hourly fee to be stated? What if Sammy decides to raise his fees the next week? What if Sammy asks Ruth to hand out regular business cards?

5. Thomas Tucker is a paralegal working for Victoria Vernon, who handles workers' compensation cases. Victoria wants to produce a television ad about her services and asks Thomas to play the part of an injured client who gets a good recovery because of Victoria's services. In the ad, Thomas would be asked to say, "I was desperate and didn't know where to go. Then I found out about Victoria. She is incredible. She got me a great settlement. I can start my life all over. She is the best workers' comp lawyer in the state." During one part of this statement, Thomas is seen in a factory with a large machine falling on him. During the other part, he is seen standing in front of the U.S. Court House. Should Thomas participate in this ad? What might be objectionable about it under current ethics rules discussed in this chapter? What do some states require on such ads?

DISCUSSION QUESTIONS AND PROJECTS

1. Locate the rules governing advertising and solicitation in your jurisdiction. Compare them to the ABA Model Code and ABA Model Rules.

2. Using the *Bates* case, make a list of the reasons that support banning lawyer advertising and a list of those that support minimal restrictions on lawyer advertising. Which side of the argument do you find more persuasive?

3. Collect examples of as many different kinds of lawyer ads as you can find in your area. Check the Yellow Pages, billboards, television, radio, and so on. Rate these ads according to their (1) usefulness and information value, (2) effectiveness in recruiting clients to a firm, and (3) degree of dignity or offensiveness.

4. Call five local law firms and find out what they are doing to bring in clients, including what methods of advertising they use. Collect their firm brochures, newsletters, and other advertising materials and rate them the same way you did the ads in question 3.

5. Do you think advertising has hurt or helped the public image of lawyers? Has it made legal services more accessible?

6. Do you think that dramatizations in television and radio ads should be restricted? Why or why not? How?

7. Do you think testimonials should be prohibited? Why or why not?

8. May an ad say that an attorney is an "expert"? "Highly qualified"? "Competent"? Why or why not?

9. May an ad say that a firm specializes in "quickie divorces"? "Guaranteed visas"? Why or why not?

10. May an ad say the fee is $150 an hour without any additional information? Why or why not?

11. May a firm in a jurisdiction that allows trade names have the name "Public Law Firm"? "Legal Defenders"?

12. May a law firm print its name and phone number on pens that are given out to clients? On shirts donated to the local Little League team? On city maps sent to new residents?

13. Go on the Internet and find sites that offer legal advice or information and that match lawyers with prospective clients. What ethics rules are implicated in these sites? Did you find any sites that you believe are operating unethically? What potential ethics violations do you see?

14. Check your state's ethics rules and advisory opinions and find out what they say about Web sites, advertising on the Internet, chats, etc.

15. Write an ethics rule that covers advertising and solicitation on the Internet and is constitutional under *Bates* and its progeny.

16. Do you think restrictions on in-person and telephone solicitation are appropriate? Can you think of a way to allow direct solicitation

while addressing concerns about overreaching and intimidation? Read the *Edenfield v. Fane* case for guidance.

17. Should political and public interest organizations be excused from restrictions on in-person solicitation? Why or why not?

SELECTED CASES

Bates v. State Bar of Arizona, 433 U.S. 350 (1977) (struck down state rules prohibiting advertising of legal services).

In re Cartmel, 676 N.E.2d 1047 (Ind. 1997) (paralegal placed ad that violated rules and lawyer was suspended).

Edenfield v. Fane, 507 U.S. 761 (1993) (struck down restrictions on CPAs that prohibited solicitation of business clients).

Florida Bar v. Went For It, Inc., 515 U.S. 618 (1995) (upheld restrictions on direct mail advertising to accident victims).

Ohralik v. Ohio State Bar Association, 436 U.S. 447 (1978) (upheld restrictions on lawyer solicitation).

Peel v. Attorney Registration and Disciplinary Commission of Illinois, 496 U.S. 91 (1990) (struck down restrictions on advertising of certification and state licenses).

In re R.M.J., 455 U.S. 1991 (1982) (struck down restrictions that prohibited advertising of a lawyer's practice areas).

Shapero v. Kentucky Bar Association, 486 U.S. 466 (1988) (struck down restrictions on direct mail advertising).

Zauderer v. Office of Disciplinary Counsel of Supreme Court of Ohio, 471 U.S. 626 (1985) (struck down restrictions that prohibited advertising a picture of an IUD).

SELECTED REFERENCES

ABA Model Rules 5.3, 7.1-7.5
ABA Model Code DR 2-101 through 2-105, 9-101 ABA Model Guideline 1
NALA Canon 3(c)
NALA Guideline 1.3
NFPA DR 1.3

6

Fees and Client Funds

This chapter examines the role that financial matters play in the attorney–client relationship and the ethics rules and cases that guide conduct in this area. Paralegals are involved in financial matters in many of their functions, from handling client trust funds to billing clients for their time. Chapter 6 covers:

- fee arrangements made with clients, including fixed fees, contingency fees, and hourly fees
- alternative fee arrangements
- factors in determining if a fee is unethically excessive
- unethical billing practices
- communication of fee agreements with clients
- terms included in fee agreements
- award of attorney's fees under fee-shifting statutes
- inclusion of paralegal fees in fee awards
- fee-splitting and referral fees
- partnerships between lawyers and nonlawyers
- client funds and client trust accounts

A. Fee Arrangements with Clients

Several different methods are used to charge clients for legal services. The method selected depends mostly on the nature of the services being rendered. The most common methods of billing are fixed fees, contingency fees, and hourly fees.

1. Fixed Fees

Fixed fees
Fee for legal services based on a set amount

Fixed fees (also known as *flat fees*) usually are used for **routine legal services**, ones for which the attorney knows the length of time needed to complete the work. In this instance, the client is paying for the attorney's expertise as much as for the time expended. Typical services for which a fixed or flat fee is charged are filing a default divorce, forming a corporation, or handling a simple wage-earner bankruptcy.

A variation on the fixed fee is a fee that is based on the **percentage of the worth** of the matter being handled, either by statute or by practice. In probate matters, for example, the fee usually is based on a percentage of the value of the estate, according to statute. It is common practice in some states for an attorney to charge a percentage of the value of a real estate transaction. Although calculated as a percentage, these kinds of fees are not to be confused with contingency fees, in which the attorney is taking the risk of not collecting a fee in the event he or she loses the case.

2. Contingency Fees

Contingency fees
Fee depends on the successful outcome of a case and is based on a percentage of the recovery

Contingency fees are usually based on a **percentage of the recovery** in a case. Sometimes a fixed fee is made contingent on the outcome in a case, giving it the most important attribute of a contingency fee — risk. Contingency fee arrangements typically are used by plaintiffs' attorneys in civil litigation, such as personal injury or medical malpractice. The risk to the attorney in handling a case on contingency is that he or she will lose the case, thus receiving no compensation for the time spent on the case.

Although the contingency fee is now well accepted in the United States (it is not used in England or Canada), it was resisted by the American bar until early in this century. Contingency fees were thought to stir up litigation and to encourage attorneys to engage in unethical conduct to win cases. Gradually, the bar came to recognize the value of the contingency fee as a means to provide access to legal services to those who have a legal claim but who cannot otherwise afford legal services.

Despite the widespread use of contingency fees in **personal injury and medical malpractice** cases, ethics rules still place some limitations on their use. Contingency fee arrangements are not permitted in any state in **criminal defense** cases because they are thought to encourage corruption and discourage plea bargaining (ABA Model Rule 1.5(d)(2)). Most jurisdictions also have rules prohibiting contingency fees in **family law** matters where the fee is contingent on securing the dissolution of the marriage or on the amount of support, because such fee arrangements are thought to discourage reconciliation and settlement. In addition, a contingency arrangement in such cases may not be necessary to provide access to legal services because the court may award attorney's fees to the spouse without the means to pay them (ABA Model Rule 1.5(d)(1)).

Other limitations on contingency fee arrangements have been codified into state ethics rules or statutes that restrict the **percentage** of the fee. For example, the Federal Torts Claims Act, 28 U.S.C.A. §2678, places the maximum fee at 25 percent. Some state statutes, including California's Business and Professions Code §6146, limit the percentage that can be charged in medical malpractice cases.

Some jurisdictions have special ethics rules relating to the communication with the client of the terms of a contingency fee arrangement. Many of these rules require contingency fee agreements to be in **writing** even though other fee agreements in most states are not required to be in writing. State rules have been upheld requiring ads that mention contingency fees to disclose that clients are liable for costs even if they lose their case. Finally, contingency fees are subject to special judicial scrutiny for reasonableness and are disallowed if the percentage is considered exorbitant or the fee is well out of proportion to the work done or the risk taken by the attorney.

Contingency fees are a perpetual subject of debate within the legal profession. There are regular initiatives to prohibit them altogether in some jurisdictions or to limit the amount of fees if a case is uncontested or is settled before trial. Despite this controversy, contingency fees are gaining in popularity in new ways as clients explore **alternative fee arrangements**. For example, more corporate clients are requesting contingency arrangements in business litigation, even on the defense side, and some states use contingency fees for lawyers working to collect overdue child support.

While a typical contingency fee in a personal injury matter is one-third of the recovery, some lawyers charge on a **sliding scale** that reflects both the amount of risk to the attorney and the time and effort expended by the attorney as the case moves forward. For example, an attorney might charge 25 percent if the case settles before trial, one-third if it goes to trial, and 40 percent if it is appealed.

Sliding scale
Method for determining contingency fee based on both the amount of risk to the attorney and the time and effort expended

109

3. Hourly Fees

Hourly fees
Fee based on hourly
rates and the amount
of time actually
expended

Hourly fees are the most common method of billing in matters other than plaintiff civil litigation. Charging for time was not always so common in the legal profession but has become deeply ingrained in law practice during the past 30 years. Most large firms bill mainly by means of **hourly rates**, with every lawyer and paralegal keeping close track of the time spent on client matters, usually in increments of either six or ten minutes.

Hourly rates are based on the **expertise** and other **qualifications** of the person billing, the nature and complexity of the services performed and, of course, the **market**. For example, a senior partner in a major law firm who handles complex securities transactions may have a billing rate of $750 an hour. The time of a mid-level associate with five years' experience, however, may be charged at $150 to 300 an hour, while that of a five-year paralegal may be charged at $100 an hour.

Recently, there has been some movement away from hourly billing as the norm. Part of the impetus for this move is attributed to the increased efficiency of law firms through specialization and the use of technology. Firms that have developed highly valuable expertise and means of producing documents quickly and efficiently want to avoid being penalized for their efficiency and receive fair compensation, not just for their time, but also for the value of their services. Clients are also calling for changes in the way legal services are priced as they seek ways to lower legal fees and structure fee agreements in ways that allow them to plan and budget more accurately, and assess the value and productivity of the services. Some large corporations and government entities are issuing requests for proposals to law firms, asking them to bid for the legal work on projects.

Many firms are beginning to use **alternative methods** of structuring fee arrangements, such as charging a percentage of the value of a transaction, charging a premium for achieving results that are especially beneficial to the client, or charging a fixed fee that reflects the value of the services to the client without regard to the time expended. Fees that are capped at a predetermined amount, discounted hourly rates for major clients or merging companies, blended hourly rates arrived at by averaging rates for all firm lawyers and paralegals, contingency fees in defense matters, and hybrids of several different billing methods are now all commonly used. Another innovation is task-based billing, in which clients are charged a predetermined flat fee for a specific function, such as taking a deposition or representing a client at a particular kind of hearing.

More changes in billing practices are on the horizon as law practice changes in response to the market and new technology. The effect on paralegals is significant: paralegals must be proficient in technology and demonstrably efficient and productive in all their work. Paralegal managers and lawyers who supervise paralegals must be certain that paralegals are well trained and are assigned to perform work that matches their degree of expertise.

It is well accepted that **paralegal time** may be charged directly to clients just as attorney time is. When utilized properly, paralegals are engaged in legal work that, were it not for the paralegal, would have to be done by an attorney. And because paralegal time is billed to clients at lower rates than attorney time is, the cost to the client is lower. Guideline 8 of the ABA Model Guidelines for the Utilization of Paralegal Services (ABA Model Guidelines) provides that lawyers may charge for paralegal services. Most state guidelines specifically endorse this customary practice, which was validated by the U.S. Supreme Court in *Missouri v. Jenkins*, 491 U.S. 274 (1989) (with regard to statutory fee awards). The comment to NALA Model Guideline V also discusses the practice of billing clients for paralegal time and fee awards that include compensation for paralegal work. (Section C below discusses this topic further.)

B.   Ethics Rules About Fees

Most states' ethics rules prohibit lawyers from agreeing to, charging, or collecting an **unreasonable** fee. Some states use the term "**excessive fees**" instead of unreasonable fees; at least one state, California, prohibits *unconscionable* fees. **Illegal** fees are also prohibited. A fee is usually found illegal if it exceeds statutory limits such as those set by the Federal Torts Claims Act, mentioned above. The ABA Model Code, which speaks in terms of "clearly excessive," and the ABA Model Rules, which prohibit "unreasonable" fees, both list several factors used to determine whether a fee is unethically high:

Unconscionable
So unreasonable as to render a contract unenforceable, usually because the terms are so favorable to one party

1. the time and labor required, the novelty and difficulty of the questions involved, and the skill requisite to perform the legal service properly
2. the likelihood, if apparent to the client, that the acceptance of the particular employment will preclude other employment by the lawyer
3. the fee customarily charged in the locality for similar legal services
4. the amount involved and the results obtained
5. the time limitations imposed by the client or by the circumstances
6. the nature and length of the professional relationship with the client
7. the experience, reputation, and ability of the lawyer or lawyers performing the services, and
8. whether the fee is fixed or contingent

Model Code DR-2-106 and Model Rule 1.5.

A proposal to add "the degree of risk assumed by the lawyer" was not adopted in the recent Model Rules revisions.

The reasonableness of fees has been litigated extensively, mainly in cases involving statutory fee awards and cases where fees were awarded under the provisions of a contract (discussed below in Section C). Guidelines can be drawn from litigation over fees and from disciplinary cases. While all the factors on the ABA list are generally considered by courts and disciplinary bodies in determining if a fee is unethical, the **amount of time spent** still tends to be the most important. In fee dispute cases and disciplinary matters, the client's understanding of the fee agreement is also a critical factor.

Probably the most widespread ethical problem relating to fees is one that is not addressed directly by either ethics codes or case law. It is also one that paralegals may face during the course of their careers. It is the practice of **inflating the figures** for time spent on client matters.

In firms that depend on hourly billing for their revenue, the pressure to bill an ever-increasing number of hours is tremendous. The value of a fee-generating attorney or paralegal is measured largely by how much revenue that person produces for the firm. Expectations of billable hours rose dramatically in the 1980s and '90s. In the early 1980s, 1,200 billable hours a year was common in a large firm; now, the expectation is closer to 2,000 hours a year in many large firms.

While most of the pressure to bill falls on highly compensated associates trying to make partner, paralegals feel it too. Firms have learned that they have to delegate and monitor work carefully to ensure that their use of paralegals is profitable. Many firms, especially those that utilize paralegals extensively and bill by the hour, have also adopted strict **guidelines on paralegal billable hours** too. The pressure to bill has created an incentive to engage in improper billing practices, such as double billing, billing full rates for recycled work product, over-billing, over-staffing, billing for overhead costs, padding hours, doing unnecessary work for clients, and spending excessive amounts of time on matters that do not warrant it, sometimes called "churning."

In the past decade, several cases of prominent attorneys who engaged in **over-billing** and billing of personal expenses to clients have given this issue a high profile. Some cases involved padding hourly bills in corporate, insurance defense, and criminal defense cases; others have involved charging personal expenses, including clothes, travel, meals, and gifts, to clients. Examples abound in the press, with new scandals coming to light with some frequency. Disciplinary cases on excessive fees have involved overcharging for legal research and driving time to an unnecessarily distant library, doubling the costs of process servers and independent contractors, billing clients for more than 24 hours a day, charging fees and costs that were agreed in advance not to be charged, and multiplying the time spent by billers (e.g., by 1½) to ensure a profit.

These incidents have caused much speculation about the actual preva-
lence of abuses and the extent to which they can be attributed to fraud
or sloppy timekeeping and lack of management oversight.

Finally, it should be noted that **corporate clients** have taken
proactive steps to prevent themselves from becoming the victims of
unscrupulous billing practices and high legal bills. Many such clients
have requested firms to make proposals for services, established budgets
beyond which a firm may not bill, and demanded task-based billing, all
of which provide detailed information on the cost of services so that
clients can evaluate services and negotiate future billing arrangements.
Some corporations have restricted the costs they will pay. For example,
corporations reimburse for coach airfare only and refuse to pay surcharges on computerized legal research or for secretarial overtime or
computer use. Some corporate clients and some law firms are conducting **audits** of their billing to turn up errors and improper practices.
Many lawyers object to outside audits on two important ethical grounds:
it violates confidentiality to have outsiders review client files and bills,
and it may interfere with the lawyer's independent professional judgment for someone else to dictate that the lawyer must handle a case in
a certain way that minimizes costs. This last factor has particular rele-
vance when the client is a person who is insured and the insurance company is paying the lawyer's fees. Remember that a third-party payer
cannot dictate how representation is handled, as this would constitute
interference with the exercise of the lawyer's independent professional
judgment. (See Chapter 4 on Conflicts of Interest, section C.8.)

The ABA and several other bar associations have issued ethics opinions addressing billing practices. Among the practices found objectionable
are: **double billing** (that is, billing more than one client for the same
hours—such as travel time when making court appearances for more
than one client on the same day); **surcharges** on services contracted
with outside vendors, such as expert witnesses and freelance paralegals;
and **charges beyond reasonable costs** for in-house services like pho-
tocopying and computer searches. Some opinions call for full disclosure
of the basis for charges when the fee agreement is made and subsequently
when the client is billed. Some emphasize that the charges must also be
reasonable, which covers the situation in which charges are made for
unnecessary work or for hours not actually worked.

Paralegals have been implicated in some cases. For example, paralegals in one case billed deposition summaries at the rate of four to five
pages an hour, about a fourth of the average speed. In another case, a
paralegal billed 43 hours in one day. In some cases, paralegal billing rates
were double the market rate or the time was billed for routine clerical
work such as copying and filing. A few well-publicized cases in the
insurance industry have forced insurance defense law firms to rethink
what work they assign to paralegals because insurance companies refuse
to pay paralegal rates for work they consider to be clerical.

Double billing
Billing more than one
client for the same
hours

Billing abuses are not only inherently dishonest and unethical, but also detrimental in the long run both to the one who engages in them and to the firm. Good firms do not send bills to clients without first examining the bills to see that the amount fairly reflects the services rendered. If the bill is excessive, the partner who is responsible for billing the client should adjust it and "write off" excessive time. The written-off time is usually allocated back to the person who billed it and deducted from his or her total billable hours.

The firm that does not **review bills** or adjust them in this fashion is running the risk of having a dissatisfied client or of losing a client. Egregious abuses may result in disbarment and malpractice suits. Some commentators believe that excessive legal fees caused by dishonest billing practices have been a leading factor in the revolt by clients against the high cost of legal services and in the lowered esteem in which lawyers are held by the public.

Paralegals should not themselves engage in such unethical billing practices and have an obligation to report others' such conduct to a supervising attorney. A paralegal should not continue to work in a firm that encourages such conduct. The NFPA Model Code calls attention to the proper paralegal role in billing under DR 1.2. EC-1.2(c) and (d) tell paralegals to prepare thorough, accurate, and honest timekeeping and billing records and specifically call attention to billing abuses such as those mentioned in this chapter.

C.   Terms and Communication of Fee Arrangements with Clients

As soon as possible after a lawyer and client agree to representation, the lawyer should fully explain the terms of the fee agreement to the client. Many states (including New York and California) require that the scope of representation and information on fees and costs be communicated to the client in writing. A proposal to add this requirement to the Model Rules was rejected.

The ABA Model Code does not have a disciplinary rule requiring **written fee agreements** but advises lawyers to reach a "clear agreement" about fees, reduce the agreement to writing, especially in the case of contingency fees, and fully explain the reasons for the fee arrangement. ABA Model Rule 1.5(b) states that the scope of representation and the fee agreement should be communicated within a reasonable amount of time, "preferably in writing." Contingency fee agreements must be in a written form and signed by the client and must include the method and percentage(s) by which the fee is to be calculated and provision for payment of costs (that is, whether they are deducted before or after calculation of the fee and whether the client is liable for them if the case is lost). A written statement showing the calculations is required at the conclusion of the matter (ABA Model Rule 1.5(c)).

Written fee agreements are favored because they promote clear **communication** between the attorney and client and prevent disputes over the fee later on. In addition, they protect both parties in the event of a dispute, especially attorneys who might have any misunderstanding about the fee arrangements construed against them. Some state bars have standard forms that attorneys are encouraged to use.

As indicated in Chapter 2, discussing the unauthorized practice of law, paralegals should be alert to the **traps** in discussing fees directly with new clients. Only an attorney can agree to represent a client and in doing so to set and communicate the fee arrangement and meet the ethical obligation to explain the arrangement fully to the client. The role of the paralegal as a liaison to the client may include answering questions about fees and costs but cannot include entering into the contractual agreement with the client on the lawyer's behalf.

The ABA Model Guidelines state that **establishing a fee** is one of the few specified functions that a lawyer cannot delegate to a paralegal. Guideline 3(b) advises that a lawyer may not delegate "responsibility for establishing the amount of a fee to be charged for a legal service." The NALA Code of Ethics and Professional Responsibility provides in Canon 3(b) that "a paralegal must not . . . establish an attorney-client relationship [or] set fees."

The fee agreement or letter of engagement should cover fully:

- the **scope** of the firm's services
- **responsibilities** of the client and the firm
- the method of determining the **fee** (that is, hourly, fixed, contingency, or some other method)
- **rates** for different professionals if services are billed hourly
- **costs** the client is obligated to pay and when (that is, out of the client's recovery after the attorney's fee is calculated, in the case of contingency arrangements, or at specified regular billings)
- **termination** rights for both parties; disposition of **client files** at the end of the matter
- the method and **time of fee payment**
- **the procedure** for and frequency of billings, if applicable

It is critical that the agreement make clear if the client will be paying for paralegal time and at what rates(s). At least one court has held that a fee agreement that does not mention billing for nonlawyer time is ambiguous. An ambiguous agreement could give rise to a dispute or be used to deny payment if the client refuses to pay.

The agreement should also contain a provision indicating that it is **privileged**. It is wise to include language indicating that the firm is not guaranteeing a particular result. If the client does not speak or read English proficiently, the agreement should be in a **language** that the client does understand. The signature clause should include an acknowledgment that the client has read and understood the terms of the agreement, and the client should be given sufficient time to read and reflect on the agreement before signing it. If the lawyer is providing limited services, this matter should be carefully addressed to ensure that the lawyer does not become responsible for work that is not contemplated to be part of the representation. Finally, fee agreements may contain provisions indicating how fee **disputes** and malpractice claims will be handled—for example, by mediation or arbitration.

In some instances, attorneys may require a *retainer* or *advance,* which is paid at the commencement of the agreed-upon work. While frequently called "retainers," *advanced fees* are usually refundable, in that the attorney earns the fee as the work progresses and will refund to the client whatever portion is unearned when, for whatever reason, the services stop. *Retainer fees* are nonrefundable, in essence acting as a minimum fee regardless of the amount of work done and as a guarantee that the attorney will be available to handle the representation. A nonrefundable retainer is ethically acceptable so long as the client fully understands the arrangement and the fee is not excessive, considering the factors previously discussed. Advances must be deposited into a *client trust account* until earned, while nonrefundable retainers may be deposited directly into a firm operating account. (Client trust accounts are discussed below in Section G.) Matters for which an hourly fee is charged represent a higher potential for disputes with clients because, without an **estimate** of the number of hours a project will take, the client will have no idea what the ultimate bill for services might be. It is good practice for the attorney to provide the client, if at all possible, with an estimate or several estimates depending on how the matter might play out, and to update the estimate if the situation changes as the matter proceeds.

Payment of **costs** requires special clarity in fee agreements, as clients may not realize what costs can arise in a matter or may resent paying many small charges when they are already paying high fees. The kinds of costs that are billed directly to clients vary somewhat from firm to firm. As a rule, all lawyers expect clients to pay direct expenses that the firm pays to an entity outside the firm, such as filing fees paid to courts and government bodies, transcripts of depositions and trials, experts' reports and testimony, out-of-the-area travel expenses, outside printing, and messengers. Most firms also charge for copying done within the firm and for long-distance telephone calls. Some firms also charge the client for costs that might ordinarily be thought of as part of overhead, such as secretarial overtime, computer use, and even air-conditioning in the event the firm must work extra evening and weekend hours for a client. Generally, costs are itemized on a client's bill.

Retainer
Fee paid at the commencement of agreed-upon work to assure the availability of the lawyer to handle specified matters

While not in widespread use, the majority of jurisdictions permit lawyers to accept payment of legal fees by **credit card**. Some state rules have limitations, including one that the attorney not increase fees to cover expenses of participating in such a plan. Some states also permit attorneys to help clients work out financing for the payment of fees with a bank. Some attorneys accept property or an **interest in a client's business** in payment of fees. When doing so, attorneys must pay special attention to the value of the property and the reasonableness of the fee under the conflict of interest rules. (See Section C.2 in Chapter 4.)

D.   Statutory and Other Court-awarded Fees

As a general rule, litigants in the United States must pay their own attorney's fees. This practice is different from that in England, Canada, and most other European countries, all of which have some form of *fee shifting*. In England and Canada, for example, attorney's fees in litigation are awarded to the prevailing party.

Fee shifting
Award of the attorney's fees to the prevailing party

Efforts have been made to reform the American system, and some progress can be seen in court decisions, contracts, and legislation. Courts have awarded attorney's fees in cases in which a **common fund** that benefits persons other than the parties has been created as a result of the litigation; in which the litigation resulted in a common benefit to the public or some portion of the public, even though no fund was created; similarly, in which the plaintiff acted as a "private attorney general" vindicating a legal right that also benefits others and for which the plaintiff's actual damages are relatively small; and, finally, in actions for malicious prosecution, for abuse of civil process, or for those taken in bad faith. This last category of fee shifting is also supported by legislation in some states. **Contract provisions** for attorney's fees are relatively common and are generally enforced by the courts.

Fee-shifting statutes have proliferated in recent years, and now hundreds of state and federal statutes provide for the award of attorney's fees in specified kinds of litigation. These fee-shifting statutes generally apply to the kinds of litigation that the legislature wants to encourage as a matter of public policy (for example, protecting civil rights) and award fees only to prevailing plaintiffs, not to defendants. Like contingency fees, statutory fees enable plaintiffs who might not otherwise be able to afford an attorney to bring legal action to vindicate their rights. And as with contingency fees, the attorney is accepting the risk of not being compensated if he or she does not prevail.

Conflict of interest problems may arise in cases involving statutory fees when the interests of the client clash with the interest of the attorney in maximizing the fee award. For example, an offer to settle may satisfy the client but not include sufficient fees for the attorney, or may satisfy the attorney as to the fee award but not the client because the recovery to the client is too low. Lawyers must always be aware of the potential for this kind of conflict and keep the client's best interests in mind when advising whether to accept an offer.

Most important to paralegals in the area of statutory fees is the landmark decision of *Missouri v. Jenkins,* 491 U.S. 274 (1989), in which an award of attorney's fees that included **compensation for paralegal work** under the federal civil rights statute was upheld. The lower court had awarded fees that included compensation for paralegal time at hourly market rates. The state of Missouri contended, first, that the statute provided only for attorney's fees, not paralegals'; second, that if paralegal time was compensable, it should be compensated at cost, not at a market rate that includes a profit to the law firm. In upholding the award, the Court construed the attorney's fee statute broadly, finding that it did include paralegals' fees and that the recognized measure of market value was the appropriate one for setting paralegals' fees.

This was a critical decision for paralegals: a court decision that had gone the other way would have acted as a disincentive to the utilization of paralegal services by firms that work in statutory fee cases and cases where fees are awarded under the provisions of a contract. Thousands of cases awarding paralegal fees as part of attorney's fee awards have been decided in state and federal trial courts since *Missouri v. Jenkins.* This case was also the first U.S. Supreme Court decision in which the role of paralegals was discussed at any length. The Court endorsed the use of paralegals as a praiseworthy innovation and an effective means of containing the costs of legal services. Finally, *Missouri v. Jenkins* resolved an issue that had been in dispute throughout the country: several state and some federal appeals courts had interpreted attorney's fees statutes not to include paralegal fees at all or had used the cost of paralegals (i.e., their compensation), not market rate, to calculate the awards.

After *Missouri v. Jenkins,* several states **amended statutes and/or court rules** to clarify that attorney's fee awards include paralegals' fees at market rates. A few states continued to resist interpreting their statutes the way that the Supreme Court did in *Missouri v. Jenkins.* For example, Michigan and Idaho courts held that general attorney's fee statutes should not be read to allow an award that includes compensation for paralegal time. The courts in those cases generally called on the legislature to amend statutes to allow market rate compensation for paralegal time. As a result, Michigan adopted a court rule allowing court-awarded attorney's fees to cover paralegal work, and Idaho finally amended its Rules of Civil Procedure in 1999 to allow paralegal fees to be included in attorney fee awards (I.R.C.P. 54(e)(1)).

An important issue in fee-award matters involves the kind of information that must be supplied in fee petitions to the court to justify the

award of paralegal fees. Some trial courts have denied paralegal fees on the grounds that the work done by paralegals was clerical in nature, not the kind of work intended to be covered by an award of attorney's fees, or because there was inadequate information as to the qualifications of the paralegals, the nature of their work, the customary practice of billing separately for their services, and the market rates charged for their services. Other courts have reduced the amounts requested for paralegal work because the work was not sufficiently documented and justified or the petition contained what appeared to the court to be too high a profit margin.

Documentation supplied to the court when seeking fees should include:

- **credentials and experience** of the paralegals
- detailed **descriptions** of the work performed, including the number of hours spent on each discrete task
- information on paralegal **compensation**, overhead allocated to paralegals, and hourly rates
- **market data** on practices and rates in the legal community

Additionally, it is preferable for a firm to have a **range of rates** for paralegals, depending on their experience and the level of work they are performing. As with attorney work, not all paralegal work requires the same level of sophistication and expertise, and some judges are keen on matching the rate to the task.

Some court rules specify what is required for the award of paralegal fees. For example, California Bankruptcy Court Rules for the Northern District allow fees only if (1) the services they rendered would have to have been done by a lawyer if the paralegal had not performed the services, (2) paralegal has special training and is not primarily a secretary or clerical worker, and (3) the fee application has a resume or summary of the paralegal's qualifications.

Finally, a few courts have reduced fee awards for an attorney's time when the work billed at the attorney's rate could have been done by a paralegal. These cases demonstrate the growing appreciation within the judiciary of the contribution paralegals make to improving the cost-effectiveness of and access to legal services.

In at least one case, a fee award that included paralegal time that was volunteered was upheld based on the reasoning of *Missouri v. Jenkins* that the compensation should be based on market rates, not actual pay to the paralegal.

In 1993, the ABA House of Delegates adopted a resolution "support[ing] the award of paralegal/paralegal fees to law firms or attorneys who represent prevailing parties in a lawsuit where statutes or current case law allow for the recovery of attorney fees." This resolution parallels Guideline 8 of the ABA Model Guidelines for the Utilization of

119

Paralegal Services, which endorses both recovery for paralegal time in statutory attorney fee matters and the billing of clients for paralegal time.

E. Fee-Splitting and Referral Fees

Ethics rules in every state carefully control the way in which lawyers and nonlawyers are compensated. These rules are designed with a number of important policies in mind: to prevent the **unauthorized practice of law,** to guard against interference with the lawyer's **independent professional judgment,** and to discourage unethical direct **solicitation** of clients by agents of the lawyer.

Ethics codes have long limited the splitting of fees **between or among lawyers** who are not members of the same firm; however, these rules are gradually giving way to some fee-sharing arrangements among lawyers. The ABA Model Code and Model Rules (DR 2-107 and Model Rule 1.5(e)) allow fee splitting between attorneys, but only under certain conditions, including client consent, proportionate division of fees to services, and a reasonable total fee.

The older rules, followed in some states, mean that an attorney may not pay a referral fee or a portion of a client's fee to another attorney simply for referring a case. Referral fees in either of these forms have long been thought to be unprofessional and to increase the cost to the client. However, a growing number of states have in recent years revised rules to permit *forwarding fees* and to omit the requirement that the fee division be proportionate to services, thereby effectively allowing referral fees. Proponents of referral fees say that they serve the client's interests by encouraging a thoughtful referral to a competent attorney, and point out that clients are protected because the rules require the fee to be reasonable.

Forwarding fees
Fee paid by one lawyer to another for referring a case

Fee splitting with nonlawyers, including paralegals, is absolutely prohibited because of concerns of unauthorized practice, interference with the lawyer's independent professional judgment, and direct solicitation. The ABA Model Code and Model Rules (DR 3-102 and Model Rule 5.4) prohibit fee splitting with nonlawyers except when a lawyer dies and fees are paid to his or her estate, and to compensate nonlawyer employees through bonuses and profit-sharing arrangements. The Model Rules also make an exception that allows a lawyer to pay for the purchase of the practice of a deceased, disabled, or disappeared lawyer. All states have some version of the prohibition on fee-splitting and referral fees with nonlawyers. In addition, such agreements are unenforceable because of illegality.

The ABA Model Guidelines follow the standard prohibitions against fee splitting with nonlawyers in Guideline 9. Most state guidelines on paralegal utilization specifically prohibit fee splitting but emphasize that **retirement plans and bonuses** based in part on a firm's overall profitability are acceptable. Neither NALA nor NFPA has a specific prohibition against fee-splitting or referral fees in its code of ethics.

An early ABA ethics opinion endorsed the inclusion of non-lawyers in **profit-based compensation** and retirement plans, and other state and local ethics opinions have followed suit. Bonus plans that compensate paralegals and associates whose billable hours exceed a set minimum and bonuses based on firm profitability have been approved. Other ethics opinions advise that lawyers may not compensate paralegals on a contingent basis, and may not compensate them only when fees are collected from a client, or only when there is a recovery in a case.

The ethics rules and the opinions interpreting them make it clear that it is not acceptable for an attorney to pay a paralegal for **referring a case**, either directly or by means of a bonus, increase in compensation, or payment of a portion of a fee received from the client. They also make it clear that an attorney may not pay a paralegal, under any circumstances, a percentage of a fee from a specific client or case. Several cases in which lawyers were disciplined for unethical fee arrangements with nonlawyers make clear that a "bonus" tied to a particular client or case is not acceptable. However, it is appropriate to pay bonuses and other compensation based on overall firm profitability. This kind of arrangement breaks the direct link between a paralegal's action and a specific client, thereby eliminating concerns about unauthorized practice and incentives to solicit clients by unethical or overly aggressive methods. Such bonus plans are commonly used by firms who want to reward paralegals for their contribution to making the firm profitable. It should be noted that a few states, however, still have ethics opinions that appear to prohibit compensation to nonlawyer employees based on overall firm profitability.

A few other exceptions to the prohibition against fee splitting with nonlawyers do exist. As mentioned above, fees may be paid to the **estate of a deceased lawyer**. A lawyer may pay a fee to an approved **lawyer referral service**. Lawyer referral services are regulated by ethics rules and usually must be approved by the state bar or some other entity. Many are run by local bar associations. Lawyer referral services charge either a flat fee or a percentage of fees. Another exception is the prepaid legal plan, under which a member pays a fee for entitlement to a range of services, and the fee is divided between the lawyer and the plan sponsor. All jurisdictions permit such fee splitting when the plan is nonprofit; some jurisdictions specifically prohibit lawyer participation in profit-making prepaid legal services plans. Lawyers may also split a court-awarded fee with a nonprofit organization that employed, retained, or recommended the lawyer in the matter (ABA Model Rule 5.4(a)).

F. Partnerships Between Lawyers and Nonlawyers

The same theories underlying the prohibitions on fee splitting with nonlawyers form the basis for rules prohibiting lawyers from entering into partnership with nonlawyers for the purpose of practicing law. The ABA Model Code and Model Rules both prohibit a lawyer from forming a partnership with a nonlawyer if any of the activities of the partnership consist of the practice of law (DR 3-103 and Model Rule 5.4(b)).

This rule is sometimes implicated when lawyers are disciplined for aiding in the unauthorized practice of law, fee splitting, and unlawful solicitation if the arrangement with the nonlawyer looks like a partnership or business venture where the nonlawyer has a meaningful voice in the operation of the firm. Virtually all jurisdictions have a rule prohibiting such arrangements, and most states that have guidelines for the utilization of paralegals reiterate this rule as it applies to paralegals.

However, because of the changing nature of law practice and the desire of law firms, especially large law firms, to be full-service providers for their clients, a movement to modify this prohibition has been gaining strength in the last two decades. This movement in support of *multidisciplinary practice* has not been endorsed by the ABA, whose latest internal effort to allow it failed. Most opponents within the organized bar cite a loss of professionalism and threat to client confidentiality as the primary reasons for opposing changes.

Some states are nonetheless making changes to accommodate these new ways of practicing law that would allow lawyers to combine forces with all kinds of other professionals, like accountants, economists, psychologists or psychiatric social workers, and lobbyists. Some law firms have contracted to work collaboratively with other kinds of nonlawyer professionals in ways that skirt the ethical prohibition on partnerships with nonlawyers. However, the corporate scandals implicating big accounting firms in recent years have slowed the move of law firms to join with them.

Multidisciplinary practice
A business model under which law firms and other professionals form partnerships to deliver legal and other related services to clients

G. Client Funds and Property

1. Client Trust Accounts

The **mishandling of client funds** is probably the leading cause of disciplinary sanctions imposed on attorneys. A typical scenario is a sole practitioner with cash-flow problems who "borrows" funds from a client trust account to pay bills until a big settlement comes in. A shortfall in a client trust account can also result from sloppy bookkeeping and management practices. The attorney will sooner or later find that a client's money just isn't there, and the client will report this to the state or local bar and possibly to the local prosecutor's office.

The most important ethics rule related to client funds is the requirement to keep the client's money separate from the attorney's — in other words, not to commingle client and law firm funds. The rule against *commingling* also applies to funds from third parties held by the lawyer. This means that lawyers must have a separate bank account for client funds. Some clients may warrant having their own individual **client trust account** if the lawyer handles large amounts of funds or transactions for them. Both the Model Code and Model Rules and every jurisdiction require separate client trust accounts (Model Code DR 9-102(A) and Model Rule 1.15(a)). Some ethics rules specify that the client trust account must be in the state where the lawyer is situated; others allow another location with client consent.

Commingling
The mixing of client funds with lawyers' funds

Client trust account
Bank account set up by a lawyer in which funds are kept that belong to one or more clients

Lawyers hold client funds for many reasons. Typically, funds in client trust accounts are estate or trust distributions, funds to be distributed at a real estate closing or on settlement of a matter, advanced fees, and awards of which the attorney is owed a portion under a contingency fee agreement.

In the case of funds that are to be **divided between the client and the attorney**, the funds must remain in the client trust account until they are earned by the lawyer and she or he prepares an accounting for the client indicating how the funds are to be divided under the fee agreement. In the event a dispute arises over the fee, the amount in dispute must be kept in the client trust account until the dispute is resolved. A minority of jurisdictions allow advanced fees to be deposited into a lawyer's operating account. Remember that advances are different from retainers, which are nonrefundable and paid directly to the lawyer.

Commingling of funds is a separate grounds for disciplinary action than is *conversion* of funds, a much more serious breach. Commingling refers only to mixing client funds with those of the attorney and does not require any intent to harm the client or actual harm to the client. Conversion is the misappropriation of the client's funds for the attorney or firm use. Conversion may take place when the attorney draws funds from the client trust account for personal use, for payment of firm expenses, or — more rarely — to cover another client's shortfall.

Conversion
The tortious deprivation of another's property without justification or authorization

Disciplinary bodies are not sympathetic to most defenses that an attorney might use in such cases, including the intention to return the funds or the actual restoration of the funds. An attorney's personal or financial problems or the mismanagement of the firm are also not excuses; in fact, they may be considered aggravating circumstances as they may lead to repeated incidents of mishandling of client funds. Blaming office personnel is also an ineffective defense.

The lawyer should be the only person who can sign checks drawn on a client trust account. Some states specifically prohibit nonlawyer personnel from serving as a signatory.

Interest on Lawyers' Trust Accounts and Client Security Funds

IOLTA
Interest on Lawyers'
Trust Accounts

Nearly all jurisdictions in the United States have a program under which the interest on certain client trust accounts is used to fund the bar disciplinary system, client security fund, or legal services for the poor, specified by the state's bar, legislature, or supreme court. Over $100 million a year is raised annually through these programs, known as *IOLTA* (Interest on Lawyers' Trust Accounts). These plans can be **mandatory, voluntary, or "opt-out."** A voluntary program is one in which a lawyer must affirmatively decide to participate; an opt-out program means that all lawyers participate unless they affirmatively declare *not* to. The plans ordinarily cover only client funds that are too small in amount or are to be held for too brief a period to earn interest for the individual client. The majority of jurisdictions have voluntary or opt-out plans, or some hybrid of the two, although a growing number of plans are being converted to mandatory status.

Client security fund
Fund set aside to reimburse clients who have lost money or property due to lawyer misconduct

IOLTA plans are different from *client security funds*, which reimburse clients who have lost money or property as a result of lawyer misconduct. Almost all states have some kind of client security fund. Funding of these plans usually comes from bonding insurance or, in a few states, from IOLTA funds.

The **constitutionality of IOLTA** programs has been challenged in the courts on the grounds that individual clients have property rights in the interest generated in these accounts, rights that are violated when the interest, however small, is not paid to the clients. So far, all the cases have upheld the plans.

2. Other Client Property and Files

The lawyer and paralegal have a duty to protect client property in addition to the duties to protect client funds. This duty to **safeguard** usually requires that property be placed in a safe deposit box. Property covered by these rules typically includes titles to real estate or valuable personal property, jewelry, and securities. If a safe deposit box is shared with other clients, the items must be identified and labeled.

Lawyers have a duty to keep **accurate and complete records** of client funds and property. The ethics rules also state a specific number of years, ranging from five to seven, that records must be kept. Some states have very specific requirements for record keeping. A few jurisdictions provide for random audits of client trust accounts and some for annual certification or verification of compliance with record-keeping rules. Many states conduct **audits** in conjunction with disciplinary actions.

The kinds of bookkeeping mechanisms that a firm uses to comply with ethics record-keeping rules vary from firm to firm. Several state bars have adopted model guidelines or standards, which usually require cash receipts journals for each account, disbursement journals for each account (with separate ledgers for each client showing monthly trial balances), monthly reconciliations of balances, bank statements, cancelled checks, and records of other client property received and distributed. Other duties regarding client property are to:

- **notify** the client on the receipt of funds or property
- **deliver** client funds or property promptly
- provide a full **accounting** to the client on request

Model Code 9-102 and Model Rule 1.15(d).

When these duties are breached, it is most often because of lax **office procedures**; sometimes it is a more egregious violation such as **conversion**. Sometimes a third party will have a claim against the client funds; in this situation the lawyer may have a duty not to turn over the funds to the client until the various parties' rights are clarified. The notion of what is "prompt" delivery can become an issue in disciplinary actions. The best practice certainly requires action within the month in which funds are received, if not more quickly. And, finally, although neither the ABA Model Code nor the Model Rules require them, regular periodic accountings to clients (monthly or quarterly) are advisable rather than accountings only on a client's request.

All jurisdictions also have some special rules that require attorneys to **turn over** papers, funds, money, and unearned advanced fees on termination of representation. These rules emphasize the lawyer's obligation to protect the client's interest, with the extension of the lawyer's duty after representation ends.

One final matter in this area is the handling of **client files** after work on a matter is completed. Firms should have policies on retention of files, turning files over to clients, destroying files, and security for files maintained in off-site storage. Since the client file is the property of the client, the attorney cannot destroy old files without first informing the client and getting permission, and/or giving the client the chance to keep the file. Care should always be taken to retain important papers such as wills, deeds, securities, and tax returns. It is good practice to include a provision about the handling of client files in the agreement for representation.

The rules governing the handling of client funds and property are especially important to paralegals because they often must implement attorneys' instructions relating to client funds and property and may be delegated substantial responsibility for handling these matters. Checks and property are likely to come directly to the attorney, who will instruct the paralegal how to proceed. In small firms, a paralegal may perform some of the bookkeeping and record keeping functions. The paralegal must know the rules well enough to identify improprieties and either rectify them or inform the supervising attorney. It is not unusual for an attorney in trouble to blame the nonlawyer employee for poor office practices that have resulted in disciplinary action against the attorney, or worse. While such excuses do not mitigate the attorney's misconduct, they can harm the paralegal's reputation. NALA's Code does not address client property and funds directly. NFPA's ethics rules calls on paralegals to be "scrupulously thorough and honest" in handling client assets (NFPA EC 1.2(e)).

REVIEW QUESTIONS

1. What are fixed fees? For what kinds of work are they typically used?
2. What are contingency fees? When are they usually used?
3. What are the traditional objections to contingency fees? What are the most important modern limitations on contingency fees? What is a sliding-scale contingency fee?
4. What are hourly fees? In what kinds of legal matters are they typically used?
5. What is the authority for paralegal time to be billed separately to clients? What is the advantage to the client?
6. Why are some firms starting to use alternatives to hourly billing? What kinds of new fee arrangements are being developed as firms move away from hourly billing? How do these affect paralegals?
7. What factors may be taken into account in determining if a fee is excessive?
8. What is an example of an illegal fee?
9. What kinds of billing abuses sometimes take place in law firms, and why? What are some of the risks of these abuses?
10. What is double billing? Is it ethical?
11. What are a lawyer's duties relating to the fee arrangement when he or she undertakes representation?
12. Under what circumstances must a fee arrangement be in writing?
13. May a paralegal tell a client what the firm's fee schedule is? Do the rules permit a paralegal to negotiate a fee arrangement with a client?
14. What is the difference between a retainer and an advanced fee? How are they treated differently when received by the firm?
15. What provisions should a written fee agreement contain?
16. What kinds of costs are usually charged directly to the client?
17. What is the purpose of "fee shifting"?
18. Give some examples of fee-shifting statutes.

19. What was the holding in *Missouri v. Jenkins?* Why is this decision so important for paralegals?
20. What information should be included in a request to the court for paralegal fees as part of an award of attorney's fees?
21. What are the rules about referral fees? What is the basis for these rules? Do the same rules apply to lawyers and paralegals?
22. What are the rules about fee splitting?
23. What kinds of retirement, bonus, and profit-sharing plans for paralegals are permitted under the ethics rules?
24. Why do the ethics rules prohibit lawyers from being partners with nonlawyers in a law practice?
25. What are the duties of lawyers and paralegals regarding client funds?
26. What is IOLTA? Do many states have such a program? Are such programs constitutional? What is a client security fund? How are the funds from these programs used?
27. Describe the difference between the commingling and the conversion of funds. Which is more serious?
28. Is mishandling of client funds common? Why?
29. How might a paralegal violate ethics in the handling of client funds?
30. When a lawyer receives a check for a judgment or settlement and the case was taken on contingency, what should he or she do with the check?
31. Do the facts that an attorney is very busy, has high staff turnover, and has not had a bookkeeper in months mitigate against charges of commingling of funds?
32. What are the lawyer's duties with regard to client property held for the client?
33. What are the lawyer's duties pertaining to client funds, files, and property when representation ceases?

HYPOTHETICALS

1. Wendell Wilson is a paralegal with a small law firm, Xavier & Young, that handles family law matters and criminal defense work. The firm just took on a new case involving the divorce of a wealthy couple, the Applebys. The firm is representing the wife, Anna Appleby. Wendell is asked to prepare an agreement with the client concerning the representation with the following provisions:
   1. The firm agrees to represent the client only concerning the divorce matter.
   2. The client agrees to pay the firm an amount equal to 25 percent of the annual spousal support that the firm gets for the client.
   3. The client agrees to hold the firm harmless for any errors its paralegals make in the handling of the matter.
   Are these provisions ethical? Why or why not?

2. During the divorce proceedings, Ms. Appleby becomes increasingly distraught about her husband's conduct. One day in a rage she attacks him with a fireplace poker. He is not badly injured but the police are called and Ms. Appleby is charged with assault and battery. The firm agrees to represent her in this matter too, but wants a separate agreement under which the firm will be paid hourly rates ranging from $85 an hour for paralegals to $500 for the trial lawyer involved, and a $10,000 bonus if the firm can get the charges dismissed. The second agreement is reached during a conference with the client but is not put in writing. Are there any ethical problems with this agreement?

3. Wendell gets disgusted with the ethics at Xavier & Young and decides to go to work for a large law firm that has a civil litigation department handling major lawsuits. This firm, Allison & Beals, has billing guidelines that require paralegals to put in 1,800 billable hours a year. If it takes eight hours on the job to produce seven billable hours, how many hours a week will Wendell have to work to reach the firm goal? After the first month on the job, Wendell gets a report showing that he billed 150 hours but that 20 hours were written off as being duplicative of the work that an associate did. What should Wendell do? Wendell becomes concerned toward the end of the year that he will not meet the required quota. He does not have enough work to warrant working overtime to make up for the hours. What can he do? Another paralegal, Zina Zumbrun, tells Wendell that she sometimes adds a tenth of an hour to each hour's work in order to make up for the time written off. What should Wendell do about this? Can he ethically do the same thing?

4. Carl Carlsmith is a paralegal working on some major civil rights litigation. He and his firm have spent years on the case and have finally prevailed. The firm's senior partner, Danielle Dupree, asks Carl to draft a request for fees that includes his time. The petition he drafts contains the following language: "Compensation is also requested for paralegal time spent by Carl Carlsmith, paralegal, who spent 1,000 hours drafting pleadings and correspondence, summarizing depositions, filing and organizing documents, and locating and interviewing witnesses. $200,000." Will the court grant this fee award? Why or why not? Be sure to look for more than one reason. Redraft this petition, adding all the requisite information and correcting anything else that is in error.

5. Emily Emerson, paralegal, works for a medical malpractice firm, Freed & Gant. A friend of hers knows someone whose surgery was botched. Emily suggests that the person call the firm to talk to the senior partner about taking the case. This prospective client, Horace Hanson, calls Emily first and asks, "What does your firm normally charge for this kind of case?" Has Emily done anything wrong at this point? Can Emily answer Horace's question? What is she permitted

to say? Later, Horace comes in and meets Fred Freed and the firm decides to take the case. The next day at work, Emily is greeted with a dozen roses and a check for $500. May Emily keep the flowers and money? Why or why not? Another paralegal in the firm, Inga Inglewood, comes in to see the flowers and says casually to Emily, "Wait until you see what you get when the case is over!" What should Emily do now?

6. Emily leaves Freed & Gant after a few months for the firm of Kranston & Knight. Kranston offers Emily a signing bonus, a salary that is $500 a month higher than her pay at Freed & Gant, great benefits, and a bonus plan based on the following formula: 1 percent of the firm's net revenue annually, plus 5 percent of her monthly salary as of the end of the year, plus 5 percent of the net recovery in every litigated matter that Emily has worked on. Is Emily's compensation package acceptable? What about the bonus plan? Be sure to look at each element of the plan.

7. Larry Langsford is a paralegal working for a sole practitioner, Martha Monroe. Larry handles all the bookkeeping for the office in addition to all the paralegal work in a variety of practice areas. One day Martha comes in very distraught and asks Larry for all the firm checkbooks. She leaves and does not come back the rest of the day. The next day, Larry notices that a check from the client trust account is missing. What should be do? The following day, a settlement check comes in on a big case. Martha instructs Larry to deposit the check in her operating account, to pay all the office bills, and to pay the client his share of the recovery. What should Larry do? Later, Larry is filing some documents in files in Martha's office and discovers several checks in the bottom of a file cabinet. These undeposited checks appear to be from clients and insurance companies. What should Larry do?

8. Nancy Nussbaum is a paralegal for Overton & Price, a firm that handles estate planning and real estate transactions. A wealthy client, Ronald Roland, comes in one day and asks Nancy to keep some jewelry for him for safekeeping while his house is being remodeled. Should she do this? If the firm agrees to do this, where should the jewelry be kept? Suppose that one day Nancy is looking for a file in Oliver Overton's office and comes across the jewelry in a file cabinet. What should she do?

DISCUSSION QUESTIONS AND PROJECTS

1. Contact five local law firms and find out:
   a. what kinds of fee arrangements they use for legal work (for example, contingency fee for personal injury, fixed fee to form a corporation, hourly fee to negotiate a deal)

    b. their hourly rates for lawyers and paralegals

    c. what costs they bill directly to clients

    d. whether they require that fee agreements be in writing (ask if you may have a copy of a standard fee agreement if the firm has one)

2. Do you believe that the special restrictions on contingency fees (for example, in criminal and divorce cases) are warranted? Why or why not?

3. Do you believe the ethics rules should require all fee agreements to be in writing? Why or why not?

4. Should the percentage of attorney's fees in contingency cases be limited by statute or ethical codes? Why or why not? What do you think is the reason for limiting the amount of contingency fees in medical malpractice cases?

5. Do you think the trend to use alternative methods of fee structures — for instance, task-based, value, or premium billing — in lieu of traditional hourly rates is a good one? Why or why not?

6. What would you do if the supervising attorney in a matter continually wrote off your time as excessive, diminishing your billable hours?

7. What would you do if a client called and wanted to know the firm's hourly rates to handle certain kinds of legal work?

8. What would you do if a prospective personal injury client with a good case came into the office seeking representation and the attorney was out of town for two weeks?

9. What would you do if an attorney was inflating the costs on clients' bills?

10. You are flying across country for client X and en route do some work for client Y. How do you bill your time?

11. Do you think the United States should have the kind of two-way fee shifting that England and Canada have? Why or why not?

12. Outline the arguments in the *Missouri v. Jenkins* majority opinion and dissent on the award of paralegal fees in attorney's fee awards. Which side do you find more convincing and why? Outline the arguments for charging paralegal fees at market rate as opposed to cost. Which do you find more convincing and why?

13. Are there cases on paralegal fees in your state? Are these supportive of paralegal fee awards?

14. Are there any statutes or court rules in your jurisdiction that provide for paralegal fees awards as part of attorney's fees awards?

15. Do you think the rules prohibiting fee splitting are well founded? Why or why not? Do you think the rules should be different for lawyers and nonlawyers?

16. Do you think the rules prohibiting referral fees are well founded? Why or why not? Does your jurisdiction allow attorneys to pay or receive referral fees? Is it common practice?

17. May a personal injury firm pay a $500 bonus for every case a paralegal brings in? May a paralegal be paid one-third of the fee when the case is settled?

18. Call five local law firms and find out if they have pension or profit-sharing plans for their paralegals or pay bonuses to their paralegals. Ask them how the amount of the bonus is determined.

19. Do you think the rule prohibiting paralegals from becoming partners in law firms is well founded? Why or why not? Do you think this rule should be changed? Ask some lawyers and practicing paralegals what they think. Has your jurisdiction considered adopting a rule that would allow multidisciplinary practice?

20. Is it ethical or acceptable for an attorney to keep the deed of trust to a client's real estate in the attorney's desk? In the client file? Under the floor board in the attorney's attic? Why or why not? What if the property were a valuable diamond ring? Stock certificates?

21. What is wrong with an attorney putting client funds in the firm's account if he or she plans to replace them in two days? Would it make any difference if the period were two weeks? If the client owed fees to the attorney? If the attorney were doing this for the benefit of another client and did not benefit himself or herself in any way?

22. What kind of IOLTA does your state have — voluntary, opt-out, or mandatory? How do attorneys pay the fund? What are the funds used for? How much money is currently in the fund?

23. Does your state have a client security fund? How is it funded? How much money is in the fund? What kinds of payments have been made from the fund?

24. What would you do if your attorney-employer is very careful about handling client funds but keeps no records other than bank reports and withdrawal slips?

25. What would you do if you discovered that a settlement check had come in and had been deposited six months ago and the client had never been notified?

26. Draft a provision on handling of client files after the matter is closed.

27. Does your state or local bar have rules on how long lawyers should retain client files?

SELECTED CASES

Absher Construction Co. v. Kent School District, 79 Wash. Ct. App. 841, 917 P.2d 1086 (1995) (appellate court case upholds fee award with paralegal fees and sets forth list of criteria for determining if fees should be awarded).

Doe v. Condon, 341 S.C. 22, 532 S.E.2d 879 (S.C. 2000) (State Supreme Court adopts ethics opinion that prohibits lawyer from allowing paralegal to give estate planning seminars for public and from paying the paralegal under a plan that is based on the number and value of cases the paralegal handles.)

F.D.I.C. v. Singh, 148 F.R.D. 6 (D. Me. 1993) (no paralegal fees in Maine attorney's fee statute).

First NH Banks Granite State v. Scarborough, 615 A.2d 248 (Me. 1992) (paralegals are covered by attorney's fee statutes).

Hines v. Hines, 129 Idaho 847, 934 P.2d 20 (1997) (legislature must change attorney's fee statute to include paralegal time).

In re Bass, 227 B.R. 103 (Bankr. E.D. Mich. 1998) (petition for fees with clerical tasks, the role of the paralegal, and an improper compensation plan).

In re Hessinger & Associates, 171 B.R. 366 (Bankr. N.D. Cal. 1994) (bankruptcy court sanctions attorney for fee splitting, excessive fees, and partnership with nonlawyers).

Kansas v. Barrett, 207 Kan. 178, 483 P.2d 1106 (1971) (attorney disciplined for client trust account violations; blaming staff is no defense).

Joerger v. Gordon Food Service, Inc., 224 Mich. App. 167, 568 N.W.2d 365 (1997) (appellate court refuses to award compensation for paralegal time under attorney's fees statute and calls on legislature to amend statute).

Missouri v. Jenkins, 491 U.S. 274 (1989) (landmark U.S. Supreme Court case upholds award of attorney's fees that included compensation for paralegal time at market rates).

Sundance v. Municipal Court, 192 Cal.App.3d 268, 237 Cal.Rptr. 269 (1987) (Court upheld award of fees that included time paralegal had volunteered).

Taylor v. Chubb, 874 P.2d 806 (Okla. 1994) (Oklahoma Supreme Court case upholds award of attorney's fees with paralegal fees at market rates).

Vitac Corp. v. Workers' Compensation Appeal Board, 578 Pa. 574, 854 A.2d 481 (Pa. 2004) (attorney fee statute in workers' compensation matter includes reasonable fees for paralegals).

SELECTED REFERENCES

ABA Model Rule 1.2 [scope of representation]

ABA Model Rule 1.5 [fees] ABA Model Rule 1.15 [safekeeping property]

ABA Model Rule 5.4 [fee-splitting and referral fees, and partnerships with nonlawyers]

ABA Model Code DR 2-110, 9-101 [scope of representation]

ABA Model Code DR 2-106, 2-107 [fees]

ABA Model Code DR 5-103, 9-102 [safekeeping property]

ABA Model Code DR 2-103, 3-102, 5-107 [fee-splitting and referral fees]

ABA Model Code 3-103 [partnerships with nonlawyers]

ABA Formal Opinion 93-379 (1993) [cites certain billing practices as unethical]

ABA Informal Opinion 875 (1965) [lay employees may not make fee arrangements or agree to undertake representation on the lawyer's behalf]

ABA Informal Opinion 1440 (1979) [nonlawyers can be included in profit-sharing and retirement plans]

ABA Formal Ethics Opinion 338 (1974) [endorses the use of credit cards for legal fee payments] Federal Bankruptcy Law (11 U.S.C. §330) [act amended to allow paralegal compensation in attorney fee award]

NFPA Ethics Opinion 95-4 [the ethics of billing for nonprofessional clerical work]

Competence

This chapter addresses competence, one of the essential elements of lawyers' and paralegals' professional responsibilities. Failure to perform competently is grounds for both legal and disciplinary remedies. Chapter 7 covers:

- definitions of lawyer and paralegal competence
- key components of competence for paralegals, including

  - knowledge
  - skills
  - thoroughness and preparation
  - diligence and promptness
  - communication with clients

- sanctions for incompetence, including disciplinary actions and malpractice suits
- trends in malpractice, including the growth in claims and in third-party actions against lawyers
- common dilemmas confronting paralegals in the area of competence, including those related to delegation, supervision, and attorney review of work
- factors in the work environment that affect competence

A.   Introduction

Lawyers are bound to represent clients competently by both **ethics codes** and common law rules of tort liability for *professional negligence*. The duty to represent a client competently also makes the lawyer responsible for the work of paralegals and others in the law firm; the ultimate responsibility for the competent handling of a client matter rests with the lawyer.

However, paralegals must consider their own competence one of their highest duties, both because they desire professional status and treatment and because they share with the lawyer the moral and ethical responsibility for providing quality legal services. As discussed in Chapter 1, paralegals should also be mindful of their own personal tort liability in the event a client brings a malpractice case.

Because competence cannot be defined quantitatively and the range of incompetent acts is virtually limitless, competence seems like an amorphous notion. Most definitions begin with the requisite legal knowledge and skill.

B.   Legal Education

Legal knowledge for lawyer competence generally means, at a minimum, a **law school** education of three or four years followed by a bar examination, which primarily tests substantive legal knowledge and judgmental-analytical ability. While slow to change, law schools have made changes in the last several years to make the education of aspiring lawyers more practical. Clinical programs along with courses on lawyering skills, mediation training, and trial techniques have been added to the traditional law school curriculum. The bar examination has been modified to include performance testing along with multiple-choice and essay questions.

In addition to formal legal education, the requisite legal knowledge and skills to practice competently encompass many things not covered in school. Newly admitted lawyers learn **on the job** from more experienced lawyers in the firms that hire them. Some of this training is informal: learning by example, by models available in the firm, and by trial and error. Some on-the-job training is more formal: some large firms and governmental agencies, such as prosecutors and public defenders, have formal in-house training and mentoring programs.

A lawyer must continue to develop legal knowledge and skills throughout his or her career. Formal **continuing education** programs are offered by firms, bar associations, and private entities. Forty states have mandatory continuing legal education. Ideally, attorneys are committed to keeping abreast with changes in the law and to developing their talents to the fullest. Such is the aspiration of the professional—it is not predicated on mandates from the state, but is a matter of commitment and integrity: the lawyer is driven by the sense of personal satisfaction derived from doing one's job well.

C. Paralegal Education

Paralegals share a lawyer's commitment to education and skill development. Because paralegals are not forced to comply with educational standards mandated by the state in most jurisdictions, the responsibility for achieving and maintaining competence through education and skill development rests firmly with paralegals and the lawyers who employ them.

Paralegal education programs are as new as the profession itself—only about 40 years old. The first programs were established around 1970, with an estimated half dozen scattered across the country. There are now approximately 1,100 paralegal programs situated in a wide variety of institutions, including two- and four-year colleges (both public and private), multidisciplinary and freestanding proprietary institutions (some of which are vocationally oriented), correspondence schools, and some institutions offering programs entirely on-line. Unlike the law school curriculum, the paralegal curriculum is not standardized, and offerings vary widely in length, content, format, level of sophistication, and degree of specialization. Good programs of all types teach an appropriate balance of substantive law and practical job skills.

About 250 of these paralegal programs are approved by the **ABA**, which means they have met guidelines on curriculum, admissions, faculty, administration, staff, facilities, finances, library, and support services, such as counseling and placement. ABA approval, first granted in 1975, is the only kind of specialized accreditation or approval of paralegal educational programs available. It is purely voluntary and is not formally recognized by the federal government. The ABA has never sought such recognition. The American Association for Paralegal Education also promotes quality in paralegal education through education, model curricula and courses, networking, and best practices.

Formal paralegal education is gradually becoming a minimum requirement for entering a paralegal career, although firm hiring standards vary throughout the country. States considering regulation of paralegals may require paralegal education. For example, one of two ways that one can qualify as a paralegal in California under state statute is to complete a program of at least 24 semester credits of paralegal courses. Not all legal employers require formal paralegal education, but most favor candidates who have formal training over those who do not. In some cities, a baccalaureate degree alone is the hiring standard in large law firms. Smaller firms often require previous legal work experience rather than formal education.

Because a lawyer who utilizes a paralegal's services is responsible for determining that the paralegal is competent to perform the tasks assigned, lawyers should require high levels of education and training. Whether or not employers require it, paralegals should acquire the appropriate formal education to meet their professional obligation of competence. This education should include not only a basic paralegal program, but also regular and frequent **continuing education** that covers new practice areas, updates paralegals in their area of practice, and enhances paralegal skills. Continuing education is available to paralegals in many forms, especially because paralegals may take courses that are designed for lawyers and courses offered specifically to paralegals. Continuing education for lawyers is readily available through state and local bar associations and independent providers. Courses for paralegals are provided by paralegal programs; local, regional, and national paralegal association and a few independent organizations. State regulatory schemes will probably mandate continuing education for paralegals, as does the recently enacted California legislation.

Certified Legal Assistant or Paralegal
Certification for paralegals offered by NALA for passing the Certified Paralegal examination

Both NALA and NFPA promote competence and education to their members. NALA's Code of Ethics Canon 6 requires paralegals to maintain a high degree of competency in the legal profession. NALA has translated this ideal into action by offering its **Certified Legal Assistant/Paralegal** (CLA or CP) and CLA Specialist examinations, discussed in Chapter 1. Educational and experiential requirements must be met to sit for the examination, and CLAs must also meet continuing education requirements to maintain their certified status. NFPA Model Code DR 1.1 contains a strong statement concerning competence and education. This statement tells paralegals that it is their professional responsibility to maintain competence through education, training, and work experience. NFPA offers the PACE examination to candidates with a degree and two years of experience. **Registered Paralegals** who pass the PACE test must participate in continuing education. Both NALA and NFPA hold annual national educational seminars and encourage their local chapters to provide frequent continuing education courses.

Registered Paralegals
Certification offered by NFPA for passing the Paralegal Advanced Competency Examination

D. A Definition of Competence

Competence cannot be defined solely in terms of formal education and professional skills, although these are essential preconditions to competence. Competence itself has full meaning only when it is applied to the tasks at hand—to the specific legal work to be done. At this point, factors other than knowledge and skill determine whether work will be carried out competently. Most state ethics codes follow the ABA Model Rule in defining competent representation as requiring:

- **legal knowledge, skill, thoroughness, and preparation;**
- reasonable **diligence and promptness**; and
- **communication with clients** to keep them informed about the status of their matters, to comply with reasonable requests for information and to explain matters so that clients can make informed decisions.

Ethics rules and cases interpreting them can be synthesized into a list of qualities that comprise competence for lawyers and paralegals alike.

1. Knowledge

Both lawyers and paralegals must have appropriate **formal education**, both legal and general, that enables them to communicate well in both oral and written form; that provides them with knowledge of substantive law and procedure; that has developed their analytical and judgmental abilities; and that has provided them with the information and skills needed to resolve legal issues.

The bodies of knowledge needed by the lawyer and the paralegal naturally differ because the lawyer exercises independent professional judgment in deciding how to proceed, while the paralegal participates in the practical steps preliminary to these decisions (for example, by interviewing clients and conducting legal and factual research) and later to implement these decisions (for example, by drafting a document).

Increasingly, the legal knowledge needed to be competent is highly **specialized**. The law has become more complex, and most practitioners emphasize no more than a few areas of practice. This trend away from general practice is also evidenced by the growing number of states that have specialized certification programs for lawyers, by the departmentalization of large firms, and by the proliferation of "boutique" firms that devote themselves to one or two very specialized areas of law. As a result of specialization, a lawyer has a duty to refer complex, specialized cases to an attorney with appropriate expertise if he or she doesn't have that expertise. Paralegals, especially in urban areas where highly specialized legal services are needed by clients, must also be specialists in order to act competently. Most paralegal education programs, unlike law school, include specialty courses, and most paralegal continuing education programs are devoted to specialized or advanced coursework. NALA offers advanced specialty examinations in a variety of practice areas, as does the State Bar of Texas in its certification program for paralegals.

Orientation and formal **on-the-job training** have become important elements of legal training. Many large law firms offer formal in-house training programs for lawyers and paralegals, which not only orient them to the firm's "way of doing things," but also cover substantive knowledge and skills as well. Many firms have courses for lawyers on advocacy skills and trial techniques; courses have been developed for paralegals on topics such as doing legal research, managing databases, and handling document productions.

Keeping abreast with changes in law and practice is critical in the application of **technology**. There are ample opportunities for errors to be made on documents by anyone who is not careful while working on a computer. For example, key documents or entries might be lost; errors can be made by selecting the wrong form, using the wrong paragraphs, or changing some but not all names, numbers, or provisions. Evolving standards of competence may now require that lawyers perform Web-based electronic research, which yields more up-to-date and accurate results.

2.   Skills

Skills are acquired through formal education and through training and experience on the job. The term "skills" refers primarily to the **execution of tasks** and the implementation of decisions about how to proceed in a legal matter, as opposed to the mastery of a body of substantive principles and information. Lawyers and paralegals both must have the ability to apply their skills to the resolution of legal problems in carrying out their respective roles. Skills needed most by paralegals include drafting and analyzing documents, summarizing information, handling procedural matters, gathering and organizing information, and conducting legal research. Lawyers need different skills, such as trial advocacy and negotiating. Studies on the utilization of paralegals show that lawyers retain the most complex and sophisticated tasks and delegate to paralegals more basic legal functions and duties that require strong organizational and oral and written communication skills.

3.   Thoroughness and Preparation

In applying knowledge and skills to any legal problem, both lawyers and paralegals must be careful and complete in their information gathering, analysis, application of judgment, and actions. Neglecting to learn all the facts, to fill out forms properly, or to be **meticulous about every detail** can have devastating consequences for the client. Because paralegals are especially valued for their knowledge of the facts in the cases they work on and for their attention to detail, thoroughness is one of the most critical aspects of paralegal competence. An example of failing to act competently in this area is omitting a necessary and important provision in a legal document, which may be grounds for a malpractice suit.

Related to thoroughness is **preparation**. Most successful lawyers credit much of their success to their careful and thorough preparation. Paralegals play an important part in this because they are often delegated considerable responsibility for preparation — for example, by organizing documents and other information before trial, or by drafting and organizing documents for a real estate closing. The paralegal, attorney, and other law firm personnel must work together as a team in preparation. The attorney relies on the preparation done by the paralegal while readying for his or her distinct role (representing the client in court, for instance).

4. Diligence and Promptness

Legal knowledge and skills are not of any value unless applied to a client's case in a timely and attentive manner. Diligence in this context requires **persistent attention to the legal matter** to ensure that it is resolved with the best possible outcome for the client. A lack of diligence or promptness is evidenced by delays that may cause harm to a client's case or cause the client unnecessary anxiety. Examples of failure to act diligently and promptly include missing court dates or appointments, frequently needing continuances, missing a statute of limitations, not pursuing discovery, or in general taking an unnecessarily long time to act. Implied in the duty of diligence is the necessity for firm management that ensures against the missing of critical deadlines, scheduling of conflicting court dates, and so forth. Often, these important organizational tasks are delegated to a paralegal.

5. Communication with Clients

The importance of clear and complete communication with clients cannot be underestimated. The good work of a competent lawyer and paralegal will not be recognized if the client is not fully informed about the status of a case at each step of the process. It may not matter how successfully the client's case is resolved if the firm does not return the client's phone calls or e-mails promptly. **Ongoing communication** with clients is an important and potentially large role for paralegals. Attorneys, especially trial attorneys, often are too busy to return clients' calls immediately or to make regular calls or written reports on how matters are proceeding. Paralegals are ideally situated to handle these tasks and can be very effective in keeping clients informed and satisfied that the lines of communication are open.

E. Sanctions for Incompetence

Malpractice
Improper conduct in the performance of duties by a professional, either intentionally or through negligence

Incompetence can be fatal to a client's rights and to a lawyer's or a paralegal's career. Failing to act competently in the handling of a case is the most common basis for *malpractice* actions against attorneys and for **disciplinary proceedings**—albeit when the incompetence is particularly egregious or persistent. Incompetence in the malpractice context is defined as the failure to exercise the level of care commonly observed in other professionals. The remedy is compensation for the loss of the client's legal rights—in other words, damages for losing a case in which the client would have prevailed if the lawyer had acted competently. Some cases also permit recovery to third persons who are damaged by an attorney's failure to act competently.

As discussed in Chapter 1, paralegals, including freelance paralegals, also may be named in legal malpractice actions. Most lawyers carry **malpractice insurance** that covers the actions of their employees, including paralegals; such insurance is mandatory in some states. Paralegals should be certain their employer has adequate malpractice coverage that also covers them.

Insurance carriers report that the most common bases for claims are:

1. substantive incompetence
2. management incompetence
3. poor communication skills and practices
4. fee misunderstandings
5. substance abuse and stress

Incompetence as grounds for disciplinary action against an attorney must normally be **severe or repeated** before sanctions are imposed. Frequently in disciplinary matters, lack of competence is coupled with other ethical violations, such as commingling or conversion of client trust account funds or failure to turn over client papers after representation is terminated. The incidents of discipline for competence-related violations have increased substantially in recent years, including cases in which attorneys were found incompetent for failing to supervise paralegals properly and for aiding in the unauthorized practice of law by allowing nonlawyers to give legal advice and to prepare legal documents without supervision or review. In recent years, some former clients have successfully used violations of ethics rules as a basis for malpractice suits. Since paralegals are not subject to discipline by the bar and not usually named in malpractice suits, the most likely consequence of a paralegal who fails to act competently is to lose a position and perhaps **employability** in the field.

Many malpractice and disciplinary cases involving competence relate to **procrastination** or to a lack of promptness, thoroughness, or communication. Typical scenarios include missing statutes of limitations, failing to proceed on a client's case after agreeing to representation, and not returning phone calls for an extended period, usually because the lawyer has not taken proper actions in a matter. These allegations are sometimes tied to financial improprieties as well, such as not returning advanced fees, not turning over settlement checks or clients' files promptly, or "borrowing" from client trust accounts. Some cases of this type are the result of mismanaged law offices—some, troubled attorneys.

Personal problems—such as financial, marital, or health problems—often interfere with the ability to function competently. A significant number of attorneys with disciplinary records have alcohol or drug dependency problems or emotional and personal problems that prevent them from operating in an ethical and effective manner. Most state bars now have programs to help attorneys with these problems, either voluntarily before they begin to affect the lawyer's professional actions or as part of the sanctions imposed on a lawyer who has been disciplined.

F.   Trends in Legal Malpractice

Recent years have seen a tremendous increase in the number and size of malpractice claims made against attorneys. Some of this increase is from **third-party claims** by nonclients who were harmed by the actions of clients from whom they could no longer recover. Corporate **securities work** carries a high risk of third-party malpractice actions because of the additional duties to the purchasers of securities imposed by federal law. Under the securities laws, attorneys may be liable when material false or misleading statements are included in offerings. The result is the imposition upon counsel of heightened duties of due diligence and fact checking. Private investors who lose money look to the lawyers who represented the promoters as possible defendants, especially when the promoters have no money.

> **Third-party claims against lawyers**
> Claims by nonclients against lawyers whose acts in representing clients may have caused harm to the third person

The principles underlying third-party liability in securities cases have been applied in other business situations as well. They were broadly used during the **savings and loan** crisis in lawsuits by the federal government against firms who represented failed thrift institutions. Most suits claimed that firms failed to advise their clients properly; in many cases, firms relied on information provided by clients. In some suits, the lawyers served on their clients' boards, exacerbating the malpractice issue because of the possible conflict of interest and exposure to details about questionable transactions. Similar cases have been brought in matters relating to environmental compliance. Unresolved issues still exist about the extent of an attorney's duty to disclose information to the government or the public and the impact of this duty on the attorney-client privilege.

Another area where third-party plaintiffs have become common is in **estate planning** work. When a gift to an intended beneficiary fails because of an attorney's negligence in drafting, the intended beneficiary may seek damages from the attorney, even though the attorney represented the testator, not the beneficiary. Similar cases have held attorneys who represented sellers in real estate transactions liable to buyers for making misleading statements that the buyer relied on in making the purchase.

When plaintiffs look for a "deep pocket," attorneys with malpractice insurance coverage make attractive defendants. More extensions of third-party liability are likely in the future, especially in areas heavily regulated by the government, such as environmental law. More and more cases are being filed against lawyers by former clients on the basis of conflicts of interest. Some cases have revolved around a firm's representation of two clients who ultimately became adversaries. Some have concerned conflicts that arose when an attorney did business with clients or served on a corporate client's board of directors. Finally, several recent suits have been brought against lawyers for giving poor advice on settling claims, when the client later discovered that the claim was worth much more money.

Another trend that merits mention is an increase in lawsuits against lawyers that are being brought under consumer fraud statutes. The states who have addressed this issue are split — some allowing lawsuits when the lawyer acted unconscionably, others finding that lawyers are not subject to these regulations.

A recently released ABA study shows that there has been a huge increase in the number of "big ticket" lawsuits against major law firms, most rising from the corporate scandals of the last five years. The growth in lawsuits against lawyers has resulted in high rates for malpractice insurance and in a flood of literature and continuing education programs designed to warn how to avoid malpractice suits. The advice given in these programs is as valuable to paralegals as it is to lawyers. A summary of the typical advice follows:

1. Lawyers should use carefully drafted **letters of engagement** as well as **letters terminating or declining representation**. These documents must spell out and limit the extent and nature of the representation and the expectations and responsibilities of the law firm and the client, and should clearly indicate that the lawyer is not guaranteeing a particular outcome.
2. **Clients should be selected carefully**. Difficult personalities and questionable cases should not be accepted.
3. Lawyers and clients should enter into complete and well-drafted **fee agreements** for each representation. The agreements should cover all the terms noted in Chapter 6. Fee agreements should be entered into as soon as possible in the representation and should be followed meticulously.

4. Clients should be charged **reasonable fees** that are in accord with the fee agreements. Bills should be detailed and should be reviewed before being sent. Excessive, duplicative, and inappropriate charges should be removed before sending bills. Billing should be done regularly and timely.

5. Clients' **phone calls and e-mails should be returned promptly**, preferably the same day. The attorney and paralegal should take the time to educate the client about relevant law and procedures and show that they care about clients' concerns. Clients should be sent copies of documents and work product. Correspondence and other materials from clients should be promptly acknowledged.

6. Lawyers and paralegals should **listen to clients** carefully and try to understand their goals and expectations. Unrealistic expectations should be addressed immediately and thoughtfully.

7. Lawyers should exercise **independent judgment** on clients' behalf and should **respect clients' decisions**.

8. Law firms should have **good management systems** and well-trained personnel in place, especially concerning the following matters:

   - conflicts checking and establishing screens
   - protecting client confidentiality
   - calendaring deadlines, court dates, and the like
   - billing and time keeping
   - handling client property
   - managing client trust accounts

9. Lawyers and paralegals should be scrupulous in the handling of **clients' funds** in keeping with the rules set forth in Chapter 6. Client trust accounts and related records must be perfectly maintained, with no commingling or other irregularities. Client files must be turned over promptly upon termination, and settlements must be paid promptly after receipt.

10. Lawyers and paralegals should know the **limits of their competence** and should seek guidance and consultation when in doubt about how to proceed on a matter.

Paralegals play an important role in helping lawyers to **avoid disputes** with clients. Communication with clients is greatly improved when an attorney delegates to a paralegal responsibility for keeping clients informed, in writing and by phone. When clients call and the lawyer is unavailable, the paralegal can take or return the call. Paralegals can keep the lawyer informed of client concerns and keep clients informed of progress in the handling of the matter. Keeping accurate and detailed time records and alerting the lawyer to potential problems in time and billing matters are also valuable paralegal functions. Paralegals often have responsibility for monitoring deadlines and handling client funds, especially in small law firms.

G. Factors Affecting Paralegal Competence

Paralegals need to be cognizant of not only the meaning of competence and how it is embodied in their work, but also the factors that may either enhance their competence or detract from it. Because paralegals work under the direction and supervision of lawyers, they are not usually in a position to establish the quality standards for the firm or to set the professional tone that determines the attitude that employees at all levels take toward their work. Paralegals, especially those in small firms, do have influence over firm standards and culture, but in many employment settings, they are subject to the environment established by the lawyers. Given this situation, paralegals should seek out firms that have high standards of quality and encourage competence and professionalism. It is unlikely that a paralegal will be able to function in a competent fashion in a firm that does not demand competence of its professional and support staff.

Paralegals are sometimes faced with competence-related ethical dilemmas. Perhaps the most common is being asked to perform a task that the paralegal does not have the **requisite knowledge or skill** to perform. This presents an especially difficult dilemma for paralegals who want to do challenging, interesting work and who know their value is in relieving the attorney from tasks that he or she would otherwise have to perform. A conflict thus may arise between the paralegal's desire to take the assignment and his or her ability to handle the assignment competently. A new paralegal, just like a lawyer just out of law school, must learn on the job. With a strong education, good research and drafting skills, and self-confidence and motivation, a paralegal can usually learn how to perform the assigned task on his or her own by conducting research, finding a model in firm files, and so forth. A paralegal may ask for some guidance from the attorney who assigned the task or seek out assistance from another lawyer or a more experienced paralegal. Paralegal colleagues in other firms may be able to guide the paralegal to the necessary sources. In any event, the supervising lawyer should be made aware that the paralegal has not previously undertaken such a task, so that the lawyer will evaluate the work fairly and review it carefully.

A related concern is the proper **delegation, supervision, and review** of paralegal work by attorneys. The ethics and agency rules discussed above and in Chapter 1 make it clear that the lawyer is ultimately responsible for the work of the paralegal. This responsibility is described in ABA Model Guideline 1 and its comment and in ABA Model Rule 5.3. For a variety of reasons, attorneys do not always carry out their supervisory responsibilities as well as they should. Many lawyers are not skilled delegaters; they often do not give adequate information and instructions when assigning work to paralegals and others. Many lawyers are overloaded and simply don't take the time to delegate and review thoroughly. Proper delegation requires selecting the appropriately skilled person for the task and giving sufficient direction so that the finished product meets expectations. Information given to the one performing the task includes background on the matter and/or reference to appropriate files that contain relevant information; an exact description of the end product desired; references to sources that may be of assistance; deadline dates; and, if possible, an estimate of the time the task should take. If paralegals are assigned work without this information, they may spend too much time on the work, the end product may not be what was desired, or the project may be late, all of which reflect poorly on the paralegal's competence. The paralegal who works for a poor delegater must take the responsibility for getting the information and instructions necessary to complete the project correctly and on time by asking the appropriate questions, repeating back instructions to make sure that they have been understood, and reducing oral instructions to writing, usually in a short confirming memorandum sent back to the attorney.

Paralegals also find that **attorney review** of their work is not always as thorough as it should be, especially when the paralegal is a long-term, trusted employee whose competence has been proven. Even if the paralegal is confident in his or her work product, the lawyer must review it. If a paralegal is aware that the lawyer is not reviewing adequately, the paralegal has an obligation to discuss the matter with the lawyer to encourage more careful review. The problem of inadequate review is exacerbated when a paralegal is working for an inexperienced attorney or for an attorney who does not have expertise in the area of law in which he or she is working. If the paralegal is very experienced, the lawyer may rely too heavily or even completely on the paralegal's expertise. Paralegals in this situation should take steps to ensure that their work is properly reviewed.

Attorney review
Responsibility of supervising attorney to review work of paralegals

A **heavy workload** often interferes with the performance of lawyers, paralegals, and other law firm employees. Many factors can make for an unreasonably heavy workload, including taking on too many cases, being poorly organized or managed, or not having adequate staff. Sometimes, especially in litigation, temporary crisis periods emerge before and during trial that require everyone involved in a case to work long hours. Paralegals must be assertive in their dealings with lawyers so that they do not take on more work than they can competently handle. Too heavy a workload causes a decline in productivity and quality and increases the likelihood of shortcuts being taken and mistakes being made. A firm that continually operates in this crisis mode is not a good place to work — the work will not be done competently, the stress will be unhealthy, and the staff will not feel personally or professionally satisfied. Paralegals should avoid working for law firms characterized by the constant pressure caused by excessive workloads. They also should be aware of the potential problems created by a temporary heavy workload. When a project or group of projects require long hours and create pressure over an extended period, the paralegal should talk to the appropriate person in the firm to see what measures can be taken to remedy the situation. Additional support staff and temporary paralegals to do the most routine paralegal and clerical work may relieve the situation, making it possible for everyone to function more effectively.

Paralegals should have a thorough understanding of their own **level of competence** and, while striving to learn and develop, should not get so far ahead of their knowledge and skills that they are no longer acting competently. This is where continuing education, in-house training programs, and mentoring can come into play. Paralegals who want long and satisfying careers are, in essence, always "in school." An honest **self-assessment** will help paralegals identify those personal characteristics that may affect their competence. Well-qualified paralegals know what particular talents and qualities they do and do not possess and they maximize strong points and minimize deficiencies accordingly. They work to improve in areas of weakness, to strengthen and emphasize natural abilities, and to seek work that matches their attributes. A paralegal who is not a good writer should strive to improve those skills but should also avoid positions that require a lot of sophisticated writing. A paralegal who works well with people should seek a position that will make use of that ability, such as a job that involves supervision of others or frequent client contact.

Paralegals who are having **personal, health, or family problems** must consider how these problems affect their work. No one functions as effectively when he or she is troubled, worried, or distracted. Paralegals who are experiencing difficulties outside the office must be alert to the potential for a decline in productivity and accuracy, and should take steps to ensure that quality is maintained. If the problems are serious or ongoing, a paralegal in this situation may want to discuss these problems with a supervisor to get both the emotional and the practical support needed to carry on competently and to make sure that his or her behavior is not misinterpreted. Paralegals who have alcohol and drug dependency problems should seek professional help, and colleagues and friends in the workplace should encourage them to do so.

REVIEW QUESTIONS

1. What are the elements of competence?
2. Are lawyers responsible for the conduct of their paralegals?
3. If lawyers are responsible for the professional actions of their paralegals, why should paralegals be concerned about competence?
4. Describe and compare legal and paralegal education.

5. What education do lawyers and paralegals need in addition to their formal professional education?
6. What are some sources of continuing education programs for paralegals?
7. What do the NALA and NFPA ethics guidelines say about competence?
8. How do ethics rules define competence?
9. Do lawyers and paralegals need to have the same knowledge and skills to be competent? How do they differ? What skills might they need in common?
10. How does the trend toward increasing legal specialization affect competence?
11. What do law firms do to develop their paralegals' competence?
12. How does a paralegal demonstrate competence in preparing a case?
13. What does *diligence* mean? What is the paralegal's role in ensuring diligence?
14. What are some common problems associated with a lack of diligence or promptness?
15. Why is communication with clients included in the definition of competence? What role can a paralegal play in this area?
16. What are the possible consequences of a lawyer's incompetence? What are the possible consequences of a paralegal's incompetence?
17. Give some examples of common grounds for malpractice claims.
18. What is third-party liability? How does it affect lawyers who work in government-regulated areas of practice?
19. What kinds of cases might give rise to third-party malpractice claims?
20. Name some steps that a firm can take to prevent malpractice claims.
21. How should a paralegal respond if he or she is asked to perform a function in which he or she has no expertise?
22. What steps should a paralegal take if his or her supervising attorney gives incomplete instructions on a project?
23. What should a paralegal do if the supervising attorney is not carefully reviewing his or her work?
24. What should a paralegal do if his or her workload is too heavy and cannot be handled in a timely, competent manner?
25. How should a paralegal react upon learning that another paralegal has a substance abuse problem that is affecting work?

HYPOTHETICALS

1. Anna Anderson just graduated from paralegal school, where she focused on probate and real estate work. Her best job offer is from a big firm, Billings & Conroy, which has asked her to work in the litigation department until there is an opening in probate or real

estate. She is assigned to work for a first-year associate, Bob Brown, on a new antitrust case that just came in. Bob asks Anna to draft a motion to dismiss the case. Anna has no idea how to begin and knows little about litigation, let alone the intricacies of federal court and antitrust law. What should she do? Anna figures out how to draft the motion and gives a very rough draft to Bob for guidance. He says it is fine and asks her to file it as is. Anna knows it is not very good and is concerned that Bob has not reviewed it carefully and may not know any more than she does about the law and procedure in the case. What should she do? Is Bob acting competently?

2. Carl Carlson is a freelance paralegal. He has been working in the probate area for 15 years and has a regular client base of lawyers with whom he works. Carl gets a call from a lawyer, Debby Dunton, who wants to meet him about handling some probate matters for her. At the meeting, Debby says, "I really don't know much about probate, but I need to take these few cases until I can build up my family law practice." What should Carl do? Can he put procedures in place to make sure that there are no problems working with Debby? Assume that Carl goes to work with Debby. She hands him a file of papers and asks him to organize it and to do whatever needs to be done. What should he do?

3. Ellen Ellerby, a paralegal with Franklin & Gainsborough, works closely with another paralegal, Harry Henderson. In the last few months, Ellen has noticed that Harry is late to work a lot and is getting behind in his workload. He seems a little forgetful and disoriented. When they have time to talk during lunch one day, Harry confides that his marriage is rocky and he has been going out drinking every night with his buddies because he doesn't want to be at home. What should Ellen do? A few more weeks pass without change. One day, Ida Imerson, a lawyer in the firm, calls for Harry and he isn't in. Ida is looking for a complaint that Harry was supposed to draft in a small personal injury matter. Ellen searches through Harry's files and sees that the complaint has not been done and the statute of limitations runs the next day. What should Ellen do now?

4. Jan Jones is a paralegal for a small firm, Kingfield & Knowlton. The firm has grown dramatically in the last year, and everyone is working 60 or 70 hours a week to keep up with the workload. Jan is at her limit of stress and believes that she cannot handle one more client matter. As Jan is leaving the office one day at 5 P.M. to pick up her child from child care, Kent Kingfield passes her in the hall and hands her a phone message from a new client and says, "Call this guy back and tell him that we will have the contracts ready tomorrow. Find the Smith file and draft the contracts, using the Smith contracts as a model. I need them by 9 in the morning." What should Jan do?

What should the firm do to change the way it is working? Assume that Jan drops everything, calls the client, arranges for a friend to pick up her child, and drafts the contracts that night, working until midnight. In her exhaustion, she transposes some numbers and the consideration for the contract is stated incorrectly. She sees this after the contracts have been signed and sent to the other contracting party. What should she do?

DISCUSSION QUESTIONS AND PROJECTS

1. Check the local ethics code in your jurisdiction to see what provisions it contains on competence.
2. Get a listing and description of the disciplinary actions recently taken against attorneys in your state or county. (This information may be published in the local legal newspaper or state bar magazine.) What kinds of ethics violations appear? To what extent do these relate to competence?
3. Do you think states should set minimum levels of education for paralegals? Why or why not?
4. What would your model of paralegal education be if you were required to set minimum standards? Consider how much general college education and paralegal education should be included. How would your model look if it were an ideal model, rather than a minimum standard? Do you think that continuing education should be required?
5. Do you think paralegals should have to take a licensing examination to demonstrate their competence? Why or why not?
6. Call five local law firms and find out:

   a. their hiring standards for paralegals
   b. whether they have in-house orientation or training programs for paralegals
   c. whether they have a mentoring program for paralegals
   d. whether they pay the cost for their paralegals to take continuing education or other job-relevant courses

7. Call your local paralegal association and get a listing of its continuing education programs for the upcoming year.
8. Obtain the current informational materials on NALA's CLA program and NFPA's PACE program. What are the requirements for taking these examinations? What is tested on these exams? What percentage of the paralegals in your area are certified by one of these organizations? Ask paralegals who are certified why they took the exam and how it has affected their careers.
9. To what extent is legal specialization important in your area? Does your jurisdiction have a certified specialist program for attorneys? If

so, in what areas of law? How many lawyers are certified? Do most
paralegals "specialize"?

10. Interview five paralegals who work in five different areas of the law.
Ask them to list the functions they perform and the functions their
attorney-supervisors perform. Compare the lists and look for common functions. Is there a difference in the competence needed by
lawyers and paralegals? What generalities can you draw about the
differences and commonalities?

11. How can you tell whether a law firm encourages competence and
quality?

12. Describe the extent to which an attorney should review the following work prepared by a paralegal:

a. a form complaint
b. articles of incorporation
c. a trial notebook
d. answers to interrogatories
e. deposition summaries
f. abstracts of documents in a computerized retrieval system

13. What would you do if you worked for a firm that was always in an
overworked, crisis mode?

14. What would you do if you knew that attorneys in your firm frequently took short cuts, such as not gathering facts carefully or not
researching legal issues thoroughly?

15. Name three of your personal strengths that may help you in your
career as a paralegal. Name three weaknesses that might interfere
with your competence or success. Considering these, what should
you do to maximize your strengths and minimize your weaknesses? What kind of work is best suited to you? What kind of
work environment?

16. Look for articles in the local legal newspaper and bar journals about
malpractice cases and bring them to class to discuss.

SELECTED CASES

Biakanja v. Irving, 49 Cal. 2d 647, 320 P.2d 16 (1958) (nonlawyer who
drafted will and had it improperly witnessed held liable to heir who
did not receive his intended inheritance under the invalid will).

Busch v. Flangas, 837 P.2d 438 (Nev. 1992) (malpractice case against law
clerk who handled matter without lawyer supervision).

De Vaux v. American Home Assurance Co., 387 Mass. 814, 444 N.E.2d
355 (1983) (misfiled letter results in missed statute of limitations).

In re Gillaspy, 640 N.E.2d 1054 (Ind. 1994) (failing to act competently
by allowing a nonlawyer bankruptcy service to prepare petitions
and other documents without lawyer review).

Pincay v. McCarron, 389 F.3d 853 (Cal. 2004) (court held that delegating calendaring of deadlines to a paralegal was not per se negligent).

Webb v. Pomeroy, 8 Kan. App. 2d 246, 655 P.2d 465 (1983) (malpractice case against nonlawyer who acted as a lawyer in a real estate transaction).

SELECTED REFERENCES

ABA Model Rules, Rule 1.1 [competence]

ABA Model Rules, Rule 1.3 [diligence]

ABA Model Rules, Rule 1.4 [communication]

ABA Model Code, DR 6-101(A) [competence]

ABA Model Code, DR 6-101(A)(3), DR 7-101(A) [diligence and communication]

ABA Model Code, DR 9-102(B)(1) [communication]

8

Special Issues in Advocacy

This chapter describes the most critical of the many dilemmas that confront litigation paralegals during the adversarial process and the ethics principles that govern advocacy. Chapter 8 covers:

- the duty to represent clients zealously
- unmeritorious claims, delay, and abuse of discovery
- disruptive courtroom tactics and sanctions for those actions
- sanctions for disobeying court orders
- the court's contempt power and its use
- candor and honesty in areas involving paralegals
- relationships and communications with judges
- contact with jurors
- contact with represented parties
- contact with unrepresented persons
- contact with witnesses
- trial publicity
- special rules for prosecutors

A. Introduction

The practice of law has changed over the past 50 years in response to the proliferation of laws, their increased complexity, and their pervasive impact on so many areas of modern life and business. One aspect of this change is that **most lawyers no longer go to court regularly**. The majority of lawyers in this country do not litigate matters, either civil or criminal, and many lawyers never go to court. The areas of law in which these lawyers practice are many, including corporate, tax, business transactions, real estate, estate planning, probate, environmental law, and intellectual property.

At the same time, some commentators contend that **society is too litigious**, as people look to the courts to handle all kinds of disputes not necessarily suited for judicial resolution. Some have argued that there is a litigation explosion; others argue that this claim is not borne out by empirical research. Politicians blame the rising cost of medical services and insurance on the growth in litigation against doctors and hospitals. Punitive damage awards have been vigorously attacked. Judges and lawyers have worked to streamline the litigation process and to encourage, or mandate, alternative dispute resolution. This environment dictates that litigation paralegals must not only be diligent in their efforts to meet high standards of competence and ethics, but that they must stay current with the ever-changing ethics rules and court rules and decisions that govern conduct in litigation.

Unlike lawyers, the **majority of paralegals work in litigation**. And, contrary to the commonly held perception of litigation, most of the work is done out of court, before trial. The role of the paralegal in litigation is expansive, including fact gathering, interviewing clients and witnesses, drafting pleadings and motions, conducting legal research, drafting discovery requests and motions and responding to discovery, preparing for trial by summarizing and indexing documents and depositions, organizing and overseeing the maintenance of databases, locating and preparing expert witnesses, and preparing demonstrative evidence. Many litigation paralegals accompany their attorney-employers to court and assist in court by taking notes, making observations about jurors' reactions to the proceedings, handling logistics and emergencies, and doing last-minute research. As the discovery experts in cases, paralegals frequently have a mastery of the facts and evidence that is of tremendous help to the attorney, who must concentrate his or her attention on presenting the case, examining and cross-examining witnesses, and making objections.

Because paralegals play such a major role in litigation, they need a strong understanding of the ethics rules governing advocacy. Violations of these rules are often not committed by an attorney acting alone; the attorney may act through an agent or may involve an unwitting paralegal.

All attorneys have an ethical **duty to represent clients zealously** (Model Code Canon 7 and Model Rule 1.3). Zealous representation entails exercising one's best efforts on the client's behalf within the boundaries of law and ethics. The duty to represent clients zealously has special meaning in the context of the lawyer's role as an advocate. It sometimes clashes with other legal-ethical duties or moral imperatives, such as the **lawyer's duty of candor to the court** and the proper administration of justice, the rules of client confidentiality, and the search for the truth that forms the basis of the adversary system. The following sections will cover some of the situations where ethical prerogatives clash and concentrate on the ethics rules on advocacy that affect paralegals most directly.

B.   Unmeritorious Claims, Delay, and Discovery Abuse

The ethics rules, statutes and court rules prohibit lawyers from bringing **unmeritorious** or **frivolous claims** or **defenses** (Model Code DR 7-102 and Model Rule 3.1). Two specific kinds of acts fall into this category: (1) actions that only serve to harass or to injure another maliciously and (2) claims or defenses that are unwarranted under existing law unless the lawyer has a good faith argument to change the law.

Violations of this rule most commonly occur when an attorney brings an **unwarranted action** to gain some advantage over the opposition, to force a party to expend funds to defend the action, or simply to earn fees. Sometimes a lawyer will bring an action based on inaccurate information supplied by the client without conducting any investigation. If the action is in fact unmeritorious, the attorney may be found to have violated ethics rules, court rules, or statutes. In general, lawyers should make a sufficient reasonable inquiry before taking action. An emergency might require action before there is time to investigate. Lawyers are not advised to proceed on the basis of the truth of a client's story alone.

An example of an unmeritorious claim is a plaintiff who sues his competitor without proper grounds under the law merely for the purpose of driving him or her out of business.

The ethics rules on unmeritorious claims do provide an important exception to the general rule against making claims or defenses that are not warranted by the law, that is, if the client is seeking to extend, modify, or reverse the law.

Related to unmeritorious claims are **abuses of the discovery process**. Conducting excessive or unnecessary discovery can be employed as a strategy to delay litigation, to burden the opposing counsel, to raise the cost to the opposition and, generally, to wear down the opposing party and counsel. Manipulation of discovery rules to gain tactical advantage, although not uncommon, causes judicial ire and increases the public's disdain for lawyers. All states and the federal courts have addressed discovery abuse by adopting statutes and court rules to streamline discovery, to expedite the pre-trial stage, and to discourage excessive and unnecessarily lengthy discovery. Common rules set limits on the number of interrogatories that can be served on a party, establish strict deadlines for completion of discovery, and mandate alternative dispute resolution and pre-trial settlement procedures. Judges can and do issue sanctions for discovery abuse.

Discovery abuse is also prohibited by ethics rules (Model Code DR 7-102(A) and Model Rule 3.4(d)). Most states' ethics rules specifically forbid making frivolous pre-trial discovery requests and failing to comply with proper discovery requests. Violations of this rule occur, for example, in requesting discovery that is beyond the scope of the case; flooding the opposition with irrelevant interrogatories; giving incomplete answers to interrogatories; requesting discovery of confidential, sensitive, or embarrassing information; or making unfounded objections to discovery. Or an attorney may respond to discovery, such as a demand for document production, by providing much more than what was requested and perhaps "hiding" a key incriminating document in volumes of unrequested documents. In a recent case involving a prominent California law firm, a court imposed a substantial fine for failing to name more than 20 witnesses in a sexual harassment case.

The ethics rules also prohibit a lawyer from **delay** of litigation (Model Code DR7-102(A)(1) and Model Rule 3.2). These rules cover delaying pre-trial procedures or the actual trial and require lawyers to make reasonable efforts to expedite litigation consistent with clients' interests. Some examples of unethical delays are delays for a lawyer's personal convenience, deliberate frustration of the opposition's legitimate goals, and financial gain. Unethical delays for which attorneys may be sanctioned by judges are: an attorney's refusing to respond to communications of opposing counsel; repeated failure to appear at hearings, settlement conferences, and depositions; unnecessary delays in filing motions to disqualify counsel; and failing to complete discovery in accordance with court rules, court orders, or statutes.

Sometimes violations of the rules against delay are caused by **incompetence**; disorganized or impaired lawyers may miss deadlines or not be able to keep up with their cases. But sometimes lawyers create intentional delays to gain a tactical advantage over the opposition.

Discipline by the bar for bringing unmeritorious claims or defenses, abusing discovery, or causing unnecessary delays is relatively rare. When discipline does occur, it is usually in a particularly egregious case, such as a multiplicity of frivolous lawsuits, or abuse or delay that is coupled with incompetence or failure to obey a court order. Because judges see the effects of ethics violations like these in the moment, the usual remedy is a swift sanction by the court under the court's **contempt power**. (See more on contempt in Section C below.)

Contempt power includes the imposition of **monetary sanctions**. Under federal statutes and procedural rules and under court rules or statutes in every jurisdiction, courts are granted authority to impose sanctions against lawyers, clients, or both for actions that are unwarranted, or for delaying or harassing conduct. The most frequently used rule in federal court is **Federal Rule of Civil Procedure 11**, which provides for appropriate sanctions against attorneys, clients, or both for filing unwarranted or other objectionable pleadings and papers. Rule 11 is supplemented by several provisions of the Federal Rules of Civil Procedure such as Fed. R. Civ. P. 37, which provides for sanctions for failure to respond to discovery and 26(g), which provides for sanctions for acting in bad faith in discovery. Rule 11(b) provides that the lawyer's signature on the document verified that the facts in the pleading have evidentiary support, that the complaint is not being made for an improper purpose, and that the claims or defense are warranted under existing law or by a non-frivolous argument to change the law. Sanctions include fines paid to the court and attorney's fees to the opposing party or parties. A judge may also dismiss a complaint with prejudice under Rule 11.

Rule 11 was adopted to help alleviate unnecessary delays and paperwork in federal court, and has been widely used by federal judges. The **amount of sanction** awards is sometimes quite substantial. Recent examples of cases in which sanctions were awarded under Rule 11 are using abusive language in a motion, filing an action unwarranted by law for purely political reasons, asking for an inflated amount of damages, and filing a motion to disqualify counsel purely to delay the proceedings.

Rule 11 applies only to pleadings, motions, and other documents filed with the court. Other federal statutes, however, provide for sanctions for abuses that do not fit into this category of actions. The U.S. Code authorizes federal judges to impose sanctions against an attorney who "multiplies the proceedings in any case unreasonably and vexatiously" (28 U.S.C. §1927). Section 1928 and Federal Rule of Appellate Procedure 38 provide for damages awarded to the prevailing party for delays caused by frivolous appeals.

Every state has specific court rules and/or statutes authorizing sanctions for the conduct described in this section, and case law recognizes the inherent authority of a court over its proceedings as the basis for imposing sanctions.

One other important remedy available to the victims of such conduct is a civil suit against the client, the lawyer, or both for **malicious prosecution** or **abuse of process**. Grounds for malicious prosecution exist

Malicious prosecution/abuse of process
Improper use of a civil or criminal process

159

when a civil lawsuit or criminal prosecution has been brought, without probable cause and with malice, after the defendant prevails in the action. Limited immunity for attorneys exists in some states if it is shown that the lawyer acted in good faith. An abuse of process action may be brought when the legal process is misused to achieve a purpose other than a legitimate legal purpose, such as filing a criminal complaint to force the defendant to pay a debt.

C. Disruption in the Courtroom and Disobeying Court Orders

Trial lawyers are bound by ethics rules to conduct themselves in a dignified and courteous manner in court (Model Code DR 7-106(C)(6)) and Model Rule 3.5(c)). Most interpretations of these two rules have found that the Model Rule requires intent to disrupt, whereas the Model Code does not.

Frequently, conduct that judges may consider disruptive is the result of a lawyer's efforts to represent a client zealously. Sometimes a lawyer's zeal is transformed into an enthusiasm that oversteps the bounds of acceptable conduct. Lawyers may also employ tactics in court that are designed to influence the jury or to throw the opposing counsel off track.

Some examples of **disruptive conduct** or dirty tricks in the courtroom are raising an unfounded objection to break opposing counsel's train of thought; making faces or gestures to the judge or the jury; asking a question that alludes to evidence known to be inadmissible; insulting the judge or opposing counsel—for example, by calling them names or accusing them of collusion, racism, incompetence, or bias; referring to the proceedings in an insulting or rude manner; and making unsupportable, inflammatory, or prejudicial side remarks to the jury.

Disobeying a court order is categorized as disruptive conduct because it interferes with the smooth administration of proceedings and demonstrates disrespect for the tribunal (Model Code DR 7-106(A) and Model Rule 3.4(c)).

Contempt
An act that obstructs the administration of justice, impairs the dignity of the court, or shows disrespect for the authority of the court

While acts reflecting a lack of respect for the court may subject an attorney to disciplinary action, the acts are more likely to elicit an immediate response from the judge. Judges may hold an attorney in **contempt** for offensive courtroom conduct and for disobeying a court order. The judges' contempt power is reserved for situations in which the administration of justice and orderly proceedings are immediately and substantially threatened. Generally, the court will warn a lawyer repeatedly before citing him or her in contempt. Contempt is punishable by jail time and may give rise to disciplinary proceedings.

Judges have imposed the contempt sanction on attorneys for a wide variety of disruptive actions, including continued argument of a point on which the court has ruled; continued mention of inadmissible evidence or prohibited arguments; absence from or tardiness for scheduled court dates; presentation of false evidence; the use of abusive, vulgar, and obscene language; disrespectful, irrelevant, or unjustified criticism of the court; implying that the defense attorney is unethical and dishonest; and engaging in a shouting match with the judge. Insults, sarcasm, and the like are not punishable by contempt unless they also obstruct the proceedings.

While most paralegals are not often in a situation in which they would have the opportunity to engage in this kind of conduct, they should honor this important prohibition. Many paralegals working in civil litigation and criminal law attend court proceedings and must be aware of and abide by these rules governing conduct in court. NFPA Model Code EC 1.3(a) calls on paralegals to refrain from "conduct that offends the dignity and decorum" of the courts.

D. Candor and Honesty

All ethics rules call for lawyers to be **honest** in their representation of clients. However, an important distinction exists between being honest and disclosing everything that the lawyer knows. Lawyers are not obligated to disclose evidence that is prejudicial to their client unless such information is not privileged and is requested through proper discovery or the lawyer is obligated by some special rule of law.

The ethics rules specifically prohibit a lawyer from making a **false statement of law or fact**; offering **false evidence**; and not disclosing **adverse controlling authority** when opposing counsel fails to do so (Model Code 7-102, 7-106 and 7-109, and Model Rule 3.3(a) and 3.4(a) and (b)). A lawyer who discovers that false evidence has been submitted to the court must correct the fraud. The lawyer must call on the client to rectify the fraud or must reveal the fraud to the court unless the information is privileged. A nonclient's fraud on the court must be promptly revealed to the court. Some states' ethics rules allow or require disclosure even if the information is protected by the privilege. Finally, lawyers may not obstruct access to evidence; alter, destroy, or conceal evidence; or falsify or allow others to falsify evidence.

Some **examples** may be instructive. In one disciplinary case, an attorney was censured for failing to disclose to arbitrators that a doctor had changed his diagnosis of the condition of the client. In another case, a court ordered a default judgment against a defendant whose attorney refused to produce a witness who had avoided service. In another, a federal court ordered a default in a race discrimination case against a corporate defendant for altering and destroying key documents, leaving critical information out of affidavits, blocking access in court to relevant information, and intimidating a witness. A corporate defendant was sanctioned more than a million dollars for withholding documents that were favorable to the plaintiff's case. The same company was sanctioned for discovery abuses in more than 15 cases in a three-year period, for violations that included altering a training tape, destroying photographs of a scene, and refusing to produce training manuals and security tapes. Other recent cases have involved a lawyer requesting that his client be released from custody to attend his mother's funeral after it had already been held, an attorney providing false information on the value of a client's property, and a lawyer conveying property with the intent to defraud a creditor.

Perjury
Criminal offense of making false statements under oath

Client perjury has been a difficult legal and ethical dilemma for lawyers. The courts have not been uniform in their handling of this area, and ethics rules and their interpretations also vary from one jurisdiction to the next. As a general rule in a civil case, the lawyer who knows that his or her client intends to commit perjury should not call the client to testify. Most courts either recommend or mandate withdrawal from representation or disclosure to the court if the client testifies dishonestly.

Criminal cases present even more difficult problems because of the client's right to testify and to be represented by competent counsel. The U.S. Supreme Court has held that withdrawal is the appropriate action (*Nix v. Whiteside,* 475 U.S. 157 (1986)). However, withdrawal may not be permitted by the court at the time of trial, and authorities are split on whether the lawyer in this situation should disclose the client's intended perjury as the basis for withdrawal. Some courts endorse the attorney allowing the defendant to testify in narrative form without the attorney's help. After the perjury has occurred, most courts require the lawyer to seek withdrawal. If withdrawal is not granted, some require disclosure of the perjury. The ABA Model Rules require the lawyer to take remedial measures, including disclosure to the court if necessary (Model Rules 3.3 (a)(3) and 3.3(b)).

Many lawyers believe that **client and witness perjury** is widespread and on the rise. Cases in which judges referred conduct to prosecutors for investigation of perjury have involved relatives testifying falsely as alibi witnesses; spouses hiding assets in marital dissolution cases; and police lying under oath about the circumstances of an arrest, a search and seizure, or an informant. Some commentators believe that this dishonesty is a natural consequence of the adversarial system. Judges and most lawyers lament this situation but believe that it is unlikely to stop because perjury is so hard to prove and so rarely prosecuted.

The aspect of the duty of candor that paralegals most often see in their work is the requirement that **adverse controlling authority** be disclosed to the court. A paralegal who finds adverse authority while conducting legal research must report the authority to the attorney and must include it in appropriate documents filed with the court. Even without the ethics rule mandating that it be revealed to the court, it is wise to cite and either criticize it or distinguish it legally or factually from the client's case because otherwise the opposition will cite it and it will go unchallenged. Judges who discover that controlling authority was not disclosed may sanction the lawyer and report him or her to the disciplinary authorities, whether the omission was intentional or the result of a lack of competence in research or drafting.

Remedies for destroying, altering, or suppressing evidence imposed by disciplinary bodies and the courts are supplemented by **obstruction of justice** statutes at both state and federal levels. In addition to criminal charges being brought against the attorney, client, or both, these statutes often provide for sanctions in the pending case, such as default, fines, dismissal, legal fees and costs, and civil causes of action by the injured party. Destruction of evidence also gives rise in some jurisdictions to a civil cause of action for **spoilation**, in which the injured party can collect damages for substantial interference with the ability to prove a claim or defense because the evidence is no longer available. And in some states, courts allow an adverse inference to be drawn from a party's failure to produce the evidence.

Spoilation
Destruction of evidence that may result in a civil cause of action for damages for interference with the ability to prove a claim or defense

E. Relationships and Communications with Judges

Making false statements about the qualifications or integrity of a judge or making such statements with reckless disregard for the truth is a violation of ethics. This rule covers false accusations against a judge (Model Code DR 8-102(A) and Model Rule 8.2(a)). In most jurisdictions, the courts have held that the First Amendment does not protect lawyers who criticize judges inappropriately because of the strong state interest in protecting public officials and in maintaining respect for the courts. However, in a few notable cases, discipline of lawyers who criticized judges has been struck down on appeal. In one such case, the lawyer called a judge an anti-Semite and a drunk. In the other, the lawyer called a local judge "a midget among giants" in a letter to a newspaper. In a recent Ohio case, a lawyer was suspended for implying to a client that he could influence a judge.

Ethics rules prohibit lawyers from attempting to **influence** judges or from implying that they can influence a judge. A lawyer may not give or lend anything of value to a judge except a campaign contribution in jurisdictions where judges are elected, and may not seek to influence a judge by any illegal means, which constitutes the crime of **bribery**. Knowingly assisting a judge in violating the law or the judicial canons is also an ethical violation in states that follow the ABA Model Rules

Bribery
The crime of giving or receiving something of value as payment for an official act

(Model Rule 8.4(f)). Implying or stating that one can influence a judge (or other public official) is forbidden by ethics rules (Model Code DR 9-101(C) and Model Rule 8.4(e)). Judges are bound by their own ethical canons and rules of conduct in every jurisdiction, and provisions of these judicial canons parallel the lawyer's rules governing their relationships with judges.

Ex parte
Action taken by or on behalf of a party without the presence of the opposing party

One rule that paralegals working in litigation need to know is the prohibition on *ex parte* **communications** with judges. To ensure fairness in the adversary process, lawyers and paralegals are prohibited from having contact with the judge in a case without the presence of the opposing counsel. Such secret communications might give the communicating party an unfair advantage or give an appearance of influence or favoritism (Model Code DR 7-110(B) and Model Rule 3.5(b)). Exceptions to these rules are made for special **ex parte proceedings** that legally do not require opposing counsel's presence, such as petitions for a temporary restraining order. The NFPA Model Code calls attention to the rules regarding ex parte communications in EC 1.2(b).

F.   Contact with Jurors

Ex parte communications with jurors and prospective jurors, before and during trial, are expressly prohibited by ethics rules to prevent influence and bribery (Model Code DR 7-108(A), (B) and Model Rule 3.5(a) and (b)). Lawyers are prohibited from such communications even if they are not involved in the case. A lawyer may not circumvent these rules by using an agent such as the client or a paralegal.

Mistrial
Trial terminated and declared void prior to the return of a verdict

In addition to disciplinary action for such conduct, a *mistrial* is likely to be declared if ex parte communications with jurors come to light. The lawyer's intent or lack of intent to influence a juror is not relevant. A lawyer's research on prospective jurors by using an investigator to contact them and ask them questions from a standard questionnaire has been held to be impermissible and led to the criminal conviction and disbarment of the lawyer in one case. Even simple socializing during a break in a trial has been held to be grounds to declare a mistrial or a new trial, and to disqualify counsel.

Jury tampering is, of course, a crime in every jurisdiction and under federal laws. For example, 18 U.S.C. §§1503 makes it a crime to attempt to influence a juror.

Communicating with jurors after the conclusion of a trial is forbidden in some states. Other states do not prohibit **post-trial communications**, which attorneys may desire to help them evaluate their presentation, to find out what influenced the jurors, and to ascertain whether the jury deliberated appropriately. Most states' ethics rules allow post-trial communications with the conditions that communications may not be made if prohibited by law or court order, if made merely to harass or embarrass the juror, or to influence his actions in future jury service (Model Code DR 7-108(D) and Model Rules 3.5(c) and 4.4(a)).

Finally, some states' ethics codes require a lawyer to reveal to the court improper conduct toward or among jurors (Model Code DR 7-108(G)).

G.   Contact with Parties and Represented Persons

Attorneys are prohibited from **communicating with parties who are represented by counsel** and may communicate directly with the represented person's counsel only (Model Code DR 7-104(A)(1) and Model Rule 4.2). This rule is based primarily on concerns about overreaching conduct designed to gain advantage over an opponent by disrupting the trust between the attorney and client or influencing the client when he or she is vulnerable because counsel is not present. Unethical solicitation is also a concern. There are two generally accepted exceptions to the general prohibition against such communications: when the party's lawyer consents to the communication or when a court order or law authorizes the communication.

Exceptions to the general rule prohibiting communication with represented parties are also made for certain situations: (1) when the represented party is not truly adverse, (2) when the represented person is seeking a second opinion or new counsel, and (3) when the represented person is dissatisfied with his or her lawyer over the representation or fee and is considering taking action against the lawyer. It should be noted that this prohibition does not restrict the parties themselves, who are free to speak to each other, although most lawyers warn their clients not to do so because of the potential for such conversations interfering with the representation and strategy in the case. Finally, the restriction applies even if the party is the one who initiates the contact. Remedies during proceedings may include **suppression of evidence** and **disqualification** of counsel. Ethical sanctions would likely follow, especially if the conduct has involved blatant dishonesty.

A lawyer may not circumvent the rules prohibiting contact with represented parties by asking a paralegal to communicate with represented persons in violation of these rules, and paralegals should be aware not to have such communications, whether on their own initiative or at the instruction of a lawyer.

H. Contact with Unrepresented Persons

Ethics rules restrict the communications a lawyer may have with a **party not represented by counsel**. Lawyers are prohibited from giving advice to such a person if there is a possibility that this third person's interests may conflict with the client's. The ABA and most states' rules also prohibit lawyers from **misrepresenting** their interest in the matter and require lawyers to clarify any misunderstanding about their role. (See Model Rule 4.3.) If a lawyer is opposing a person who is representing himself or herself, the lawyer may, of course, communicate with that person directly, but should take special care not to take advantage of the situation.

Applying rules about communications with unrepresented persons in a corporate environment requires special care. Paralegals sometimes need to interview **employees and former employees** about matters that are being litigated or may be litigated in the future. Most cases hold that a lawyer may speak to unrepresented former employees of a corporation on the opposing side of litigation unless the employees were privy to privileged information. Current employees may be classified as represented persons if the corporation provides counsel to them. Members of a class in a class action are also considered to be represented parties.

Since a lawyer may not circumvent these rules by **using an agent**, a paralegal should be very careful when speaking with unrepresented persons — for example, persons who are potential witnesses or parties. Paralegals must refrain from inadvertently or intentionally misleading persons not represented by counsel about their interest in a matter and from giving them advice. An ABA Formal Ethics Opinion has concluded that a lawyer is responsible for the improper ex parte contacts of an investigator under his or her supervision if the lawyer did not try to prevent the improper contacts, told the investigator to make them, or failed to tell him or her not to make them once the contact came to light (ABA Formal Opinion 95-396 (1995)).

I. Contact with Witnesses

A few special rules govern lawyers' contact with witnesses. Like most other rules related to advocacy, these provisions are intended to protect the integrity of the adversary system.

The first category of witness-related rules concerns the communication between the attorney and the witness. A lawyer is forbidden from **advising or causing a witness to flee the jurisdiction** or to hide to avoid testifying (Model Code DR 7-109(B) and Model Rule 3.4(f)).

In addition to violating ethics rules, such conduct constitutes **obstruction of justice** and violates statutes that make it a crime to tamper with a witness or to delay, hinder, or prevent a witness from testifying.

An attorney may not advise a witness to testify falsely (Model Code DR 7-109(A) and Model Rule 3.4(b)). Giving **false testimony** under oath constitutes the crime of *perjury*, and counseling a witness to do so is also a crime, called *subornation of perjury*.

Subornation of perjury
Criminal offense of encouraging another to commit perjury

Lawyers and their employees can and do interview witnesses in depth to ascertain as exactly as possible the content and consistency of the witnesses' testimony and their credibility. If a witness's story changes, opposing counsel may use the inconsistency to attack the accuracy of the information and to impeach the credibility of that witness.

Ethics rules do not prohibit lawyers from **preparing witnesses**, including clients, to testify effectively. A witness who is familiar with courtroom procedure and who knows what questions counsel and opposing counsel will ask is more likely to be consistent and clear and less likely to become confused when being examined by opposing counsel. However, paralegals who handle witness preparation must be careful not to inadvertently encourage witnesses to give false testimony and not to overcoach witnesses, with the result that their testimony seems "prepared."

Coaching witnesses too much can backfire. For example, in a large asbestos case, one of the plaintiffs' law firms prepared a detailed memorandum to clients telling them how to testify, including what to say about their injuries. When the defense counsel was inadvertently given a copy of this memorandum and exposed it to the court, the firm stopped sending it to the plaintiffs and blamed an overzealous paralegal for writing it. The judge reported the matter to the state bar, but no action was taken against the lawyers involved.

The line between preparing witnesses to give their testimony effectively and encouraging them to testify untruthfully must not be crossed, and paralegals who play a part in preparing witnesses must be careful not to cross it. As noted, **perjury** is rarely prosecuted and hard to prove. Perjury is even harder to prove when the witness is also a client because communications between the lawyer and paralegal and the client are protected by the privilege. But judges and juries may perceive the deception and will, at the very least, discount the witness's testimony.

Lawyers and paralegals are prohibited from **harassing witnesses**, both inside and outside the courtroom. Lawyers may not engage in any conduct with the sole purpose of embarrassing, harassing, degrading, or burdening a third person (Model Code DR 7-106(C)(2) and DR 7-102(A)(1); Model Rule 4.4(a)).

Related to these ethics prohibitions about communicating with nonclients are statutes that prohibit the **tape recording** of a person without his or her permission. For example, a federal statute provides criminal and civil remedies for interception and disclosure of wire, oral, or electronic communications (18 U.S.C. §2511 and 2520) and prohibits the use of such communications as evidence in any court (18 U.S.C. §2515). Not all jurisdictions prohibit secret tape recording of conversations, and some states have endorsed the practice. However, an ABA advisory opinion recommends against it on ethical grounds (ABA Formal Opinion 331 (1974)). Attorneys and paralegals must consult state statutes and rules before engaging in such conduct.

Lawyers may **pay witnesses for expenses** related to testifying. The usual and permissible expenses are travel and lost wages. **Expert witnesses** may also be paid a reasonable fee for their professional services. No witness may be paid a fee or bonus that is contingent on the outcome of a case, as this would obviously provide an incentive for false testimony (Model Code DR 7-109(C) and Comment [3] to Model Rule 3.4(b)).

As discussed in Section D above, with regard to client perjury, a lawyer has special duties to prevent the introduction of **false testimony** and to take corrective measures if a witness gives false testimony. The ethical dilemma presented by a witness's false testimony is not difficult to resolve when the witness is not a client. The lawyer does not have an ethical duty to a witness, even if the witness's testimony would favor the client, that outweighs the lawyer's duty of candor to the court. A lawyer who knows that a witness intends to testify falsely should advise the witness not to do so and should refuse to call the witness if he or she persists in intending to commit perjury. Once a witness gives false testimony, the lawyer must inform the court (Model Code DR 7-102(A)(4); Model Rule 3.3(a)(3)).

J.   Trial Publicity

Balancing the **right of free expression** and the **right to a fair trial** is a precarious and constant struggle. The public interest in big cases and the pervasiveness of the modern media have frequently clashed with the smooth administration of the court system and assurance of a fair trial, especially in criminal cases. This conflict most visibly presents itself in sensational cases, especially those in which the press seeks a presence by having cameras in the courtroom or when a judge issues a *gag order*.

Gag order
Court-imposed order that restricts information or comment about a case

The ethics rules on trial publicity have been hotly debated among trial lawyers and in the press and the courts. Early Model Code provisions were found **unconstitutional**, and new Model Rules provisions were adopted in the 1980s and revised in the 1990s. All states have some version of these new rules. The rules vary from state to state but, in general, provide that a lawyer must not make a public statement "if the lawyer knows or reasonably should know that it will have a **substantial likelihood of materially prejudicing** an adjudicative proceeding."

The ABA and most state ethics rules have a list of the kinds of information that presumably would or would not be prejudicial in the comment to this rule. Many states have adopted a provision that permits lawyers to make statements to protect their clients in response to publicity not generated by the lawyer or the client (Model Rule 3.6).

While **disciplinary actions** against lawyers for violations of these provisions are relatively rare, they do occur, usually in sensational cases that are closely covered by the media. For example, the lawyer representing underworld figure John Gotti was held in contempt for statements made in his media campaign, particularly for statements perceived by the court as intended to frighten potential jurors. The defense lawyers in the O. J. Simpson case were investigated for statements made to the media about Los Angeles police officers framing their client and then covering up their effort to frame him, but no charges were brought. Some courts impose gag orders to prevent lawyers from making any statements but, when challenged, these gag orders are sometimes struck down as unconstitutional prior restraints on speech.

The debate over lawyer conduct in high-profile cases continues to be heated. Discussions cover not only the ethics rules on trial publicity, but the impact of such lawyers' conduct on the public's opinion of lawyers. Polls have shown that a majority of people view lawyers more negatively because of their high profile in the media. Most people believe that lawyers use the media to influence **public opinion** about their cases, and many believe that this conduct is inappropriate and unethical. However, there is ample evidence that jurors are not influenced by the "trial in the press." Realistically, jurors cannot be easily influenced if they are sequestered and do not have access to the daily barrage of statements by lawyers and lawyer-commentators.

Paralegals should not allow themselves to be used by lawyers to circumvent the rules on trial publicity. Some states ethics codes have a provision that requires lawyers to exercise reasonable care to prevent employees and associates from making prohibited statements. Model Code 7-108(J) and Model Rule 3.8(f) set forth prosecutors' duties to prevent employees from making unethical extrajudicial statements. A lawyer is responsible for such conduct under the general rules governing a lawyer's responsibility for acts of employees (Model Rule 5.3).

K. Special Rules for Prosecutors

As representatives of the government and the people, prosecutors have a **special duty of truth and fairness** in the administration of justice.

Prosecutors must seek not only to convict, but also to seek justice and to ensure that all citizens are afforded their rights. Ethics rules in all jurisdictions establish these obligations, and local laws frequently impose additional requirements.

One critical duty of the prosecutor is to not institute unsupported criminal charges and to not continue to pursue an unsupported action. **Probable cause** is required (Model Code DR 7-103(A); Model Rule 3.8(a)). This limitation also prevents prosecutors from abusing their discretion in prosecuting cases by singling out someone for prosecution on a discriminatory basis. Prosecutors are also required to **disclose information** that tends to negate or mitigate guilt or to reduce punishment (Model Code DR 7-103(B); Model Rule 3.8(d)).

Most states have ethics rules that require prosecutors to make reasonable efforts to see that accused persons know of their **right to counsel** and have an opportunity to secure counsel; not to obtain a waiver of rights from an unrepresented accused; and to exercise reasonable care to prevent employees and others involved with the prosecution from making prohibited *extrajudicial* statements (Model Rule 3.8(b) and (c)). Rules also limit a prosecutor's right to subpoena a lawyer to testify about a client or former client. A prosecutor may subpoena a lawyer only if the information sought is not privileged, is essential to the case and not otherwise available, and there is no other feasible way to obtain the information sought (Model Rule 3.8(e)). For additional guidance on ethical issues in the criminal area, see the ABA Standards for Criminal Justice, which include separate sections on the prosecutorial and defense functions.

In addition to disciplinary sanctions for violations of the special rules for prosecutors, courts may impose remedies in a pending case if the defendant's constitutional rights have been violated. A court may reverse a conviction, suppress evidence, dismiss charges, or order a new trial. For example, a murder conviction was reversed on appeal when the appellate court found extensive prosecutorial misconduct, including misrepresenting the law and the facts and intimidating witnesses. The prosecutor was reassigned to a desk job.

Extrajudicial
An act that takes place outside the presence of the judge or jury

---

REVIEW QUESTIONS

1. Why do paralegals have to know about the rules governing advocacy?
2. What is zealous representation, and what other ethics rules does it sometimes conflict with?
3. Define unmeritorious or frivolous claims, and give examples.
4. When can a lawyer make a claim that is not warranted under existing law?
5. What is the duty to investigate a client's story before filing an action?

6. Give examples of abuses of the discovery process. What are the possible consequences for the lawyer?

7. Give an example of an unethical delay. What other ethics violations might be involved in an unnecessary delay?

8. Name the remedies or sanctions that might result from bringing unmeritorious claims, abusing discovery, or causing unnecessary delays.

9. Under what circumstances may an action for malicious prosecution be brought? Abuse of process?

10. What kinds of sanctions may a court impose for unwarranted, delaying, or harassing actions? On whom are they imposed?

11. Give examples of actions by lawyers that would be disruptive in the courtroom. What do the ethics rules prohibiting such disruptions say? For what reasons might a lawyer be disruptive?

12. What is the most immediate remedy for disruptive conduct in the courtroom or disobedience of a court order?

13. What kinds of actions are prohibited and required by a lawyer's duty of candor?

14. What must a lawyer do if he or she discovers that a nonclient witness has given false testimony? What if the false testimony is given by a client in a civil case? In a criminal case?

15. What should a paralegal do if he or she discovers adverse controlling authority in the course of research?

16. What might happen if a lawyer presents false evidence or permits false testimony in court?

17. What are the rules governing lawyers' relationships with judges?

18. May a lawyer give a judge a gift? What if they are good friends?

19. Why are lawyers and their employees prohibited from having ex parte communications with judges?

20. What kinds of contact with jurors are prohibited by the ethics rules and why? What crime might be involved when a lawyer or paralegal tries to influence a juror?

21. What are the general rules about lawyers and their agents having contact with persons who already have a lawyer? Why? What are the exceptions?

22. What is the general rule about contact with persons who are not represented by counsel? What if the person makes the contact?

23. What must paralegals do when they are communicating with witnesses?

24. What actions might constitute harassing a witness? What crime (or crimes) might be committed in addition to violations of ethics rules?

25. May a lawyer pay a witness to testify? What are the applicable restrictions?

26. May a lawyer pay an expert witness? May the lawyer pay the witness more if the client wins?

27. What two important constitutional interests are being balanced in the ethics rules on trial publicity?
28. What kinds of extrajudicial statements are generally permitted by ethics rules? What kinds are prohibited?
29. May a lawyer have a paralegal speak to the press and reveal information about a pending case that the lawyer could not reveal under the ethics rules? Why or why not?
30. Why are prosecutors bound by additional ethics rules? Name four ethical duties that prosecutors have that other lawyers do not have.
31. What sanctions and remedies may be imposed for prosecutorial misconduct?

HYPOTHETICALS

1. Donna Duggan is a paralegal working for a criminal defense firm, Crane & Cook. She often interviews clients to gather facts and to assist in preparing them for trial. During one such interview, client Tommy Thorton, who has been charged with a number of crimes relating to a bank robbery, says, "I wasn't even there! Put me on the stand and I will tell the judge and jury!" Donna does not believe this because she has seen a videotape of the robbery and one of the perpetrators looks exactly like Tommy. In addition, all the bank tellers identified him in a line-up. What should Donna say to Tommy? What should she tell Calvin Crane, the lawyer handling the case? Later in the interview, Tommy says, "My mom and my sister will testify that they were with me at home watching television." What should Donna do with this piece of information?

2. Evan Eldridge is a paralegal working for Matilda Moniker, who handles lots of small lawsuits that often go to trial. Matilda asks Evan to contact opposing counsel in six cases and to tell them that she is ill and cannot take depositions as scheduled. Then she asks Evan to draft requests for continuances in three other cases, also based on her illness. Evan knows that Matilda is not ill and suspects that she is delaying the discovery process and trials because the suits are weak and she is overworked. Matilda later confides over drinks that she thinks the cases will have a better chance of settling with the delays. Is Matilda doing anything unethical? What should Evan do?

3. Fanny Franks, a litigation paralegal, is working for a large law firm defending the Oxxon oil refinery in a big toxic tort case. Fanny is in charge of the document productions and responses to discovery. George Gunderson, one of the lawyers on the case, tells her not to answer about two-thirds of the interrogatories that have been propounded and to draft objections to the rest based on irrelevance and privilege. Fanny reviews the interrogatories and sees only two that might be objectionable. She believes that George wants to make

these objections in order to wear down the opposition. Opposing counsel is a small law firm that is handling only this one case at the moment because the case is so big. Its existence depends on winning, and it currently has no other revenue. What should Fanny do? A few weeks later, Fanny is preparing the documents that will go to opposing counsel on a document production. She notices that a key internal memorandum from an employee to management about the toxicity levels at the site in question is missing from the documents she has been working with. What should she do?

4. Hanna Hanson, the chief trial lawyer for Hanson & Harding, asks paralegal James Jameson to accompany her to trial. When she arrives, she sees that the opposing counsel has two other lawyers with him. She tells James not to say anything that might reveal that he is a paralegal, not a lawyer, because she doesn't want to appear to be "outgunned." Hanna seats James at the counsel table and introduces him as her "associate." Has Hanna done anything wrong? What should James do? Hanna has a reputation for being a very zealous advocate. During the first day at trial, while the opposing counsel is making opening statements, she starts giggling and shaking her head. Later, when a damaging witness is being examined, she asks him what his IQ is and where he gets his clothes, both of which are not relevant to his testimony. Has she done anything wrong? What do you think the judge should do? What should James do? What if Hanna makes faces and rolls her eyes at James and giggles when opposing counsel is talking?

5. Larry Lemon is a family law paralegal working for Matthew & Morrison. One especially difficult divorce case they are working on is the Tyson divorce. The husband and wife don't have that much money and they have four kids. They are using all their money to pay attorneys and at this rate will be deeply in debt by the time the divorce is final. The lead lawyer, Marilyn Matthew, asks Larry to call the opposing party, Tim Tyson, to try to set up a meeting between Tim and his wife, their client, Tina Tyson. Marilyn says, "I know these two could work this out without all this expense if they just sit down without all these other people around." Should Larry do this? Later that day, while Larry is trying to decide what to do, Tim himself calls and asks for Tina's new home phone number, saying, "I just want to call and talk to her. I want to settle this thing between us without all the lawyers." Should Larry give him the number? What should he do?

6. Monica Middlebrook is a paralegal for the U.S. Attorney's office. Lawyer Nat Nottingham asks Monica to call Erik Ellington, a target in a major organized crime investigation, to see if she can sweet-talk him into meeting her for an interview. Erik has a reputation as a "ladies' man" and is always accompanied by his lawyer and bodyguards. Should Monica make the call? Later, during the trial, Nat

tells Monica to copy and mail some documents to a crime reporter for the local newspaper. Among the documents is a copy of an anonymous letter to Erik from a woman named Sunny. The letter refers to a romantic tryst between the two of them and makes allusions to their using illegal drugs. Should Monica follow Nat's instructions? If not, what should she do?

7. Shane Samuels is a litigation paralegal working for the ImTox Corporation. Shane is asked to interview some employees who may know something about improper disposal of toxic waste. During his interview with Rachel Robinson, a truck driver, Rachel breaks down and starts crying and says, "All the guys cheat on the rules when they get rid of that stuff. Lately they have been putting it in my truck and going off to have beers. I was late getting home to my sick kid last night, so I just drove to the pier and dumped it in the bay." Shane knows Rachel can be charged with a crime for this act and that the corporation has not indicated that it will represent her. He also knows that if the crime is pinned on her and other employees who acted without the corporation's knowledge, the corporation may escape liability. What should Shane do?

DISCUSSION QUESTIONS AND PROJECTS

1. Why are there proportionately more litigation paralegals than trial lawyers?
2. Are you surprised that lawyers have duties that temper their duty to represent clients zealously?
3. What would you do if you interviewed a client who told you a story that you did not fully believe, and, on telling your supervising attorney, he or she told you to draft a complaint on the client's behalf based solely on the client's story?
4. How would you respond if your supervising attorney asked you to prepare an involuntary bankruptcy petition that you knew was unwarranted and designed solely to stop a foreclosure proceeding against your client?
5. Why are court-imposed sanctions such a powerful remedy for abuses in pleading and discovery?
6. Does your jurisdiction have rules or statutes comparable to the federal rules cited in this chapter?
7. How would you respond if the supervising lawyer asked you to shred documents that you knew were discoverable?
8. What would you do if you found adverse authority in researching a case but did not believe the authority was controlling?
9. Do you believe that the adversary system encourages perjury? Contact the local federal and or state prosecutors and interview

several lawyers for their opinions on the matter and ask them how many prosecutions for perjury have been brought in recent years.

10. What would you do if your attorney-employer asked you to invite a judge who was serving in one of your cases to a social event you were planning? What would you do if your attorney-employer asked you to try to find out what a judge who was a friend of yours was thinking about a pending case?

11. Do you think lawyers and their employees should be prohibited from giving campaign contributions to judges?

12. What would you do if your supervisor asked you to give a sealed note to a juror during a recess?

13. Does your state have an ethics rule that governs communication with jurors after trial? Do you think lawyers should be able to interview jurors after a trial is over? Why or why not?

14. Why are lawyers not involved in a case prohibited from talking to jurors about the case?

15. What would you do if a co-plaintiff who was not represented by your firm contacted you to discuss changing lawyers? What if the party wanted to discuss the merits of the case? The performance of his or her lawyer?

16. What would you do if you were interviewing a potential witness who did not have an attorney, and you suddenly realized that he seemed to believe that you and your firm were representing him?

17. Suppose that one of your duties as a litigation paralegal is to prepare witnesses for trial. What would you do if you were preparing a witness and his or her story kept changing? What if the witness seemed to be changing his or her version of the facts to be more favorable to you? Suppose the witness, although generally favorable to your client, has some information that is adverse to your client. What do you tell the witness about how to handle this information while he or she is on the stand?

18. What would you do if you discovered that a client was sending anonymous threatening letters to a witness who planned to testify against her? Would it make any difference if you knew the witness's testimony would be false?

19. Does your jurisdiction have a statute that prohibits or limits the tape recording of conversations? What does it say about permission from the party or parties? About the admissibility of illegally tape-recorded conversations?

20. What would you do if your firm paid a witness, who was not an expert, a witness fee that was three times his normal salary?

21. Review the rules governing a lawyer's handling of client perjury. Do you think a lawyer should be bound to tell the court if her client commits perjury? Would you answer differently in criminal and civil cases? What does your jurisdiction's ethics rule say? Are there any cases on the issue in your jurisdiction?

22. What does your jurisdiction's ethics code say about extrajudicial statements or trial publicity? Do you think the rule strikes the right balance between free speech and fair trial? Have any lawyers in your jurisdiction been disciplined under the rule?

23. What would you do if your attorney-employer asked you to leak information to the press that you know is prohibited by ethics rules? Would it make any difference if you were certain that without press coverage of this information your client would be unfairly convicted of a serious crime?

24. Suppose you work for the local prosecuting attorney. What would you do if you uncovered information that proved a criminal defendant in a case was innocent? What if you went to the supervising attorney and he refused to drop the charges or to turn over the exculpatory evidence to the defendant's counsel?

25. What would you do if your supervisor, the prosecuting attorney, asked you to obtain a statement from a recently arrested person, and in doing so you discovered that the person had not been advised of her right to counsel? What if the accused had been advised of her right to counsel but had not yet been able to reach an attorney?

26. Obtain a copy of your state judicial canons and compare the relevant provisions to those for lawyers covered in this chapter.

SELECTED CASES

Chira v. Lockheed, 634 F.2d 664 (2d Cir. 1980) (case dismissed when lawyer and client refuse to move forward with discovery).

Crane v. State Bar of California, 30 Cal. 3d 117, 635 P.2d 163, 177 Cal. Rptr. 670 (1981) (sanctions for altering document and sending unethical threatening letter to represented party).

Gentile v. Nevada State Bar, 501 U.S. 1030 (1990) (questions constitutionality of certain provisions of ethics rules on trial publicity).

In re White, 121 Cal. App. 4th 1453 (2004) (monetary sanctions and disgorgement of fees for filing frivolous habeas corpus writs produced by a mill where law students were unsupervised and other ethical violations were rampant).

Jorgenson v. County of Volusia, 846 F.2d 1350 (11th Cir. 1988) (sanctions for intentional failure to cite controlling authority).

Massey v. Prince George's County, 907 F. Supp. 138 (D. Md. 1995) (sanctions for failure of both sides to cite controlling authority).

Mississippi Bar v. Attorney ST, 621 So. 2d 229 (Miss. 1993) (endorses secret tape recording).

Omaha Bank v. Siouxland Cattle Cooperative, 305 N.W.2d 458 (Iowa 1981) (retrial after lawyers and jurors had drinks together during trial).

SELECTED REFERENCES

ABA Model Rules 3.1 through 3.9 [advocacy]

ABA Model Code Disciplinary Rules 2-109, 5-102, 7-102 [meritorious claims and defenses]

ABA Model Code Disciplinary Rules 1-102, 7-102, 7-106, 7-109 [candor]

ABA Model Code Disciplinary Rules 1-102, 7-106, 7-109 [fairness]

ABA Model Code Disciplinary Rules 7-107, 7-108, 7-109, 7-110, 8-101 [impartiality and decorum]

ABA Model Code Disciplinary Rule 7-107 [trial publicity]

ABA Model Code Disciplinary Rule 7-103 [prosecutors]

ABA Model Code Disciplinary Rule 7-104 [communication with represented and unrepresented persons]

NFPA Model Code of Ethics and Professional Responsibility, EC 1.2(a) [ex parte communications]

NFPA Model Code of Ethics and Professional Responsibility, EC 1.2(b) [communications with represented persons]

NFPA Model Code of Ethics and Professional Responsibility, DR 1.3 and EC 1.3(a) [decorum]

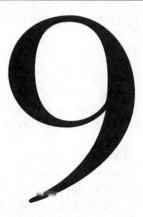

Professionalism and Special Issues for Paralegals

This chapter gives an overview of issues and challenges in professionalism that face paralegals today. Chapter 9 covers:

- the role of paralegals in the legal profession
- definition of professionalism
- special issues for paralegals, including

    - regulation of the occupation
    - paralegal education
    - utilization
    - overtime compensation
    - gender and related issues

- paralegal participation in pro bono activities

A. The State of Professionalism in the Legal Field

A poor public image has plagued the legal profession for the last three decades. The involvement of lawyers in major corporate and political **scandals** has made the legal profession the target of criticism in the media and among the public.

Society appears to have become more **litigious.** Lawyers— including what many people consider an oversupply of them—have been blamed for the tremendous increase in litigation during the past thirty years. The public looks to the law to solve many of its problems, sometimes social and personal ones, that in days past would have been dealt with in other ways. Public opinion polls show that lawyers rate well below most other occupations in the areas of honesty and integrity. Many clients polled believe that lawyers are **greedy,** unethical, hard to communicate with, and lacking in compassion and respect for others. The high salaries paid to lawyers—especially new lawyers right out of law school—have shocked and dismayed many Americans who cannot hope to achieve such salaries in a lifetime of work. The high legal fees generated in major litigation have likewise added to the perception of lawyers as overpaid and greedy.

Related is the public perception that lawyers manipulate the legal process, finding clever ways to circumvent the law in order to prevail. This goal of winning at all costs has made many lawyers seem like contentious and **overzealous** abusers of the system. Lawyers' involvement in highly publicized criminal cases and business-related scandals have validated public opinion that lawyers' knowledge and skills are for sale to the highest bidder and that lawyers will not hesitate to use their talents to line their client's or their own pockets, whatever the cost to the public. Despite the poor regard in which lawyers are held, many clients seek out and expect "attack dog" behavior when they need legal representation. A related client complaint is that lawyers are too chummy with one another; some clients complain when their lawyers extend professional courtesies such as continuances to opposing counsel.

Lawyers recognize their poor image and acknowledge problems that trouble lawyers and the practice of law. Some studies estimate that at least half the lawyers disciplined for misconduct are **"impaired,"** usually by some type of substance abuse. Law firms have become very "bottom line-oriented," building in size and salary at astronomical rates and sometimes placing horrendous pressure on lawyers to bill an unrealistically high number of hours. This pressure leads many lawyers to inflate or pad bills, especially bills of wealthy clients. Higher **legal bills** drive clients away, creating a cycle of competitiveness and ever-higher billable hours. These conditions undermine firm **loyalty,** which once held most lawyers to one firm for their entire career. Lawyers now commonly move several times before they stick with a firm. For the last twenty years, it has become increasingly common for prominent senior partners to leave their firms for better opportunities. The overwhelming sense of law practice as a business first, a profession second, has caused great turnover and instability in law firms, which themselves dissolve and merge frequently.

Finally, the competitiveness and zeal of lawyers has led to **abuses** of the system, such as those described in Chapter 8. Many lawyers view the litigation process as a game where tactics and strategy are more important than merit and substance. Bringing frivolous cases and motions, flooding an opponent with irrelevant and unwarranted discovery, and behaving discourteously and disrespectfully to other lawyers and even to judges have become the daily method of operation for some lawyers.

The bar and the press report stories monthly of lawyers charged with criminal conduct, often in relationship to their clients. Embezzlement, insider trading, and fraud by lawyers are not unheard of. One district attorney in a major metropolitan area has created a justice system integrity division to centralize prosecutions of judges, lawyers, and others working in the justice system. But lawyers are not the only ones in the legal profession to engage in improper conduct. Paralegals have been charged with embezzlement and insider trading in a couple of well-publicized cases. In one case, a paralegal and a lawyer were charged with attempting to defraud mortgage companies of millions of dollars.

Historically, there have been relatively few instances where lawyers openly reported misconduct within their law firms despite the **"snitch" rules** that are contained in most states' ethics rules. (See ABA Model Rule 8.3(a), which requires lawyers to report violations of ethics rules that raise a substantial question about a lawyer's honesty, trustworthiness, or fitness to practice.) Firms have usually handled these matters internally and as privately as possible. But this silence has been broken by billing and related kinds of scandals in recent years. Most courts that have addressed the matter hold that attorneys who report violations as required by the codes cannot be fired for these actions. A few states also have *whistleblower statutes* that protect employees from being discharged in retaliation for reporting violations. It should be noted that the NFPA Model Code requires paralegals to report ethical and legal violations under DR 1.3.

The organized bar has developed initiatives relating to **professionalism.** Disciplinary systems have been found lacking and are being revamped throughout the country. Bar-sponsored programs for impaired lawyers are found in every state. Court rules and statutes limit discovery and provide for severe sanctions against lawyers for abuse. Bar associations have launched public relations campaigns to improve their image.

Snitch rules
Rules requiring lawyers to report unethical conduct

Whistleblower statutes
Protect employees and others from retaliation for reporting violations

They have encouraged lawyers to engage in pro bono work and to support local charities and community activities. State and local bar associations and some courts have adopted codes of professional courtesy and civility or litigation guidelines, which advise lawyers how to conduct themselves.

Professionalism **guidelines** typically cover:

- client relations (including communicating frequently, advising mediation, resolving matters expeditiously, and not overcharging)
- relations with other lawyers and parties (including acting courteously, not engaging in delay or unmeritorious tactics, cooperating in scheduling and resolving disputes, not disparaging other lawyers, and not harassing the opposition)
- relations with courts (including advocating vigorously but with civility, being punctual, and being honest with the court)
- duty to the public and the profession (including keeping current in practice areas, supporting the profession, and upholding the profession's image)

Litigation guidelines usually contain rules covering continuances, extensions, service of process, communication with adversaries, discovery, and motions. They specify conduct that is courteous and honest and not designed to harass or unduly burden opponents.

Among the other recommendations to address these professional concerns coming from the organized bar are improvements in undergraduate education in **ethics,** teaching ethics and professionalism across the curriculum in law school, more aggressive judicial intervention in litigation, and more pro bono and public interest work. Some local bars offer client relations programs that attempt to alter lawyers' attitudes toward and treatment of clients. Increasingly, the conversation about these issues turns to the matter of morality and ethics in law practice. Many ethicists and bar leaders have called on lawyers to examine the ethical and moral content of their actions and to avoid separating their values and beliefs as persons from their conduct as lawyers.

Many lawyers have left the profession because of the problems that characterize law practice today. Some surveys show that as many as half the lawyers in practice would not become lawyers if they had it to do all over again. Some firms have started to deal with **quality of life issues** by creating counseling programs for troubled lawyers, providing part-time and flexible scheduling options, encouraging sabbaticals, increasing pro bono work, and establishing a firm culture that places more value on collegiality and gives lawyers and staff more time for their lives outside law practice. Legal newspapers publish surveys rating the satisfaction of associates working in the major firms, which provides incentive for firms to be good work places. Some firms have an in-house ethics specialist or committee to help lawyers with ethical dilemmas and have established one-on-one or small group mentoring for new lawyers and paralegals to mitigate the negative effects of working in isolation and to build collegiality and trust.

Many studies have shown that lawyers are much more likely than persons in other occupations to be alcoholics or substance abusers. Also, as noted in Chapter 7, there is also a strong correlation between disciplinary actions and substance abuse or emotional problems. In the last decade, many bar associations have been proactive in developing programs to identify and help lawyers who are impaired before the impairment leads to unethical and destructive conduct.

Burnout and stress are major factors in conduct that lead to discipline. The pressures of billable hours, the competitive environment of the legal world, the lack of loyalty among clients and law firms, the constant work of meeting other peoples' needs, the feeling of not having any control: all these factors contribute to burnout, detachment from relationships with others, loss of job satisfaction, and even to chronic anger and anxiety.

This troubled milieu is the one in which paralegals find themselves working. These concerns, voiced both by the public and within the profession, affect the way in which paralegals are viewed and view themselves. A paralegal can be part of the problem—working for a firm that utilizes paralegals' talents principally to abuse the legal process and to accumulate wealth—or part of the solution—working for a firm that utilizes paralegals' talents to improve efficiency, to perform work competently and ethically, and to lower the cost of legal services to its clients. In the coming years, as the problems plaguing the profession and the proposals to solve them begin to shape a new image for law practice, paralegals can help determine what their image will be in that picture.

B.   Professionalization of the Paralegal Occupation

Paralegals are in a sometimes difficult and **ambiguous position** in the legal profession. Because they are not lawyers, they may not legally engage in certain activities carved out exclusively for lawyers. But they do engage in substantive legal work that otherwise would have to be done by lawyers and that is paid for by the client. The line between permissible and impermissible conduct is not always clear. Paralegals are part of the professional staff engaging in legal work, not part of the support staff, but they can never be full and equal partners in the law firm. And, because the paralegal occupation is relatively new, the parameters of paralegal job responsibilities are undefined, evolving over time to meet client needs, new technology, and changes in the law and procedure.

Because the paralegal field is relatively new, the paralegal's role is not universally well understood, either by those in the legal profession or by the general public. Paralegals frequently must explain to lay persons what they do, even while they recognize that their role in legal services is still evolving. Complicating this situation is the increased use of the title "legal assistant" for legal secretaries and administrative assistants who do not do paralegal work. This phenomenon has driven most associations and many individual paralegals to favor the title "paralegal."

The dilemma posed by occupational ambiguity has many ramifications for the daily work lives of paralegals. The overriding question is how paralegals can forge a role for themselves — a professional role that holds them to high standards of ethics and performance while affording them the opportunity for long, satisfying, and challenging careers. Defining "professionalism" is an essential first step in this process.

Dictionaries define "profession" as an occupation that involves a special education and requires mental rather than manual labor. Sociologists define the term as an occupation whose members have the exclusive right to engage in certain activities that are intellectual in nature and require special education. Professions are bound by codes of ethics and are generally self-regulating. Philosophers tend to define *profession* as a calling that requires a special commitment to public service.

Legal paraprofessionals
Persons who perform legal work under the supervision of a lawyer

Paralegals usually are classified as ***paraprofessionals*** — that is, they perform legal work under the supervision of a lawyer but do not have the special education nor share in the societal prestige of the lawyer. Analogous to the paralegal are the many paraprofessionals in the allied health fields — for example, physical therapists, physician's assistants, and dental assistants.

The paralegal field is characterized by inconsistencies that inhibit its **professionalization.** For example, many law firms do not require formal paralegal training, adopting nonuniform and sometimes substandard hiring qualifications. On the other hand, paralegals who have a formal education, frequently a baccalaureate degree and postgraduate certificate, find themselves overtrained for many of the tasks that they perform and unable to utilize fully their knowledge and skills. Prestige for paralegals is found mainly in the reflected prestige of the lawyers for whom they work. This status may be enhanced when a law firm treats its paralegals well, affording them a meaningful career path and appropriate perquisites; alternatively, paralegal's status may be undermined by poor treatment.

Paralegals sometimes do not share a **common bond** with their paralegal colleagues, in part because they lack a shared educational experience. Aggravating this lack of bond is the fact that many paralegals view themselves as competitors within the firm for the most interesting work and highest pay. Paralegals sometimes express their primary loyalty to the firm or to their supervising attorney, not to their chosen occupation. Many paralegals work in small or mid-sized firms where they may be the only paralegal, lending to their feelings of **isolation** from others. On the other hand, paralegal associations have been quite successful in building a strong sense of camaraderie and shared interests and responsibilities among their members.

Considerable progress has been made in the professionalization of the paralegal occupation. Levels of education, both general and specialized paralegal education, are rising. The duties paralegals are performing have greatly broadened and include more client contact and more sophisticated work. More than half of law firms report that paralegal duties have expanded in the last five years. Billing rates and salaries are up. Both NALA and NFPA promote voluntary certification, and statewide certification programs exist in five states.

States are beginning to look seriously at **regulation** of the paralegal occupation. Regulation now exists under state law in California, and other states have court rules or statutes that define and limit the use of "paralegal," "paralegal," and comparable titles. Many see regulation as a necessary step in the evolution of the profession, to distinguish it from other law-related positions and to give it enhanced and deserved prestige. (See Chapter 1 for a discussion of regulation.)

Conducting oneself as a "professional" in the workplace has been a topic of much discussion in the ranks of paralegals, in paralegal publications, and professional associations. Building on ideas about the meaning of a profession that are commonly accepted in society, the following nine points comprise a list of qualities to which professional paralegals should dedicate themselves.

1.   Commitment to Public Service

Paralegals should always remember that their highest goal is to assist in the delivery of legal services to the public — legal services that are delivered ethically, competently, and efficiently. In addition to being part of their daily work lives, this commitment also requires paralegals to engage in activities, such as pro bono programs, that improve the system of delivery of legal services overall. See Section D below for more on pro bono work.

2.   Commitment to Education

Fulfilling this commitment includes participating in formal education, continuing education, and on-the-job learning that enhances knowledge and skills and continually develops the paralegal's potential. Education heightens the paralegal's ability to deliver quality legal services and enriches long-term career satisfaction.

3.   Commitment to the Highest Standards of Ethical Conduct

Paralegals must know the rules of ethics that bind lawyers and paralegals and understand how these rules apply to them. Paralegals also must develop their own personal standards of ethics and morality that reach beyond the minimums imposed by law. Paralegals must be scrupulously honest in their relations with clients, courts, attorneys, and coworkers.

4.   Commitment to Excellence

Paralegals must set high standards of performance for themselves and seek to meet those standards in all the work they undertake. They should approach each task with an attitude of seriousness and apply all their knowledge, skill, and talent to accomplish their work.

5.   Commitment to the Paralegal Profession

Paralegals must view themselves as part of a common occupation, with interests and goals that are shared by other paralegals. They must support paralegal activities organized through professional associations, bar associations, and alumni associations. Paralegals must also engender collegiality with their colleagues, mentoring new paralegals when appropriate and acting as role models and sources of information for those who aspire to the paralegal profession.

6.   Commitment to a Strong Work Ethic

Paralegals must strive to do their best on every task and serve the clients of their firms diligently. They should be meticulous and thorough, organized in their work process, prompt in meeting deadlines, and always do more than the minimum. They should take pride in their work and always do work that merits that pride.

7.   Commitment to Acting with Integrity and Honor

Paralegals must be courteous, respectful, and fair in their dealings with lawyers, other paralegals, support staff, clients, and others both within and outside their firm. They must demonstrate maturity, patience, and thoughtfulness in their actions, avoiding gossip, undue criticism of others, prejudice, and favoritism. This commitment also requires paralegals to show sensitivity to the needs and talents of others, appreciation for the differences in people's backgrounds, tolerance, helpfulness, and a sense of recognition for others' achievements.

8. Commitment to the Development of the Whole Person

Paralegals must not become so consumed by their work that they neglect the other aspects of their life, like family, friends, health, and personal interests and activities. They should seek to be well-rounded persons, with a variety of interests. Commitment to a profession need not prevent a person from leading a full life; in fact, a person who narrows his or her interests only to work will not be as effective in relations with others and will not possess the sense of proportion and balance needed to fulfill his or her commitments as a professional.

9. Commitment to Exercising Good Judgment, Common Sense, and Communication Skills

Paralegals must use their understanding of human nature as a guide in their relations with others. They must listen to others carefully and communicate, both orally and in writing, clearly and persuasively.

C. Current Issues in Professionalism

1. Regulation

One issue central to the debate about the evolution of the paralegal field is regulation. Discussed in Chapter 1, regulation is a complex question that will not be resolved without a good deal of stress on paralegals and the organizations that represent them. The debate has raised many difficult questions:

- Is there a need for regulation?
- Who should be regulated?
- Who should do the regulating?
- Should regulation be mandatory or voluntary?
- What level of regulation is appropriate?
- What educational requirements should be established?

- What kind of examination, if any, should be required?
- What, if any, tasks should paralegals be authorized to perform only if they are regulated?

The resolution of the regulation issue will determine the future of the career, the extent to which it becomes an independent "profession," and the nature and character of paralegals and their work.

2. Education

Education is another critical issue for paralegals. The lack of consistency in hiring standards and in uniformity in the paralegal curriculum prevents paralegals from having a shared body of knowledge and a shared educational experience, two important characteristics that distinguish occupations from professions. The lack of common educational experience also inhibits the development of collegiality among paralegals.

However, the diversity within paralegal education and the variety of ways that are used to enter the field have allowed the paralegal profession to flourish and to move in directions many thought impossible. Paralegals have a continuously expanding bank of job responsibilities, unhindered by a standardized, limiting education that trains everyone to perform the same tasks. The diverse work and life experiences that are brought to the profession by the wide variety of people who become paralegals have enriched both the career possibilities and legal profession itself.

As indicated earlier, educational achievement among paralegals is rising. While the ABA and the American Association for Paralegal Education endorse two years of college as a minimum for entry into the paralegal field, IPMA, representing corporate counsel offices and large law firms, favors a four-year degree. Paralegal educators and paralegal associations continue to discuss appropriate minimal and aspirational levels of education for paralegals and the competencies that should be required of them.

3. Utilization and Treatment

The ambiguity that accompanies the development of a new profession has resulted in both underutilization of paralegals and disparities in the way that paralegal services are utilized. Even now, nearly forty years after the advent of the modern American paralegal system, many lawyers still resist using paralegals' services, especially those lawyers in small firms who believe that they cannot afford paralegals. While all large law firms and many midsized ones employ paralegals, an estimated two-thirds of sole practitioners and small firms do not use the services of paralegals. Some lawyers do not understand how to utilize paralegals' talents and skills or are reluctant to delegate anything more than routine or repetitive work. Paralegals report that the lack of challenging work is one of the main reasons for leaving a job and for job dissatisfaction.

Some lawyers and law firms treat their paralegals poorly—by not compensating them fairly, by not providing appropriate working conditions and clerical support, or by not giving them recognition when deserved—but still expect professional work and attitudes. This poor treatment has resulted in a high turnover within those firms and relatively high turnover in the occupation as a whole, as paralegals leave the profession dissatisfied with working conditions, compensation, and the nature of the work. However, surveys also show that the role of the paralegal has expanded, with more sophisticated work being assigned to senior paralegals, increased responsibility and compensation, and job titles and benefits that reflect a greater appreciation of paralegals.

4. Exempt Status

Related is the question of whether paralegals should be classified as *exempt or nonexempt* employees. Recently rewritten rules on overtime pay indicate that paralegals are generally nonexempt and therefore are entitled to overtime compensation under the Fair Labor Standards Act (29 C.F.R. 541). The new rules are in keeping with earlier U.S. Department of Labor Letter Rulings, which held that paralegals as a group may not be classified as exempt because they are not required to have advanced professional knowledge acquired through prolonged specialized instruction and study (usually at least four years of college), and are not generally involved in the performance of duties that require the exercise of discretion and independent judgment. Section 541.301(7) indicates that the exemption is available for paralegals who hold advanced degrees in other professional fields that they apply to their work as paralegals, such as engineering. Paralegals, and their paralegal associations, are divided on the issue. Many believe that their classification as nonexempt is degrading and does not accurately reflect their professional work and status; others believe that they will not be fairly compensated for their long hours of work unless they get overtime pay, and that overtime pay does not lower their status or prestige in the law firm.

More than half of the paralegals in surveys report that they are paid overtime. However, not all firms have changed their policies since the new rules were adopted or pay all their paralegals in the same way. For example, many law firms that have career paths for paralegals classify the lower rungs of the ladder as nonexempt and the top level or levels as exempt, based on the nature and complexity of the specific responsibilities, including supervising other paralegals and the degree of independence exercised by the paralegal at each level. Often, senior and specialist paralegals and paralegal managers who supervise paralegals are classified as exempt.

5. Gender, Race, and Related Issues

Finally, the paralegal career continues to be a **female-dominated occupation** that serves a still male-dominated profession. Even though the proportion of women in law school has increased to almost half, only about one-third of the lawyers in this country are women. Other traditionally female-dominated professions like nursing and teaching have struggled very hard — not always successfully — to achieve status and recognition, fair treatment, good working conditions, and compensation that is based on the value, nature, and difficulty of their work.

Gender-related issues have come to the forefront in recent years in discussions about law practice. Ethics rules now bar attorneys from having **sexual relations with clients.** Some jurisdictions have experienced a rise in lawsuits against attorneys who have had sexual relations with their clients, and in some cases substantial judgments have been awarded.

High-profile **sexual harassment and sex discrimination** cases have been brought and won against several prominent lawyers and law firms. Some suits have been brought by women lawyers and some by support staff. Surveys show that half of the women lawyers in the United States believe they have been harassed. Most women do not report such incidents out of fear of retaliation and marginalization. Many firms have instituted sexual harassment policies that define prohibited conduct, establish procedures and sanctions, and include sensitivity training.

Bias in the legal profession on the basis of race, sex, or sexual orientation has been well documented. In general, women and minority lawyers make less money, are less likely to make partner, and are excluded from key committees and prestigious practice areas in their law firms. Most jurisdictions have adopted anti-bias provisions in their ethics rules that make it an ethical violation to discriminate in the operation of a practice and/or to disparage or humiliate someone on the basis of race, national origin, sex, sexual orientation, religion, age, or disability. The Americans with Disabilities Act has added new protection for disabled employees and other persons in their interactions with law firms.

D. Pro Bono Work

The fact that the legal needs of the vast majority of Americans are going unmet is undisputed. Study after study has proven that most Americans — including poor and middle-income persons — do not have access to a lawyer when they need one. Most Americans cannot afford a lawyer and would not know how to find a lawyer if they needed one. Most would not know how to go about finding a lawyer. Recent state studies show that half to three-quarters of low-income households experience a civil legal need within a year's time, and 10 to 20 percent of these sought a lawyer's help. Most of the people who try to handle legal problems on their own are ill-equipped to navigate the system. Many are afraid, face language barriers, and are unaware that there are legal aid or pro bono help for them.

To cope with this problem, the organized bar has encouraged individual lawyers to engage in *pro bono* work and has sponsored a wide variety of pro bono programs to which lawyers can contribute their time and expertise. Several states have adopted **voluntary aspirational guidelines** for lawyers to do pro bono work. Only a few have mandatory rules, which can be fulfilled by making a donation in lieu of doing the work. Some law schools have a requirement for public service or pro bono work, and many law firms have policies that encourage their attorneys and paralegals to engage in such activities.

Pro bono
For free

During the past decade, there has been an increase in voluntary pro bono work being done by lawyers and law firms. The need for legal services is still unmet, however, and paralegals have an opportunity to help fill this need. Participating in pro bono activities as part of one's professional commitment not only produces psychic rewards, but also increases career satisfaction and self-esteem.

Guideline 10 of the ABA Model Guidelines for the Utilization of Paralegal Services encourages lawyers to facilitate paralegal participation in pro bono activities. Many state guidelines on paralegals follow suit. Lawyers have a duty to provide pro bono services under ABA Model Rule 6.1 and Canon 2 of the ABA Model Code, and the ABA has called on lawyers to fulfill this duty by aspiring to do 50 hours of pro bono legal services work annually. NFPA asks paralegals to aspire to do 24 pro bono hours annually (NFPA EC 1.4(d)).

Many law firms that do pro bono work include paralegals in these activities. Paralegals who do not have an opportunity to become involved in pro bono work through their jobs should seek out activities on their own. Local bar associations and paralegal associations usually have several kinds of pro bono projects on which paralegals can work. Legal aid organizations and law clinics are always in need of volunteers.

Pro bono programs have been established in many specialized areas of law, thus affording paralegals a chance either to exercise their expertise or to learn a new area. **Examples** of some of the programs are: court-appointed special advocates in juvenile and family law, consumer disputes, landlord-tenant matters, major public interest litigation (for example, housing or employment discrimination or children's rights), immigration, indigent taxpayers, elder law, bankruptcy, family law, mental health advocacy, domestic violence restraining orders and counseling, AIDS, and homelessness projects.

Paralegals who do pro bono work often find themselves working more **independently** than they do in their law firms; they are engaged in challenging tasks that they would not be delegated on their jobs. Paralegals in legal aid settings very often have extensive client contact, as they handle intake interviews and help clients directly with matters not requiring a lawyer. Paralegals are often called on in these settings to advocate for clients before administrative agencies, to conduct in-depth research, and to draft documents and memoranda.

Besides skill development and growth, paralegals who do pro bono work derive the ultimate **satisfaction** of helping someone who needs help and who might not otherwise have gotten that help. Usually, the assistance needed and provided is of the most critical kind—for instance, keeping someone from losing a home or government benefits—and is a matter of survival to the clients.

REVIEW QUESTIONS

1. Give five reasons why the public image of lawyers is so poor.
2. What are lawyers doing to improve their public image?
3. What is a code of professional courtesy? What kinds of conduct does it require?
4. How can a paralegal make a difference in improving the professionalism and public image of the legal field?
5. Why are paralegals in an ambiguous position in the legal environment? Give at least three reasons.
6. How is *profession* defined?
7. What is a *paraprofessional*?
8. What is collegiality? Why is it difficult for paralegals to have collegiality?
9. To what extent are paralegals overtrained?
10. Describe the nine professional commitments that paralegals should make.
11. Name and discuss some of the issues facing today's paralegals.
12. What is the basis for classifying a paralegal as an exempt or nonexempt employee? What is the law currently?
13. Does the fact that paralegals are predominately female affect the career? How?
14. What is the current state of legal services for poor and middle-income Americans?
15. Have pro bono activities increased or decreased in the last decade?
16. What kinds of pro bono activities do lawyers and paralegals engage in?
17. What are the benefits to a paralegal of doing pro bono work?
18. How can a paralegal get involved in pro bono work?
19. What are some of the gender-related issues that paralegals face?

HYPOTHETICALS

1. Ann Arista works for the law firm of Smith & Tory. Ann is a first-year paralegal. She is paid a monthly salary and a bonus at the end of the year. She works on document preparation for large lawsuits with a team of other paralegals and case clerks. She does not supervise anyone and has little discretion in her duties. She is hopeful that she will be promoted next year and begin doing more substantive paralegal work. Ann is not paid overtime. She often works more than eight hours a day, and for three straight months worked in excess of 50 hours a week. Is Ann being treated appropriately under the laws for exempt and nonexempt employees? Is she being treated fairly? What should she do? Suppose the firm offers her compensatory time off. Should she accept it?

2. Fred Fester is a senior paralegal with a large law firm. He works with one of the more flamboyant and successful trial attorneys, Sam Shore. Sam is known for being very flirtatious, especially with the young women in the firm. Fred walks into Sam's office one day and sees him apparently kissing a young associate, Betty Block. Fred walks out embarrassed and Betty leaves a few minutes later in tears. What should Fred do? Suppose that a few weeks later Fred finds out that Sam has recommended against Betty's being retained by the firm.

3. Martin Morrison and Pamela Polk work for a large law firm that has a career path for paralegals. They call their paralegals by different titles as they move up the ladder: "case clerk," "junior legal assistant," "senior paralegal," "supervising paralegal," and "senior paralegal specialist." The firm's secretaries are unhappy with their work and pay. Some of them lobby for changes in their treatment. As a result, the most senior legal secretaries are given the title "legal assistant." Other legal secretaries are permitted to move into senior paralegal positions without meeting the usual educational requirements for those positions, and in some cases are given higher rates of pay. Some of these persons are capable of doing the paralegal work, and some are not. Martin and Pamela are really distressed and believe these changes undermine the credibility of the paralegals at the firm. What should they do?

DISCUSSION QUESTIONS

1. Do you think the legal profession deserves its poor public image? Why or why not?
2. Read a general interest newspaper every day for a month and clip out all the articles that mention lawyers. How many are favorable? What image do they present?

3. How can the legal profession overcome its poor image?
4. Do you think lawyers' salaries are disproportionately high? Why or why not?
5. Do you think lawyers' increased mobility is a good or bad thing? Why?
6. Does your local bar association or court have a code of professional courtesy? Do you think a nonbinding code such as this is appropriate for a court or bar association to have? Why or why not? Should such a code be binding? Why or why not? Do such codes derogate the lawyer's duty of zealousness? Do they contribute to lawyers' "clubbiness"? Do they work?
7. Contact your local paralegal association and get salary surveys that ask about job satisfaction, career paths, pro bono work, and exempt/nonexempt status.
8. Contact paralegals at local law firms and ask them:

   a. if they regard their paralegal career as a profession
   b. if they are treated as professionals by their employers
   c. if they plan to continue as a paralegal indefinitely, and, if not,

   - what they plan to do
   - why they are leaving the career

   d. if they are members of the local paralegal association;
   e. if their firm does pro bono work;
   f. if they do pro bono work;
   g. if their education and training are well utilized;
   h. if they are paid overtime;
   i. if they have experienced gender-related discrimination.

9. Do you think paralegals are professionals or paraprofessionals? Is this distinction important to you? Why?
10. Do you think standardization in paralegal education would be good or bad for the career? Why?
11. How can paralegals build collegiality? Why is it important?
12. Do you think voluntary certification is good for paralegals? Why or why not? What about mandatory regulation? Why or why not?
13. Do you agree with the nine professional commitments for paralegals? Why or why not? How would you prioritize their relative importance? What would you add or delete?
14. Do you think regulation of paralegals would enhance their professional status? Why or why not?
15. Get the position papers on regulation of the major paralegal associations and compare the points of view and the rationale for the various positions. Stage a debate in your class with students or local paralegal association members arguing the points.
16. How can paralegals help overcome lawyers' reluctance to use paralegals' services? How can paralegals encourage lawyers to use their services more effectively and fully?

17. Contact the local bar and paralegal associations and find out what kinds of pro bono opportunities are available to paralegals in your area.

SELECTED REFERENCES

ABA Model Rules of Professional Conduct, Rule 6.1 [pro bono service]

ABA Model Rules of Professional Conduct, Rule 8.3 [reporting misconduct]

ABA Guidelines for the Utilization of paralegal Services, Guideline 10 [continuing education, pro bono]

NALA Code of Ethics and Professional Responsibility, Canon 6 [education]

NFPA Model Code of Ethics and Professional Responsibility, Canon 3, EC 3.2 [reporting misconduct]

NFPA Model Code of Ethics and Professional Responsibility, Canon 1, EC 1.2 [continuing education]

NFPA Model Code of Ethics and Professional Responsibility, Canon 4 [public interest, pro bono]

Q. Johnstone & M. Wenglinsky, Paralegals: Progress and Prospects of a Satellite Occupation, pp. 183 et seq. (1985)

Green, Snell, Corgiat & Paramanith, *The Professionalization of the Paralegal: Identity, Maturation States and Goal Attainment,* 7 J. Para. Ed. & Prac. 35 (1990)

ABA Model Guidelines for the Utilization of Paralegal Services

Preamble

The Standing Committee on Paralegals of the American Bar Association drafted, and the ABA House of Delegates adopted, the ABA Model Guidelines for the Utilization of Legal Assistant Services in 1991. Most states have also prepared or adopted state-specific recommendations or guidelines for the utilization of services provided by paralegals.[1] All of these recommendations or guidelines are intended to provide lawyers with useful and authoritative guidance in working with paralegals.

This 2003 revision of the Model Guidelines is intended to reflect the legal and policy developments that have taken place since the first

---

1. In 1986, the ABA Board of Governors approved a definition for the term "legal assistant." In 1997, the ABA amended the definition of legal assistant by adopting the following language: "A legal assistant or paralegal is a person qualified by education, training or work experience who is employed or retained by a lawyer, law office, corporation, governmental agency or other entity who performs specifically delegated substantive legal work for which a lawyer is responsible." To comport with current usage in the profession, these guidelines use the term "paralegal" rather than "legal assistant," however, lawyers should be aware that the terms legal assistant and paralegals are often used interchangeably.

draft in 1991 and may assist states in revising or further refining their own recommendations and guidelines. Moreover, the Standing Committee is of the view that these and other guidelines on paralegal services will encourage lawyers to utilize those services effectively and promote the continued growth of the paralegal profession.[2]

The Standing Committee has based these 2003 revisions on the American Bar Association's Model Rules of Professional Conduct but has also attempted to take into account existing state recommendations and guidelines, decided authority and contemporary practice. Lawyers, of course, are to be first directed by Rule 5.3 of the Model Rules in the utilization of paralegal services, and nothing contained in these Model Guidelines is intended to be inconsistent with that rule. Specific ethical considerations and case law in particular states must also be taken into account by each lawyer that reviews these guidelines. In the commentary after each Guideline, we have attempted to identify the basis for the Guideline and any issues of which we are aware that the Guideline may present. We have also included selected references to state and paralegal association guidelines where we believed it would be helpful to the reader.

Guideline 1: A lawyer is responsible for all of the professional actions of a paralegal performing services at the lawyer's direction and should take reasonable measures to ensure that the paralegal's conduct is consistent with the lawyer's obligations under the rules of professional conduct of the jurisdiction in which the lawyer practices.

Comment to Guideline 1

The Standing Committee on Paralegals ("Standing Committee") regards Guideline 1 as a comprehensive statement of general principle governing the utilization of paralegals in the practice of law. As such, the principles contained in Guideline 1 are part of each of the remaining Guidelines. Fundamentally, Guideline 1 expresses the overarching principle that although a lawyer may delegate tasks to a paralegal, a lawyer must always assume ultimate responsibility for the delegated tasks and exercise independent professional judgment with respect to all aspects of the representation of a client.

---

2. While necessarily mentioning paralegal conduct, lawyers are the intended audience of these Guidelines. The Guidelines, therefore, are addressed to lawyer conduct and not directly to the conduct of the paralegal. Both the National Association of Legal Assistants (NALA) and the National Federation of Paralegal Associations (NFPA) have adopted guidelines of conduct that are directed to paralegals. *See* NALA, "Code of Ethics and Professional Responsibility of the National Association of Legal Assistants, Inc." (adopted 1975, revised 1979, 1988 and 1995); NFPA, "Affirmation of Responsibility" (adopted 1977, revised 1981).

Under principles of agency law and the rules of professional conduct, lawyers are responsible for the actions and the work product of the nonlawyers they employ. Rule 5.3 of the Model Rules of Professional Conduct ("Model Rules")[3] requires that supervising lawyers ensure that the conduct of nonlawyer assistants is compatible with the lawyer's professional obligations. Ethical Consideration 3-6 of the Model Code encourages lawyers to delegate tasks to paralegals so that legal services can be rendered more economically and efficiently. Ethical Consideration 3-6, however, provides that such delegation is only proper if the lawyer "maintains a direct relationship with his client, supervises the delegated work, and has complete professional responsibility for the work product." The adoption of Rule 5.3, which incorporates these principles, reaffirms this encouragement.

To conform to Guideline 1, a lawyer must give appropriate instruction to paralegals supervised by the lawyer about the rules governing the lawyer's professional conduct, and require paralegals to act in accordance with those rules. *See* Comment to Model Rule 5.3; *see also* National Association of Legal Assistant's Model Standards and Guidelines for the Utilization of Legal Assistants, Guidelines 1 and 4 (1985, revised 1990, 1997) (hereafter "NALA Guidelines"). Additionally, the lawyer must directly supervise paralegals employed by the lawyer to ensure that, in every circumstance, the paralegal is acting in a manner consistent with the lawyer's ethical and professional obligations. What constitutes appropriate instruction and supervision will differ from one state to another and the lawyer has the obligation to make adjustments accordingly.

Guideline 2: Provided the lawyer maintains responsibility for the work product, a lawyer may delegate to a paralegal any task normally performed by the lawyer except those tasks proscribed to a nonlawyer by statute, court rule, administrative rule or regulation, controlling authority, the applicable rule of professional conduct of the jurisdiction in which the lawyer practices, or these Guidelines.

---

3. The Model Rules were first adopted by the ABA House of Delegates in August of 1983. To date, some 43 states and two jurisdictions have adopted the Model Rules to govern the professional conduct of lawyers licensed in those states. However, because several states still utilize a version of the Model Code of Professional Responsibility ("Model Code"), these comments will refer to both the Model Rules and the predecessor Model Code (and to the Ethical Considerations and Disciplinary Rules found under the canons in the Model Codes). In 1997, the ABA formed the Commission on Evaluation of the Rules of Professional Conduct ("Ethics 2000 Commission") to undertake a comprehensive review and revision of the Model Rules. The ABA House of Delegates completed its review of the Commission's recommended revisions in February 2002. Visit *www.abanet.org/cpr/jclr/jclr_home.html* for information regarding the status of each state supreme court's adoption of the Ethics 2000 revisions to the Model Rules.

Comment to Guideline 2

The essence of the definition of the term "legal assistant" first adopted by the ABA in 1986[4] and subsequently amended in 1997[5] is that, so long as appropriate supervision is maintained, many tasks normally performed by lawyers may be delegated to paralegals. EC 3- 6 under the Model Code mentioned three specific kinds of tasks that paralegals may perform under appropriate lawyer supervision: factual investigation and research, legal research, and the preparation of legal documents. Various states delineate more specific tasks in their guidelines including attending client conferences, corresponding with and obtaining information from clients, witnessing the execution of documents, preparing transmittal letters, and maintaining estate/guardianship trust accounts. *See, e.g.*, Colorado Bar Association Guidelines for the Use of Paralegals (the Colorado Bar Association has adopted guidelines for the use of paralegals in 18 specialty practice areas including civil litigation, corporate law and estate planning); NALA Guideline 5.

While appropriate delegation of tasks is encouraged and a broad array of tasks is properly delegable to paralegals, improper delegation of tasks will often run afoul of a lawyer's obligations under applicable rules of professional conduct. A common consequence of the improper delegation of tasks is that the lawyer will have assisted the paralegal in the unauthorized "practice of law" in violation of Rule 5.5 of the Model Rules, DR 3-101 of the Model Code, and the professional rules of most states. Neither the Model Rules nor the Model Code defines the "practice of law." EC 3-5 under the Model Code gave some guidance by equating the practice of law to the application of the professional judgment of the lawyer in solving clients' legal problems. This approach is consistent with that taken in ABA Opinion 316 (1967) which states: "A lawyer . . . may employ nonlawyers to do any task for him except counsel clients about law matters, engage directly in the practice of law, appear in court or appear in formal proceedings as part of the judicial process, so long as it is he who takes the work and vouches for it to the client and becomes responsible for it to the client."

As a general matter, most state guidelines specify that paralegals may not appear before courts, administrative tribunals, or other adjudicatory

---

4. The 1986 ABA definition read: "A legal assistant is a person, qualified through education, training or work experience, who is employed or retained by a lawyer, law office, governmental agency, or other entity, in a capacity or function which involves the performance, under the ultimate direction and supervision of an attorney, of specifically delegated substantive legal work, which work, for the most part, requires a sufficient knowledge of legal concepts that, absent such assistant the attorney would perform the task."

5. In 1997, the ABA amended the definition of legal assistant by adopting the following language: "A legal assistant or paralegal is a person qualified by education, training or work experience who is employed or retained by a lawyer, law office, corporation, governmental agency or other entity who performs specifically delegated substantive legal work for which a lawyer is responsible."

bodies unless the procedural rules of the adjudicatory body authorize such appearances. *See, e.g.*, State Bar of Arizona, Committee on the Rules of Prof'l Conduct, Opinion No. 99-13 (December 1999) (attorney did not assist in unauthorized practice of law by supervising paralegal in tribal court where tribal court rules permit non-attorneys to be licensed tribal advocates).[6] Additionally, no state permits paralegals to conduct depositions or give legal advice to clients. *E.g.*, Guideline 2, Connecticut Bar Association Guidelines for Lawyers Who Employ or Retain Legal Assistants (the "Connecticut Guidelines"); Guideline 2, State Bar of Michigan Guidelines for Utilization of Legal Assistants; State Bar of Georgia, State Disciplinary Board Advisory Opinion No. 21 (September 16, 1977); *Doe v. Condon*, 532 S.E.2d 879 (S.C. 2000) (it is the unauthorized practice of law for a paralegal to conduct educational seminars and answer estate planning questions because the paralegal will be implicitly advising participants that they require estate planning services). *See also* NALA Guidelines II, III, and V.

Ultimately, apart from the obvious tasks that virtually all states argue are proscribed to paralegals, what constitutes the "practice of law" is governed by state law and is a fact specific question. *See, e.g.*, Louisiana Rules of Prof'l Conduct Rule 5.5 which sets out specific tasks considered to be the "practice of law" by the Supreme Court of Louisiana. Thus, some tasks that have been specifically prohibited in some states are expressly delegable in others. *Compare*, Guideline 2, Connecticut Guidelines (permitting paralegal to attend real estate closings even though no supervising lawyer is present provided that the paralegal does not render opinion or judgment about execution of documents, changes in adjustments or price or other matters involving documents or funds) *and* The Florida Bar, Opinion 89-5 (November 1989) (permitting paralegal to handle real estate closing at which no supervising lawyer is present provided, among other things, that the paralegal will not give legal advice or make impromptu decisions that should be made by a lawyer) *with* Supreme Court of Georgia, Formal Advisory Opinion No. 86-5 (May 1989) (closing of real estate transactions constitutes the practice of law and it is ethically improper for a lawyer to permit a paralegal to close the transaction). It is thus incumbent on the lawyer to determine whether a particular task is properly delegable in the jurisdiction at issue.

Once the lawyer has determined that a particular task is delegable consistent with the professional rules, utilization guidelines, and case law of the relevant jurisdiction, the key to Guideline 2 is proper supervision.

---

6. It is important to note that pursuant to federal or state statute, paralegals are permitted to provide direct client representation in certain administrative proceedings. While this does not obviate the lawyer's responsibility for the paralegal's work, it does change the nature of the lawyer's supervision of the paralegal. The opportunity to use such paralegal services has particular benefits to legal services programs and does not violate Guideline 2. *See generally* ABA Standards for Providers of Civil Legal Services to the Poor Std. 6.3, at 6.17-6.18 (1986).

A lawyer should start the supervision process by ensuring that the paralegal has sufficient education, background and experience to handle the task being assigned. The lawyer should provide adequate instruction when assigning projects and should also monitor the progress of the project. Finally, it is the lawyer's obligation to review the completed project to ensure that the work product is appropriate for the assigned task. *See* Guideline 1, Connecticut Guidelines; *See also, e.g., Spencer v. Steinman,* 179 F.R.D. 484 (E.D. Penn. 1998) (lawyer sanctioned under Rule 11 for paralegal's failure to serve subpoena duces tecum on parties to the litigation because the lawyer "did not assure himself that [the paralegal] had adequate training nor did he adequately supervise her once he assigned her the task of issuing subpoenas").

Serious consequences can result from a lawyer's failure to properly delegate tasks to or to supervise a paralegal properly. For example, the Supreme Court of Virginia upheld a malpractice verdict against a lawyer based in part on negligent actions of a paralegal in performing tasks that evidently were properly delegable. *Musselman v. Willoughby Corp.,* 230 Va. 337, 337 S.E. 2d 724 (1985). *See also* C. Wolfram, Modern Legal Ethics (1986), at 236, 896. Disbarment and suspension from the practice of law have resulted from a lawyer's failure to properly supervise the work performed by paralegals. *See Matter of Disciplinary Action Against Nassif,* 547 N.W.2d 541 (N.D. 1996) (disbarment for failure to supervise which resulted in the unauthorized practice of law by office paralegals); *Attorney Grievance Comm'n of Maryland v. Hallmon,* 681 A.2d 510 (Md. 1996) (90-day suspension for, among other things, abdicating responsibility for a case to paralegal without supervising or reviewing the paralegal's work). Lawyers have also been subject to monetary and other sanctions in federal and state courts for failing to properly utilize and supervise paralegals. *See In re Hessinger & Associates,* 192 B.R. 211 (N.D. Cal. 1996) (bankruptcy court directed to reevaluate its $100,000 sanction but district court finds that law firm violated Rule 3-110(A) of the California Rules of Professional Conduct by permitting bankruptcy paralegals to undertake initial interviews, fill out forms and complete schedules without attorney supervision).

Finally, it is important to note that although the attorney has the primary obligation to not permit a nonlawyer to engage in the unauthorized practice of law, some states have concluded that a paralegal is not relieved from an independent obligation to refrain from illegal conduct and to work directly under an attorney's supervision. *See In re Opinion No. 24 of the Committee on the Unauthorized Practice of Law,* 607 A.2d 962, 969 (N.J. 1992) (a "paralegal who recognizes that the attorney is not directly supervising his or her work or that such supervision is illusory because the attorney knows nothing about the field in which the paralegal is working must understand that he or she is engaged in the unauthorized practice of law"); Kentucky Supreme Court Rule 3.7 (stating that "the paralegal does have an independent obligation to refrain from illegal conduct"). Additionally, paralegals must also familiarize themselves with the specific statutes governing the particular area of law with which they might come into contact while providing paralegal services. *See, e.g.*, 11 U.S.C. § 110 (provisions governing nonlawyer preparers of bankruptcy petitions); *In Re Moffett*, 263 B.R. 805 (W.D. Ky. 2001) (nonlawyer bankruptcy petition preparer fined for advertising herself as "paralegal" because that is prohibited by 11 U.S.C. § 110(f)(1)). Again, the lawyer must remember that any independent obligation a paralegal might have under state law to refrain from the unauthorized practice of law does not in any way diminish or vitiate the lawyer's obligation to properly delegate tasks and supervise the paralegal working for the lawyer.

> **Guideline 3:   A lawyer may not delegate to a paralegal:**
>
> **(a) Responsibility for establishing an attorney-client relationship.**
> **(b) Responsibility for establishing the amount of a fee to be charged for a legal service.**
> **(c) Responsibility for a legal opinion rendered to a client.**

Comment to Guideline 3

Model Rule 1.4 and most state codes require lawyers to communicate directly with their clients and to provide their clients information reasonably necessary to make informed decisions and to effectively participate in the representation. While delegation of legal tasks to nonlawyers may benefit clients by enabling their lawyers to render legal services more economically and efficiently, Model Rule 1.4 and Ethical Consideration 3-6 under the Model Code emphasize that delegation is proper only if the lawyer "maintains a direct relationship with his client, supervises the delegated work and has complete professional responsibility for the work product." The National Association of Legal Assistants ("NALA"), Code of Ethics and Professional Responsibility, Canon 2, echoes the Model Rule when it states: "A legal assistant may perform any task which is properly delegated and supervised by an attorney as long as the attorney is ultimately responsible to the client, maintains a direct relationship with the client, and assumes professional responsibility for the work product." Most state guidelines also stress the paramount importance of a direct attorney-client relationship. *See* Ohio EC 3-6 and New Mexico Rule 20-106. The direct personal relationship between client and lawyer is critical to the exercise of the lawyer's trained professional judgment.

Fundamental to the lawyer-client relationship is the lawyer's agreement to undertake representation and the related fee arrangement. The Model Rules and most states require lawyers to make fee arrangements with their clients and to clearly communicate with their clients concerning the scope of the representation and the basis for the fees for which the client will be responsible. Model Rule 1.5 and Comments. Many state guidelines prohibit paralegals from "setting fees" or "accepting cases." *See, e.g.*, Pennsylvania Eth. Op. 98-75, 1994 Utah Eth. Op. 139. NALA Canon 3 states that a paralegal must not establish attorney-client relationships or set fees.

EC 3-5 states: "[T]he essence of the professional judgment of the lawyer is his educated ability to relate the general body and philosophy of law to a specific legal problem of a client; and thus, the public interest will be better served if only lawyers are permitted to act in matters involving professional judgment." Clients are entitled to their lawyers' professional judgment and opinion. Paralegals may, however, be authorized to communicate a lawyer's legal advice to a client so long as they do not interpret or expand on that advice. Typically, state guidelines phrase this prohibition in terms of paralegals being forbidden from "giving legal advice" or "counseling clients about legal matters." *See, e.g.*, New Hampshire Rule 35, Sub-Rule 1, Kentucky SCR 3.700, Sub-Rule 2. NALA Canon 3 states that a paralegal must not give legal opinions or advice. Some states have more expansive wording that prohibits paralegals from engaging in any activity that would require the exercise of independent legal judgment. *See, e.g.*, New Mexico Rule 20-103. Nevertheless, it is clear that all states and the Model Rules encourage direct communication between clients and a paralegal insofar as the paralegal is performing a task properly delegated by a lawyer. It should be noted that a lawyer who permits a paralegal to assist in establishing the attorney-client relationship, in communicating the lawyer's fee, or in preparing the lawyer's legal opinion is not delegating responsibility for those matters and, therefore, is not in violation of this guideline.

Guideline 4:   A lawyer is responsible for taking reasonable measures to ensure that clients, courts, and other lawyers are aware that a paralegal, whose services are utilized by the lawyer in performing legal services, is not licensed to practice law.

Comment to Guideline 4

Since, in most instances, a paralegal is not licensed as a lawyer, it is important that those with whom the paralegal communicates are aware of that fact. The National Federation of Paralegal Associations, Inc. ("NFPA"), Model Code of Professional Ethics and Responsibility and Guidelines for Enforcement, EC 1.7(a)-(c) requires paralegals to disclose their status. Likewise, NALA Canon 5 requires a paralegal to disclose his or her status at the outset of any professional relationship. While requiring the paralegal to make such disclosure is one way in which the lawyer's responsibility to third parties may be discharged, the Standing

Committee is of the view that it is desirable to emphasize the lawyer's responsibility for the disclosure under Model Rule 5.3 (b) and (c). Lawyers may discharge that responsibility by direct communication with the client and third parties, or by requiring the paralegal to make the disclosure, by a written memorandum, or by some other means. Several state guidelines impose on the lawyer responsibility for instructing a paralegal whose services are utilized by the lawyer to disclose the paralegal's status in any dealings with a third party. *See, e.g.*, Kentucky SCR 3.700, Sub-Rule 7, Indiana Guidelines 9.4, 9.10, New Hampshire Rule 35, Sub-Rule 8, New Mexico Rule 20-104. Although in most initial engagements by a client it may be prudent for the attorney to discharge this responsibility with a writing, the guideline requires only that the lawyer recognize the responsibility and ensure that it is discharged. Clearly, when a client has been adequately informed of the lawyer's utilization of paralegal services, it is unnecessary to make additional formalistic disclosures as the client retains the lawyer for other services.

Most guidelines or ethics opinions concerning the disclosure of the status of paralegals include a proviso that the paralegal's status as a nonlawyer be clear and that the title used to identify the paralegal not be deceptive. To fulfill these objectives, the titles assigned to paralegals must be indicative of their status as nonlawyers and not imply that they are lawyers. The most common titles are "paralegal" and "legal assistant" although other titles may fulfill the dual purposes noted above. The titles "paralegal" and "legal assistant" are sometimes coupled with a descriptor of the paralegal's status, e.g., "senior paralegal" or "paralegal coordinator," or of the area of practice in which the paralegal works, e.g., "litigation paralegal" or "probate paralegal." Titles that are commonly used to identify lawyers, such as "associate" or "counsel," are misleading and inappropriate. *See, e.g.,* Comment to New Mexico Rule 20-104 (warning against the use of the title "associate" since it may be construed to mean associate-attorney).

Most state guidelines specifically endorse paralegals signing correspondence so long as their status as a paralegal is clearly indicated by an appropriate title. *See* ABA Informal Opinion 1367 (1976).

Guideline 5:   A lawyer may identify paralegals by name and title on the lawyer's letterhead and on business cards identifying the lawyer's firm.

Comment to Guideline 5

Under Guideline 4, above, a lawyer who employs a paralegal has an obligation to ensure that the status of the paralegal as a nonlawyer is fully disclosed. The primary purpose of this disclosure is to avoid confusion that might lead someone to believe that the paralegal is a lawyer. The identification suggested by this guideline is consistent with that objective while also affording the paralegal recognition as an important member of the legal services team.

ABA Informal Opinion 1527 (1989) provides that nonlawyer support personnel, including paralegals, may be listed on a law firm's letterhead and reiterates previous opinions that approve of paralegals having business cards. *See also* ABA Informal Opinion 1185 (1971). The listing must not be false or misleading and "must make it clear that the support personnel who are listed are not lawyers."

All state guidelines and ethics opinions that address the issue approve of business cards for paralegals, so long as the paralegal's status is clearly indicated. *See, e.g.*, Florida State Bar Ass'n. Comm. on Prof'l Ethics, Op. 86-4 (1986); Kansas Bar Ass'n, Prof'l Ethical Op. 85-4; State Bar of Michigan Standing Comm. on Prof'l and Judicial Ethics, RI-34 (1989); Minnesota Lawyers' Prof'l Responsibility Bd., Op. 8 (1974). Some authorities prescribe the contents and format of the card or the title to be used. *E.g.*, Georgia Guidelines for Attorneys Utilizing Paralegals, State Disciplinary Board Advisory Op. No. 21 (1977); Iowa State Bar Ethical Guidelines for Legal Assistants in Iowa, Guideline 4; South Carolina Bar Ethics Op. 88-06; and Texas General Guidelines for the Utilization of the Services of Legal Assistants by Attorneys, Guideline VIII. All agree the paralegal's status must be clearly indicated and the card may not be used in a deceptive way. Some state rules, such as New Hampshire Supreme Court Rule 7, approve the use of business cards noting that the card should not be used for unethical solicitation.

Most states with guidelines on the use of paralegal services permit the listing of paralegals on firm letterhead. A few states do not permit attorneys to list paralegals on their letterhead. *E.g.*, State Bar of Georgia Disciplinary Board Opinion Number 21 "Guidelines for Attorneys Utilizing Paralegals," 1(b); New Hampshire Supreme Court Rule 35, Sub-Rule 7; New Mexico Supreme Court Rule 20-113 and South Carolina Bar Guidelines for the Utilization by Lawyers of the Services of Legal Assistants Guideline VI. These states rely on earlier ABA Informal Opinions 619 (1962), 845 (1965), and 1000 (1977), all of which were expressly withdrawn by ABA Informal Opinion 1527. These earlier opinions interpreted the predecessor Model Code DR 2-102 (A), which, prior to *Bates v. State Bar of Arizona,* 433 U.S. 350 (1977), had strict limitations on the information that could be listed on letterheads. In light of the United States Supreme Court opinion in *Peel v. Attorney Registration and Disciplinary Comm'n of Illinois,* 496 U.S. 91 (1990), it may be that a restriction on letterhead identification of paralegals that is not deceptive and clearly identifies the paralegal's status violates the First Amendment rights of the lawyer.

More than 20 states have rules or opinions that explicitly permit lawyers to list names of paralegals on their letterhead stationery, including Arizona, Connecticut, Florida, Illinois, Indiana, Kentucky, Michigan,

Mississippi, Missouri, Nebraska, New York, North Carolina, Oregon, South Dakota, Texas, Virginia, and Washington.

The Model Code of Ethics and Professional Responsibility of the National Federation of Paralegal Associations indicates that the paralegal's "title shall be included if the paralegal's name appears on business cards, letterheads, brochures, directories, and advertisements." Canon 6, EC-6.2. NFPA Informal Ethics and Disciplinary Opinion No. 95-2 provides that a paralegal may be identified with name and title on law firm letterhead unless such conduct is prohibited by the appropriate state authority.

Guideline 6:   A lawyer is responsible for taking reasonable measures to ensure that all client confidences are preserved by a paralegal.

Comment to Guideline 6

A fundamental principle in the client-lawyer relationship is that the lawyer must not reveal information relating to the representation. Model Rule 1.6. A client must feel free to discuss whatever he/she wishes with his/her lawyer, and a lawyer must be equally free to obtain information beyond that volunteered by his/her client. The ethical obligation of a lawyer to hold inviolate the confidences and secrets of the client facilitates the full development of the facts essential to proper representation of the client and encourages laypersons to seek early legal assistance. EC 4-1, Model Code. "It is a matter of common knowledge that the normal operation of a law office exposes confidential professional information to nonlawyer employees of the office. . . this obligates a lawyer to exercise care in selecting and training employees so that the sanctity of all confidences and secrets of clients may be preserved." EC 4-2, Model Code.

Model Rule 1.6 applies not only to matters communicated in confidence by the client, but also to all information relating to the representation, whatever its source. Pursuant to the rule, a lawyer may not disclose such information except as authorized or required by the Rules of Professional Conduct or other law. Further, a lawyer must act competently to safeguard information relating to the representation of a client against inadvertent or unauthorized disclosure by the lawyer or "other persons who are participating in the representation of the client or who are subject to the lawyer supervision." Model Rule 1.6, Comment 15. It is therefore the lawyer's obligation to instruct clearly and to take reasonable steps to ensure that paralegals preserve client confidences.

Model Rule 5.3 requires a lawyer having direct supervisory authority over a paralegal to make reasonable efforts to ensure that the person's conduct is compatible with the professional obligations of the lawyer. Comment 1 to Model Rule 5.3 makes it clear that a lawyer must give "such assistants appropriate instruction and supervision concerning the ethical aspects of their employment, particularly regarding the obligation not to disclose information relating to the representation of the client, and should be responsible for their work product." Disciplinary Rule 4-101(D) under the Model Code provides that: "A lawyer shall exercise reasonable care to prevent his employees, associates and others whose services are utilized by him from disclosing or using confidences or secrets of a client. . . ." Nearly all states that have guidelines for utilization of paralegals require the lawyer "to instruct legal assistants concerning client confidences and to exercise care to ensure the legal assistants comply with the Code in this regard." *See, e.g.* New Hampshire Rule 35, Sub-Rule 4; Kentucky Supreme Court Rule 3.700, Sub-Rule 4; Indiana Rules of Prof'l Responsibility, Guideline 9.10.

Model Rule 5.3 further extends responsibility for the professional conduct of paralegals to a "partner, and a lawyer who individually or together with other lawyers possesses comparable managerial authority in a law firm." Lawyers with managerial authority within a law firm are required to make reasonable efforts to establish internal policies and procedures designed to provide reasonable assurance that paralegals in the firm act in a way compatible with the relevant rules of professional conduct. Model Rule 5.3(a), Comment 2.

The NFPA Model Code of Professional Ethics and Responsibility and Guidelines for Enforcement, EC-1.5 states that a paralegal "shall preserve all confidential information provided by the client or acquired from other sources before, during, and after the course of the professional relationship." Further, NFPA EC-1.5(a) requires a paralegal to be aware of and abide by all legal authority governing confidential information in the jurisdiction in which the paralegal practices and prohibits any use of confidential information to the disadvantage of a client. Likewise, the NALA Code of Ethics and Professional Responsibility, Canon 7 states that, "A legal assistant must protect the confidences of the client and must not violate any rule or statute now in effect or hereafter enacted controlling the doctrine of privileged communications between a client and an attorney." Likewise, NALA Guidelines state that paralegals should "preserve the confidences and secrets of all clients; and understand the attorney's code of professional responsibility and these guidelines in order to avoid any action which would involve the attorney in a violation of that code, or give the appearance of professional impropriety." NALA Guideline 1 and Comment.

Guideline 7:   A lawyer should take reasonable measures to prevent conflicts of interest resulting from a paralegal's other employment or interests.

Comment to Guideline 7

Loyalty and independent judgment are essential elements in the lawyer's relationship to a client. Model Rule 1.7, comment 1. The independent judgment of a lawyer should be exercised solely for the benefit of his client and free from all compromising influences and loyalties. EC 5.1. Model Rules 1.7 through 1.13 address a lawyer's responsibility to prevent conflicts of interest and potential conflicts of interest. Model Rule 5.3 requires lawyers with direct supervisory authority over a paralegal and partners/lawyers with managerial authority within a law firm to make reasonable efforts to ensure that the conduct of the paralegals they employ is compatible with their own professional obligations, including the obligation to prevent conflicts of interest. Therefore, paralegals should be instructed to inform the supervising lawyer and the management of the firm of any interest that could result in a conflict of interest or even give the appearance of a conflict. The guideline intentionally speaks to "other employment" rather than only past employment because there are instances where paralegals are employed by more than one law firm at the same time. The guideline's reference to "other interests" is intended to include personal relationships as well as instances where the paralegal may have a financial interest (i.e., as a stockholder, trust beneficiary, or trustee, etc.) that would conflict with the clients in the matter in which the lawyer has been employed.

"Imputed Disqualification Arising from Change in Employment by Non-Lawyer Employee," ABA Informal Opinion 1526 (1988), defines the duties of both the present and former employing lawyers and reasons that the restrictions on paralegals' employment should be kept to "the minimum necessary to protect confidentiality" in order to prevent paralegals from being forced to leave their careers, which "would disserve clients as well as the legal profession." The Opinion describes the attorney's obligations (1) to caution the paralegal not to disclose any information and (2) to prevent the paralegal from working on any matter on which the paralegal worked for a prior employer or respecting which the employee has confidential information.

Disqualification is mandatory where the paralegal gained information relating to the representation of an adverse party while employed at another law firm and has revealed it to lawyers in the new law firm, where screening of the paralegal would be ineffective, or where the paralegal would be required to work on the other side of the same or substantially related matter on which the paralegal had worked while employed at another firm. When a paralegal moves to an opposing firm during ongoing litigation, courts have held that a rebuttable presumption exists that the paralegal will share client confidences. *See, e.g., Phoenix v. Founders*, 887 S.W.2d 831, 835 (Tex. 1994) (the presumption that confidential information has been shared may be rebutted upon showing that sufficient precautions were taken by the new firm to prevent disclosure including that it (1) cautioned the newly-hired paralegal not to disclose any information relating to representation of a client of the former employer; (2) instructed the paralegal not to work on any matter on which he or she worked during prior employment or about which he or she has information relating to the former employer's representation; and (3) the new firm has taken reasonable measures to ensure that the paralegal does not work on any matter on which he or she worked during the prior employment, absent the former client's consent). But, adequate and effective screening of a paralegal may prevent disqualification of the new firm. Model Rule 1.10, comment 4. Adequate and effective screening gives a lawyer and the lawyer's firm the opportunity to build and enforce an "ethical wall" to preclude the paralegal from any involvement in the client matter that is the subject of the conflict and to prevent the paralegal from receiving or disclosing any information concerning the matter. ABA Informal Opinion 1526 (1988). The implication of the ABA's informal opinion is that if the lawyer, and the firm, do not implement a procedure to effectively screen the paralegal from involvement with the litigation, and from communication with attorneys and/or co-employees concerning the litigation, the lawyer and the firm may be disqualified from representing either party in the controversy. *See In re Complex Asbestos Litigation*, 232 Cal. App. 3d 572, 283 Cal. Rptr. 732 (1991) (law firm disqualified from nine pending asbestos cases because it failed to screen paralegal that possessed attorney-client confidences from prior employment by opposing counsel).

Some courts hold that paralegals are subject to the same rules governing imputed disqualification as are lawyers. In jurisdictions that do not recognize screening devices as adequate protection against a lawyer's potential conflict in a new law firm, neither a "cone of silence" nor any other screening device will be recognized as a proper or effective remedy where a paralegal who has switched firms possesses material and confidential information. *Zimmerman v. Mahaska Bottling Company*, 19 P.3d 784, 791-792 (Kan. 2001) ("[W]here screening devices are not allowed for lawyers, they are not allowed for non-lawyers either."); *Koulisis v. Rivers*, 730 So. 2d 289 (Fla. Dist. Ct. App. 1999) (firm that hired paralegal with actual knowledge of protected information could not defeat disqualification by showing steps taken to screen the paralegal from the case); Ala. Bar R-02-01, 63 Ala. Law 94 (2002). These cases do not mean that disqualification is mandatory whenever a nonlawyer moves from one private firm to an opposing firm while there is pending litigation. Rather, a firm may still avoid disqualification if (1) the paralegal has not acquired material or confidential information regarding the litigation, or (2) if the client of the former firm waives disqualification and approves the use of a screening device or ethical wall. *Zimmerman*, 19 P.3d at 822.

Other authorities, consistent with Model Rule 1.10(a), differentiate between lawyers and nonlawyers. In *Stewart v. Bee Dee Neon & Signs,*

Inc., 751 So. 2d 196 (Fla. Dist. Ct. App. 2000) the court disagreed with the *Koulisis* rule that paralegals should be held to the same conflicts analyses as lawyers when they change law firms. In *Stewart,* a secretary moved from one law firm to the opposing firm in mid-litigation. While Florida would not permit lawyer screening to defeat disqualification under these circumstance, the *Stewart* court emphasized that "it is important that non-lawyer employees have as much mobility in employment opportunity as possible" and that "any restrictions on the non-lawyer's employment should be held to the minimum necessary to protect confidentiality of client information." *Stewart,* 751 So. 2d at 203 (citing ABA Informal Opinion 1526 (1988)). The analysis in *Stewart* requires the party moving for disqualification to prove that the nonlawyer actually has confidential information, and that screening has not and can not be effectively implemented. *Id.* at 208. In *Leibowitz v. The Eighth Judicial District Court of the State of Nevada,* 79 P.3d 515 (2003), the Supreme Court of Nevada overruled its earlier decision in *Ciaffone v. District Court,* 113 Nev. 1165, 945 P.2d 950 (1997), which held that screening of nonlawyer employees would not prevent disqualification. In *Leibowitz,* the court held that when a firm identifies a conflict, it has an absolute duty to screen and to inform the adversarial party about the hiring and the screening mechanisms. The Court emphasized that disqualification is required when confidential information has been disclosed, when screening would be ineffective, or when the affected employee would be required to work on the case in question.

Still other courts that approve screening for paralegals compare paralegals to former government lawyers who have neither a financial interest in the outcome of a particular litigation, nor the choice of which clients they serve. *Smart Industries Corp. v. Superior Court County of Yuma,* 876 P.2d 1176, 1184 (Ariz. App. 1994) ("We believe that this reasoning for treating government attorneys differently in the context of imputed disqualification applies equally to nonlawyer assistants . . ."); *accord, Hayes v. Central States Orthopedic Specialists, Inc.,* 51 P.3d 562 (Okla. 2002); Model Rule 1.11(b) and (c).

Comment 4 to Model Rule 1.10(a) states that the rule does not prohibit representation by others in the law firm where the person prohibited from involvement in a matter is a paralegal. But, paralegals "ordinarily must be screened from any personal participation in the matter to avoid communication to others in the firm of confidential information that both the nonlawyers and the firm have a legal duty to protect." *Id.* Because disqualification is such a drastic consequence for lawyers and their firms, lawyers must be especially attuned to controlling authority in the jurisdictions where they practice. *See generally,* Steve Morris and Christina C. Stipp, Ethical Conflicts Facing Litigators, ALI SH009ALI-ABA 449, 500-502 (2002).

To assist lawyers and their firms in discharging their professional obligations under the Model Rules, the NALA Guidelines requires paralegals "to take any and all steps necessary to prevent conflicts of interest and fully disclose such conflicts to the supervising attorney" and warns paralegals that any "failure to do so may jeopardize both the attorney's representation and the case itself." NALA, Comment to Guideline 1. NFPA Model Code of Professional Ethics and Responsibility and Guidelines for Enforcement, EC-1.6 requires paralegals to avoid conflicts of interest and to disclose any possible conflicts to the employer or client, as well as to the prospective employers or clients. NFPA, EC-1.6 (a)-(g).

Guideline 8: A lawyer may include a charge for the work performed by a paralegal in setting a charge and/or billing for legal services.

Comment to Guideline 8

In *Missouri v. Jenkins*, 491 U.S. 274 (1989), the United States Supreme Court held that in setting a reasonable attorney's fee under 28 U.S.C. § 1988, a legal fee may include a charge for paralegal services at "market rates" rather than "actual cost" to the attorneys. In its opinion, the Court stated that, in setting recoverable attorney fees, it starts from "the self-evident proposition that the 'reasonable attorney's fee' provided for by statute should compensate the work of paralegals, as well as that of attorneys." *Id.* at 286. This statement should resolve any question concerning the propriety of setting a charge for legal services based on work performed by a paralegal. *See also*, Alaska Rules of Civil Procedure Rule 79; Florida Statutes Title VI, Civil Practice & Procedure, 57.104; North Carolina Guideline 8; Comment to NALA Guideline 5; Michigan Guideline 6. In addition to approving paralegal time as a compensable fee element, the Supreme Court effectively encouraged the use of paralegals for the costeffective delivery of services. It is important to note, however, that *Missouri v. Jenkins* does not abrogate the attorney's responsibilities under Model Rule 1.5 to set a reasonable fee for legal services, and it follows that those considerations apply to a fee that includes a fee for paralegal services. *See also*, South Carolina Ethics Advisory Opinion 96-13 (a lawyer may use and bill for the services of an independent paralegal so long as the lawyer supervises the work of the paralegal and, in billing the paralegal's time, the lawyer discloses to the client the basis of the fee and expenses).

It is important to note that a number of court decisions have addressed or otherwise set forth the criteria to be used in evaluating whether paralegal services should be compensated. Some requirements include that the services performed must be legal in nature rather than clerical, the fee statement must specify in detail the qualifications of the person performing the service to demonstrate that the paralegal is qualified by education, training or work to perform the assigned work, and evidence that the work performed by the paralegal would have had to be performed by the attorney at a higher rate. Because considerations and criteria vary from one jurisdiction to another, it is important for the practitioner to determine the criteria required by the jurisdiction in which the practitioner intends to file a fee application seeking compensation for paralegal services.

Guideline 9:   A lawyer may not split legal fees with a paralegal nor pay a paralegal for the referral of legal business. A lawyer may compensate a paralegal based on the quantity and quality of the paralegal's work and the value of that work to a law practice, but the paralegal's compensation may not be contingent, by advance agreement, upon the outcome of a particular case or class of cases.

Comment to Guideline 9

Model Rule 5.4 and DR 3-102(A) and 3-103(A) under the Model Code clearly prohibits fee "splitting" with paralegals, whether characterized as splitting of contingent fees, "forwarding" fees, or other sharing of legal fees. Virtually all guidelines adopted by state bar associations have continued this prohibition in one form or another. *See, e.g.*, Connecticut Guideline 7, Kentucky Supreme Court Rule 3.700, Sub-Rule 5; Michigan Guideline 7; Missouri Guideline III; North Carolina Guideline 8; New Hampshire Rule 35, Sub-Rules 5 and 6; R.I. Sup. Ct. Art. V. R. 5.4; South Carolina Guideline V. It appears clear that a paralegal may not be compensated on a contingent basis for a particular case or be paid for "signing up" clients for representation.

Having stated this prohibition, however, the guideline attempts to deal with the practical consideration of how a paralegal may be compensated properly by a lawyer or law firm. The linchpin of the prohibition seems to be the advance agreement of the lawyer to "split" a fee based on a pre-existing contingent arrangement.[7] *See, e.g.*, *Matter of Struthers*, 877 P.2d 789 (Ariz. 1994) (an agreement to give to nonlawyer all fees resulting from nonlawyer's debt collection activities constitutes improper fee splitting); *Florida Bar v. Shapiro*, 413 So. 2d 1184 (Fla. 1982) (payment of contingent salary to nonlawyer based on total amount of fees generated is improper); State Bar of Montana, Op. 95-0411 (1995) (lawyer paid on contingency basis for debt collection cannot share that fee with a nonlawyer collection agency that worked with lawyer).

7. In its Rule 5.4 of the Rules of Professional Conduct, the District of Columbia permits lawyers to form legal service partnerships that include non-lawyer participants. Comments 5 and 6 to that rule, however, state that the term "nonlawyer participants" should not be confused with the term "nonlawyer assistants" and that "[n]onlawyer assistants under Rule 5.3 do not have managerial authority or financial interests in the organization."

There is no general prohibition against a lawyer who enjoys a particularly profitable period recognizing the contribution of the paralegal to that profitability with a discretionary bonus so long as the bonus is based on the overall success of the firm and not the fees generated from any particular case. *See, e.g.,* Philadelphia Bar Ass'n Prof. Guidance Comm., Op. 2001-7 (law firm may pay nonlawyer employee a bonus if bonus is not tied to fees generated from a particular case or class of cases from a specific client); Va. St. Bar St. Comm. of Legal Ethics, Op. 885 (1987) (a nonlawyer may be paid based on the percentage of profits from all fees collected by the lawyer). Likewise, a lawyer engaged in a particularly profitable specialty of legal practice is not prohibited from compensating the paralegal who aids materially in that practice more handsomely than the compensation generally awarded to paralegals in that geographic area who work in law practices that are less lucrative. Indeed, any effort to fix a compensation level for paralegals and prohibit great compensation would appear to violate the federal antitrust laws. *See, e.g., Goldfarb v. Virginia State Bar,* 421 U.S. 773 (1975).

In addition to the prohibition on fee splitting, a lawyer also may not provide direct or indirect remuneration to a paralegal for referring legal matters to the lawyer. *See* Model Guideline 9; Connecticut Guideline 7; Michigan Guideline 7; North Carolina Guideline 8. *See also, Committee on Prof'l Ethics & Conduct of Iowa State Bar Ass'n v. Lawler,* 342 N.W. 2d 486 (Iowa 1984) (reprimand for lawyer payment of referral fee); *Trotter v. Nelson,* 684 N.E.2d 1150 (Ind. 1997) (wrongful to pay to nonlawyer five percent of fees collected from a case referred by the nonlawyer).

Guideline 10: A lawyer who employs a paralegal should facilitate the paralegal's participation in appropriate continuing education and pro bono publico activities.

Comment to Guideline 10

For many years the Standing Committee on Paralegals has advocated that formal paralegal education generally improves the legal services rendered by lawyers employing paralegals and provides a more satisfying professional atmosphere in which paralegals may work. Recognition of the employing lawyer's obligation to facilitate the paralegal's continuing professional education is, therefore, appropriate because of the benefits to both the law practice and the paralegals and is consistent with the lawyer's own responsibility to maintain professional competence under Model Rule 1.1. *See also* EC 6-2 of the Model Code. Since these Guidelines were first adopted by the House of Delegates in 1991, several state bar associations have adopted guidelines that encourage lawyers to promote the professional development and continuing education of paralegals in their employ, including Connecticut, Idaho, Indiana,

Michigan, New York, Virginia, Washington, and West Virginia. The National Association of Legal Assistants Code of Ethics and Professional Responsibility, Canon 6, calls on paralegals to "maintain a high degree of competency through education and training . . . and through continuing education. . . ." and the National Federation of Paralegal Associations Model Code of Ethics and Professional Responsibility, Canon 1.1, states that a paralegal "shall achieve and maintain a high level of competence" through education, training, work experience and continuing education.

The Standing Committee is of the view that similar benefits accrue to the lawyer and paralegal if the paralegal is included in the pro bono publico legal services that a lawyer has a clear obligation to provide under Model Rule 6.1 and, where appropriate, the paralegal is encouraged to provide such services independently. The ability of a law firm to provide more pro bono publico services is enhanced if paralegals are included. Recognition of the paralegal's role in such services is consistent with the role of the paralegal in the contemporary delivery of legal services generally and is also consistent with the lawyer's duty to the legal profession under Canon 2 of the Model Code. Several state bar associations, including Connecticut, Idaho, Indiana, Michigan, Washington and West Virginia, have adopted a guideline that calls on lawyers to facilitate paralegals' involvement in pro bono publico activities. One state, New York, includes pro bono work under the rubric of professional development. (*See* Commentary to Guideline VII of the New York State Bar Association Guidelines for the Utilization by Lawyers of the Service of Legal Assistants, adopted June 1997.) The National Federation of Paralegal Associations Model Code of Ethics and Professional Responsibility and Guidelines for Enforcement, Canon 1.4, states that paralegals "shall serve the public interest by contributing to the improvement of the legal system and delivery of quality legal services, including pro bono publico legal services." In the accompanying Ethical Consideration 1.4(d), the Federation asks its members to aspire to contribute at least 24 hours of pro bono services annually.

B

NALA Code of Ethics and Professional Responsibility

A legal assistant must adhere strictly to the accepted standards of legal ethics and to the general principles of proper conduct. The performance of the duties of the legal assistant shall be governed by specific canons as defined herein so that justice will be served and goals of the profession attained. (See Model Standards and Guidelines for Utilization of Legal Assistants, Section II.)

The canons of ethics set forth hereafter are adopted by the National Association of Legal Assistants, Inc., as a general guide intended to aid legal assistants and attorneys. The enumeration of these rules does not mean there are not others of equal importance although not specifically mentioned. Court rules, agency rules and statutes must be taken into consideration when interpreting the canons.

Definition: Legal assistants, also known as paralegals, are a distinguishable group of persons who assist attorneys in the delivery of legal services. Through formal education, training and experience, legal assistants have knowledge and expertise regarding the legal system and substantive and procedural law which qualify them to do work of a legal nature under the supervision of an attorney.

Canon 1.

A legal assistant must not perform any of the duties that attorneys only may perform nor take any actions that attorneys may not take.

Canon 2.

A legal assistant may perform any task which is properly delegated and supervised by an attorney, as long as the attorney is ultimately responsible to the client, maintains a direct relationship with the client, and assumes professional responsibility for the work product.

Canon 3.

A legal assistant must not: (a) engage in, encourage, or contribute to any act which could constitute the unauthorized practice of law; and (b) establish attorney–client relationships, set fees, give legal opinions or advice or represent a client before a court or agency unless so authorized by that court or agency; and (c) engage in conduct or take any action which would assist or involve the attorney in a violation of professional ethics or give the appearance of professional impropriety.

Canon 4.

A legal assistant must use discretion and professional judgment commensurate with knowledge and experience but must not render independent legal judgment in place of an attorney. The services of an attorney are essential in the public interest whenever such legal judgment is required.

Canon 5.

A legal assistant must disclose his or her status as a legal assistant at the outset of any professional relationship with a client, attorney, a court or administrative agency or personnel thereof, or a member of the general public. A legal assistant must act prudently in determining the extent to which a client may be assisted without the presence of an attorney.

Canon 6.

A legal assistant must strive to maintain integrity and a high degree of competency through education and training with respect to professional responsibility, local rules and practice, and through continuing education in substantive areas of law to better assist the legal profession in fulfilling its duty to provide legal service.

Canon 7.

A legal assistant must protect the confidences of a client and must not violate any rule or statute now in effect or hereafter enacted controlling the doctrine of privileged communications between a client and an attorney.

Canon 8.

A legal assistant must do all other things incidental, necessary, or expedient for the attainment of the ethics and responsibilities as defined by statute or rule of court.

Canon 9.

A legal assistant's conduct is guided by bar associations' codes of professional responsibility and rules of professional conduct.

Adopted, May 1, 1975
Revised 1979, 1988, 1995, and 1998,
National Association of Legal Assistants

National Federation of Paralegal Associations, Inc. Model Code of Ethics and Professional Responsibility

Preamble

The National Federation of Paralegal Associations, Inc. ("NFPA") is a professional organization comprised of paralegal associations and individual paralegals throughout the United States and Canada. Members of NFPA have varying backgrounds, experiences, education and job responsibilities that reflect the diversity of the paralegal profession. NFPA promotes the growth, development and recognition of the paralegal profession as an integral partner in the delivery of legal services.

In May 1993 NFPA adopted its Model Code of Ethics and Professional Responsibility ("Model Code") to delineate the principles for ethics and conduct to which every paralegal should aspire.

Many paralegal associations throughout the United States have endorsed the concept and content of NFPA's Model Code through the adoption of their own ethical codes. In doing so, paralegals have confirmed the profession's commitment to increase the quality and efficiency of legal services, as well as recognized its responsibilities to the public, the legal community, and colleagues.

Paralegals have recognized, and will continue to recognize, that the profession must continue to evolve to enhance their roles in the delivery of legal services. With increased levels of responsibility comes the need to define and enforce mandatory rules of professional conduct. Enforcement of codes of paralegal conduct is a logical and necessary step to enhance and ensure the confidence of the legal community and the public in the integrity and professional responsibility of paralegals.

In April 1997 NFPA adopted the Model Disciplinary Rules ("Model Rules") to make possible the enforcement of the Canons and Ethical Considerations contained in the NFPA Model Code. A concurrent determination was made that the Model Code of Ethics and Professional Responsibility, formerly aspirational in nature, should be recognized as setting forth the enforceable obligations of all paralegals.

The Model Code and Model Rules offer a framework for professional discipline, either voluntarily or through formal regulatory programs.

§1.   NFPA Model Disciplinary Rules and Ethical Considerations

1.1   A Paralegal Shall Achieve and Maintain a High Level of Competence

Ethical Considerations

EC-1.1(a) A paralegal shall achieve competency through education, training, and work experience.

EC-1.1(b) A paralegal shall aspire to participate in a minimum of twelve (12) hours of continuing legal education, to include at least one (1) hour of ethics education, every two (2) years in order to remain current on developments in the law.

EC-1.1(c) A paralegal shall perform all assignments promptly and efficiently.

1.2 A Paralegal Shall Maintain a High Level of Personal and Professional Integrity

Ethical Considerations

EC-1.2(a) A paralegal shall not engage in any ex parte communications involving the courts or any other adjudicatory body in an attempt to exert undue influence or to obtain advantage or the benefit of only one party.

EC-1.2(b) A paralegal shall not communicate, or cause another to communicate, with a party the paralegal knows to be represented by a lawyer in a pending matter without the prior consent of the lawyer representing such other party.

EC-1.2(c) A paralegal shall ensure that all timekeeping and billing records prepared by the paralegal are thorough, accurate, honest, and complete.

EC-1.2(d) A paralegal shall not knowingly engage in fraudulent billing practices. Such practices may include, but are not limited to: inflation of hours billed to a client or employer; misrepresentation of the nature of tasks performed; and/or submission of fraudulent expense and disbursement documentation.

EC-1.2(e) A paralegal shall be scrupulous, thorough and honest in the identification and maintenance of all funds, securities, and other assets of a client and shall provide accurate accounting as appropriate.

EC-1.2(f) A paralegal shall advise the proper authority of non-confidential knowledge of any dishonest or fraudulent acts by any person pertaining to the handling of the funds, securities or other assets of a client. The authority to whom the report is made shall depend on the nature and circumstances of the possible misconduct, (e.g., ethics committees of law firms, corporations and/or paralegal associations, local or state bar associations, local prosecutors, administrative agencies, etc.). Failure to report such knowledge is in itself misconduct and shall be treated as such under these rules.

1.3 A Paralegal Shall Maintain a High Standard of Professional Conduct

Ethical Considerations

EC-1.3(a) A paralegal shall refrain from engaging in any conduct that offends the dignity and decorum of proceedings before a court or other adjudicatory body and shall be respectful of all rules and procedures.

EC-1.3(b) A paralegal shall avoid impropriety and the appearance of impropriety and shall not engage in any conduct that would adversely affect his/her fitness to practice. Such conduct may include, but is not limited to: violence, dishonesty, interference with the administration of justice, and/or abuse of a professional position or public office.

EC-1.3(c) Should a paralegal's fitness to practice be compromised by physical or mental illness, causing that paralegal to commit an act that is in direct violation of the Model Code/Model Rules and/or the rules and/or laws governing the jurisdiction in which the paralegal practices, that paralegal may be protected from sanction upon review of the nature and circumstances of that illness.

EC-1.3(d) A paralegal shall advise the proper authority of non-confidential knowledge of any action of another legal professional that clearly demonstrates fraud, deceit, dishonesty, or misrepresentation. The authority to whom the report is made shall depend on the nature and circumstances of the possible misconduct, (e.g., ethics committees of law firms, corporations and/or paralegal associations, local or state bar associations, local prosecutors, administrative agencies, etc.). Failure to report such knowledge is in itself misconduct and shall be treated as such under these rules.

EC-1.3(e) A paralegal shall not knowingly assist any individual with the commission of an act that is in direct violation of the Model Code/Model Rules and/or the rules and/or laws governing the jurisdiction in which the paralegal practices.

EC-1.3(f) If a paralegal possesses knowledge of future criminal activity, that knowledge must be reported to the appropriate authority immediately.

1.4 A Paralegal Shall Serve the Public Interest by Contributing to the Improvement of the Legal System and Delivery of Quality Legal Services, Including Pro Bono Publico Services

Ethical Considerations

EC-1.4(a) A paralegal shall be sensitive to the legal needs of the public and shall promote the development and implementation of programs that address those needs.

EC-1.4(b) A paralegal shall support efforts to improve the legal system and access thereto and shall assist in making changes.

EC-1.4(c) A paralegal shall support and participate in the delivery of Pro Bono Publico services directed toward implementing and improving access to justice, the law, the legal system or the paralegal and legal professions.

EC-1.4(d) A paralegal should aspire annually to contribute twenty-four (24) hours of Pro Bono Publico services under the supervision of an attorney or as authorized by administrative, statutory or court authority to:

1. persons of limited means; or
2. charitable, religious, civic, community, governmental and educational organizations in matters that are designed primarily to address the legal needs of persons with limited means; or
3. individuals, groups or organizations seeking to secure or protect civil rights, civil liberties or public rights.

The twenty-four (24) hours of Pro Bono Publico services contributed annually by a paralegal may consist of such services as detailed in this EC-1.4(d), and/or administrative matters designed to develop and implement the attainment of this aspiration as detailed above in EC-1.4(a) B (c), or any combination of the two.

1.5 A Paralegal Shall Preserve All Confidential Information Provided by the Client or Acquired From Other Sources Before, During, and After the Course of the Professional Relationship

Ethical Considerations

EC-1.5(a) A paralegal shall be aware of and abide by all legal authority governing confidential information in the jurisdiction in which the paralegal practices.

EC-1.5(b) A paralegal shall not use confidential information to the disadvantage of the client.

EC-1.5(c) A paralegal shall not use confidential information to the advantage of the paralegal or of a third person.

EC-1.5(d) A paralegal may reveal confidential information only after full disclosure and with the client's written consent; or, when required by law or court order; or, when necessary to prevent the client from committing an act that could result in death or serious bodily harm.

EC-1.5(e) A paralegal shall keep those individuals responsible for the legal representation of a client fully informed of any confidential information the paralegal may have pertaining to that client.

EC-1.5(f) A paralegal shall not engage in any indiscreet communications concerning clients.

1.6 A Paralegal Shall Avoid Conflicts of Interest and Shall Disclose Any Possible Conflict to the Employer or Client, As Well As to the Prospective Employers or Clients

Ethical Considerations

EC-1.6(a) A paralegal shall act within the bounds of the law, solely for the benefit of the client, and shall be free of compromising influences and loyalties. Neither the paralegal's personal or business interest, nor those of other clients or third persons, should compromise the paralegal's professional judgment and loyalty to the client.

EC-1.6(b) A paralegal shall avoid conflicts of interest that may arise from previous assignments, whether for a present or past employer or client.

EC-1.6(c) A paralegal shall avoid conflicts of interest that may arise from family relationships and from personal and business interests.

EC-1.6(d) In order to be able to determine whether an actual or potential conflict of interest exists a paralegal shall create and maintain an effective recordkeeping system that identifies clients, matters, and parties with which the paralegal has worked.

EC-1.6(e) A paralegal shall reveal sufficient non-confidential information about a client or former client to reasonably ascertain if an actual or potential conflict of interest exists.

EC-1.6(f) A paralegal shall not participate in or conduct work on any matter where a conflict of interest has been identified.

EC-1.6(g) In matters where a conflict of interest has been identified and the client consents to continued representation, a paralegal shall comply fully with the implementation and maintenance of an Ethical Wall.

1.7 A Paralegal's Title Shall be Fully Disclosed

Ethical Considerations

EC-1.7(a) A paralegal's title shall clearly indicate the individual's status and shall be disclosed in all business and professional communications to avoid misunderstandings and misconceptions about the paralegal's role and responsibilities.

EC-1.7(b) A paralegal's title shall be included if the paralegal's name appears on business cards, letterhead, brochures, directories, and advertisements.

EC-1.7(c) A paralegal shall not use letterhead, business cards or other promotional materials to create a fraudulent impression of his/her status or ability to practice in the jurisdiction in which the paralegal practices.

EC-1.7(d) A paralegal shall not practice under color of any record, diploma, or certificate that has been illegally or fraudulently obtained or issued or which is misrepresentative in any way.

EC-1.7(e) A paralegal shall not participate in the creation, issuance, or dissemination of fraudulent records, diplomas, or certificates.

1.8 A Paralegal Shall Not Engage in the Unauthorized Practice of Law

Ethical Considerations

EC-1.8(a) A paralegal shall comply with the applicable legal authority governing the unauthorized practice of law in the jurisdiction in which the paralegal practices.

Glossary

Abuse of process   The improper use of a civil or criminal process.

Administrative agency   A government body responsible for the control and supervision of a particular activity or area of public interest.

Advanced fee   A fee paid by a client to a lawyer in advance of the work being done which is earned by the lawyer as the work is done.

Associate   A lawyer in a law firm who is not a partner but is an employee.

Attorney–client privilege   The rule of evidence that protects confidential communications between a lawyer and client made in the course of the professional relationship.

Barratry   The common law crime of stirring up lawsuits and disputes.

Bribery   The crime of giving or receiving something of value as payment for an official act.

Certification   A form of recognition of an occupation based on a person's having met specified qualifications.

Champerty   An old common law agreement between a lawyer and client under which the lawyer undertakes representation and pays costs and is reimbursed and paid a fee out of the recovery; such agreements were outlawed in most states.

Chat   Discussion carried on electronically over the Internet, which can be live or asynchronous.

Chinese wall   An antiquated term for a screen. See **Screen/screening.**

Class action suit   A lawsuit brought by a representative of a group of persons on behalf of the group.

Client security fund   A fund set aside to reimburse clients whose funds have been converted or misappropriated by lawyers.

Client trust account A bank account set up by a lawyer in which funds are kept that belong in whole or in part to the client.

Commingling The mixing of the funds of a fiduciary, including a lawyer, with those of a client.

Cone of silence The silence imposed on a person with a conflict of interest when a screen is erected to protect against breaches of confidentiality.

Confidentiality agreement An agreement entered into between a law firm and an employee or other agent in which the employee or agent agrees to keep client information confidential.

Contempt An act that obstructs the administration of justice, impairs the dignity of the court, or shows disrespect for the authority of the court.

Contingency fee A fee that is contingent on the successful outcome of a case and based on a percentage of the recovery.

Control group test The test applied by some courts to determine whether communications in a corporate setting are covered by the attorney-client privilege; under this test, communications are privileged only if they are made with the management and board members.

Court facilitators Persons employed by the courts to assist lay persons who are representing themselves in their own court matters. Typically employed in family law courts.

Conversion The tortious deprivation of another's property without justification or authorization.

Deposition A method of pre-trial discovery that consists of a witness statement taken under oath in a question–and–answer format and recorded.

Disbarment The rescinding of a lawyer's license to practice law.

Discovery Pre-trial procedures designed for the parties to gain information in order to narrow the issues of fact and law.

Document production A form of discovery under which one party must provide copies of specified documents to the other side.

Ethics advisory opinions Written opinions promulgated by bar associations in which the association interprets the relevant ethical precedents in the context of a specific ethical dilemma posed to it.

Ex parte An action taken by or on behalf of a party without the presence of the opposing party.

Extrajudicial An act that takes place outside the presence of the judge or jury.

Fee-shifting statute Legislation that permits the award of attorney's fees to the prevailing party.

Fixed fees   A fee for legal services based on a set amount, usually used for standardized routine work.

Forwarding fee   A fee paid by a lawyer to another lawyer for referring a case.

Freelance paralegals   Legal assistants who work as independent contractors providing services to lawyers on an as-needed basis.

Gag order   A court-imposed order that restricts information or comment about a case.

Hourly fees   Fees for legal services based on hourly rates and the amount of time actually expended in rendering the services.

Imputed conflict/disqualification   A conflict of interest involving one person that is attributed vicariously to the entire law firm, which is disqualified from representing the party at issue.

In camera   Proceedings held in the judge's chambers without the jury or public present; the examination of documents to determine if there is privileged information is conducted "in camera."

Independent paralegals   A term sometimes used by nonlawyer legal service providers and sometimes used by freelance paralegals. See both these terms in this glossary.

Integrated bar   A bar association in which the mandatory and voluntary aspects of bar activities are combined and membership is required.

Inter vivos   During life.

IOLTA   Interest on Lawyers' Trust Accounts. A program under which the interest from lawyers' client trust accounts, which is too small to pay to clients, is collected by banks and used by bar associations and/or courts to fund law-related programs.

Issue conflict   The situation that arises when a lawyer argues opposing sides of a legal issue, the result of which may be that one client's interests are harmed, even though that client is not a party to the matter.

Jailhouse lawyers   Prison inmates who assist other prisoners in preparing writs and lawsuits.

Legal document assistants   Nonlawyer legal service providers who assist persons in preparing legal documents without giving legal advice under California statutes.

Legal malpractice   Improper conduct in the performance of duties by a legal professional, either intentionally or through negligence.

Legal technicians   A term used by some nonlawyer legal service providers.

Licensing   Mandatory governmental regulation of a profession requiring that the members meet specified qualifications.

Lien   An encumbrance or claim on the property of another as security for a debt or charge.

Malicious prosecution   An action to recover damages resulting from an unsuccessful criminal or civil action which was instituted without probable cause and with malice.

Malpractice   Improper conduct in the performance of duties by a professional, either intentionally or through negligence.

Mistrial   A trial terminated and declared void prior to the return of a verdict, often because of a jury deadlock.

Multidisciplinary practice   A business model under which law firms and other professionals form partnerships to deliver legal and other related services to clients.

Multijurisdictional practice   Engaging in the practice of law in more than one state.

Nonlawyer legal service providers   Laypersons who provide legal services directly to the public.

Paraprofessional   A person who works within a profession in a subordinate position but with special training and a degree of independence in carrying out duties.

Perjury   A criminal offense of making false statements under oath.

Pleading   Statements in written legal form that set forth the plaintiff's cause of action and the defendant's grounds of defense.

Pro bono   For free.

Professional negligence   Improper conduct in the performance of duties by a professional, either intentionally or through negligence.

Pro per   A nonlawyer representing himself or herself in a legal matter.

Pro se   A nonlawyer representing himself or herself in a legal matter.

Probation   A procedure under which someone found guilty of an offense is subjected to certain conditions and oversight by the entity involved and is released from a more serious sanction.

Pro hac vice   The permission granted by a court to an out-of-state lawyer to appear in a particular case as though admitted to practice in that jurisdiction.

Real estate closing   The consummation of the sale of real estate by payment of the purchase price, delivery of the deed, and finalizing collateral matters, such as mortgage, insurance and taxes.

Reprimand   The least serious of the sanctions that can be placed on a lawyer for unethical conduct; it may be public or private.

Reproval   Another word for reprimand, used in some states.

Retainer fee   A fee for legal services paid to assure the availability of the lawyer to handle specified matters whether or not any such matters arise during the retainer period.

Screen/screening   The isolation of a person from participation in a matter through the timely imposition of procedures within a firm that are reasonably adequate under the circumstances to protect information that the person is obligated to protect under the ethics rules or the attorney-client privilege.

Self-representation   The act of representing oneself in legal proceedings before a tribunal.

Simultaneous representation   The representation of clients in current legal matters that involve a conflict of interest.

Spoilation   Destruction of evidence that may result in a civil cause of action for damages for interference with the ability to prove a claim or defense.

Subject matter test   The test applied by some courts to determine whether communications in a corporate setting are covered by the attorney-client privilege; under this test, communications with corporate employees are privileged if they related to the legal matter being discussed.

Subornation of perjury   The criminal offense of encouraging another to commit perjury.

Successive representation   The representation of clients in a conflict of interest situation involving a current matter and a former client whose interests conflict.

Suspension   The temporary removal of a lawyer's license to practice law for a stated period.

Testamentary   Through a will.

Unconscionable   So unreasonable as to render a contract unenforceable, usually because the terms are so favorable to one party.

Unlawful detainer assistant   Title granted by the California legislature for persons who provide legal-clerical services to persons representing themselves in matters relating to evictions.

Vicarious disqualification   The imputation of a conflict to others in a firm so that the entire firm is disqualified from undertaking the representation.

Whistleblower statutes   Statutes that protect and/or reward persons who reveal unlawful practices.

Will execution   The formal process of signing and witnessing of a will.

Work product rule   The rule of evidence that protects the work done by a lawyer and his/her employees and agents in the process of representing a client in litigation.

Index